INSIDE THE GREAT MIRROR

INSIDE THE GREAT MIRROR

A CRITICAL EXAMINATION OF
THE PHILOSOPHY OF RUSSELL, WITTGENSTEIN,
AND THEIR FOLLOWERS

by

JAMES K. FEIBLEMAN
Tulane University

MARTINUS NIJHOFF / THE HAGUE

1958

TO THOSE STUDENTS WHO HAVE WORKED OVER
THIS GROUND WITH ME, THROUGH NO CHOICE
OF THEIR OWN

ACKNOWLEDGEMENTS

My thanks are due to the following journals for permission to reprint as chapters in this book articles which originally appeared in their pages: *The Journal of Philosophy*, for "Russell's Inventory of the World'"; *The Library of Living Philosophers*, Volume V, for "A Reply to Bertrand Russell's Introduction to the Second Edition of *The Principles of Mathematics*"; *Tulane Studies in Philosophy*, for "Viennese Positivism in the United States"; *The Review of Metaphysics*, for "The Metaphysics of Logical Positivism"; and *Sophia*, for "Reflections After Wittgenstein".

CONTENTS

I shall assume that there is an objective complexity in the world, and that it is mirrored by the complexity of propositions.

BERTRAND RUSSELL,
The Philosophy of Logical Atomism.

How can the all-embracing logic which mirrors the world use such special catches and manipulations? Only because all these are connected into an infinitely fine network, to the great mirror.

L. WITTGENSTEIN,
Tractatus Logico-Philosophicus, 5.511.

PART ONE

RUSSELL'S EARLY PHILOSOPHY

AN 'INVENTORY OF THE WORLD'

This book is devoted to the study of one modern revolt against realism and of how it has failed. The authors of the revolt have failed to refute realism but succeeded in gaining wide professional acceptance. Bertrand Russell, in his studies in philosophy, and in particular those in the foundations of mathematics written in the first quarter of the twentieth century, was an advocate of realism. He himself turned away from it later on; and he led his followers, especially Wittgenstein, in a movement against it, a movement which Wittgenstein's followers, in turn, accelerated into a vigorous crusade, while Russell and Wittgenstein, the inventive members of the movement, were never altogether able to shake themselves free of its influence. Their best work was made possible by realism, and it has been in the interest of the truth contained in realism that the present study was undertaken.

One subsidiary aim of this work, therefore, is to make an interpretation of Wittgenstein different from that one which has been made by the Viennese logical positivists and their American followers and by the British linguistic analysts. Wittgenstein is dead and his work must stand on what he has written, and his writings are now public property: anyone may legitimately interpret them. It is not possible to sell a copy of Wittgenstein with every copy of his books, so the books must rest on their own grounds, and this will be increasingly true as the generation which knew him dies out. Moreover, it is what his words say and not what he may have wanted to have them say that counts.

In brief, both the logical positivists and the linguistic analysts endeavor to make a nominalistic interpretation of Wittgenstein; what is here undertaken is a realistic interpretation. Where the members of these two schools interpret him as denying meta-physics altogether, he is here interpreted as denying some metaphysics and presupposing others, and it is the presuppositions which we have endeavored to bring out in our interpretation.

What it all adds up to, we may suppose, is some evidence of the importance of Wittgenstein: that he, like his master Russell, has interested rival schools and stimulated rival interpretations – and this, in the great family of philosophy, is all to the good.

Our procedure will be as follows. First, it will be necessary to say what realism is in the sense in which the term is employed here. Then we shall show in what manner Russell advocated realism. Although Russell is more important than Wittgenstein, our examination of Wittgenstein will be more extensive, since Wittgenstein's books have come to be somewhat pivotal affairs; we shall undertake to examine the first of them in all its details, so that the background of its realism, and the way in which it constituted a revolt against realism, will be made clear.

Realism in philosophy means one thing for epistemology and another for metaphysics. The two are related but they are not the same. Realism in epistemology means the existence of concrete objects independent of human perceptions. Things exist whether we perceive them or not, and would exist whether there were any human beings or not. This kind of existence includes of course the human body in so far as human beings do exist as concrete objects.

Realism in metaphysics affirms the same reality for both concrete objects and abstract objects. Abstract objects to be real must have two kinds of independence; they must be independent of human perceptions, just as concrete objects are, and they must be independent of the concrete objects which they resemble, or which, perhaps we should more properly say, resemble them.

Realism of this sort, so far as our limited knowledge of the history of philosophy goes, began with Plato. Although Plato was primarily an objective idealist in believing that the abstract objects were more real, in the sense of being more reliable, than the concrete objects, he recognized at times also the reliability of the concrete objects. Some would suppose that Aristotle was fighting the idealism of Plato's followers and was himself a realist of the Platonic variety. But we shall not try here to trace the history of realism; it is only necessary to say that Russell's realism is due to that of the nineteenth century German philosopher, Meinong, whose realism was of the Platonic variety.

Bertrand Russell was born in 1872. His early influences were Mill, whom he read in 1890, then Kant, Hegel, and Bradley at Cambridge. He found Bradley's *Logic* important. By 1898 he had become a realist, largely as a result of conversations with G. E. Moore. Hard work on Leibniz revealed that he as well as the foregoing philosophers had developed philosophies which were no stronger than the logic by which they were supported. He then returned to the study of logic, stimulated by the work of Peano and Frege [1].

So much he has himself noted. One might add that the "atomic facts" of his early philosophy of logical atomism might have come from an analogy with Leibniz' monads, and further that the metaphysical realism which he says that he learned from Moore might have been reinforced by the realism of Frege. The Russell of *The Principles of Mathematics* is the Russell of a strong metaphysical and epistemological realism. The book was written in 1900 and published in 1903. Russell's realism in this period may have been due to Frege, the published dates of whose quoted works in the *Principles* of Russell are given as 1879 and 1893 [2], and Meinong, whose quoted work is dated 1896 [3]. Somewhere between the *Principles* and the *Principia Mathematica*, atomism came in to war against realism.

The Problems of Philosophy was published in 1912, and certainly its author was by that time a well-entrenched Platonic realist, as Chapter X clearly shows. In 1924, he was still a metaphysical realist, and has so stated himself [4].

Was he a metaphysical realist when the *Principia Mathematica* appeared? Clearly yes, if he had become one, as the record shows, in 1898 and remained one as late as 1924, for the first edition of the *Principia* appeared in 1910. Yet the *Principia* contains evidence for the attempt to establish a logical nominalism,

---

[1] All of the foregoing information to be found in the first pages of "Logical Atomism" by Bertrand Russell in *Contemporary British Philosophy*, First Series, ed. by J. H. Muirhead (London 1925, Allen & Unwin), p. 359 ff.

[2] *The Principles of Mathematics*, p. 19n.

[3] *Ibid.*, p. 173n.

[4] *Contemporary British Philosophy*, p. 359.

points which some of his students – Wittgenstein in particular –
were quick to pick up.

The first published evidence for the relation between Russell
and Wittgenstein dates from the Lowell Lectures of 1914. In a
Preface, Russell acknowledged his debt to the "vitally important
discoveries, not yet published, by my friend, Mr. Ludwig Wittgenstein" later to be published as the *Tractatus* (1922). The
lectures were themselves published under the title, *Our Knowledge
of the External World*. The next published mention would seem
to be in the *Monist* articles of 1918–19. In 1918 Russell wrote,
introducing his philosophy of logical atomism, that the articles
setting it forth were "largely concerned with explaining certain
ideas which I learned from my friend and former pupil Ludwig
Wittgenstein". By 1922, the date of the publication of the
Tractatus Logico-Philosophicus, Russell was already able to
write one of those negatively critical introductions which is no
less negative for ending on an affirmative note. When Wittgenstein died in 1954 Russell wrote an obituary which is, to say the
least, less than completely flattering.

Russell's relations with Wittgenstein were complex indeed.
Russell in the course of time played the role of teacher, friend,
critic, disciple, and finally adversary. It is evident that each
learned from the other; but since the influence to other philosophers has spread out from Wittgenstein rather than from
Russell, in one direction at least, we shall follow the early
influence which Russell exerted on Wittgenstein.

The logic in some sense but not the realistic metaphysics was
transferred from Russell to Wittgenstein. The realistic metaphysics was transferred from Russell to Whitehead, presumably at
about the time when they were working together on the writing
of the *Principia*. Subsequently, Whitehead developed the metaphysics of realism into a comprehensive and systematic philosophy, which he called the philosophy of organism.

We shall be more concerned in this place to follow the influence of Russell on Wittgenstein. But before we do so, it might
be advisable to be clear about the metaphysical realism. When,
and how, did it become modified?

It may be best to start by distinguishing between metaphysical and epistemological realism. Many philosophers who

hold the one also hold the other, but not all. In particular, it is possible to hold epistemological realism without accepting metaphysical realism; the materialists, for example, do so. Russell at one time accepted both. He may have acquired epistemological realism first, for he finds it in Leibniz [1]. In 1900 the study of Leibniz was published, and in it Russell set up five premises, the fifth of which is that of epistemological realism. In Chapter X of *The Problems of Philosophy* already referred to, Russell avowed metaphysical realism. This was in 1912. Then somehow during this period the elements of a logical nominalism (though not, to be sure, under that name) crept into the picture, for they are there in the *Principia Mathematica* of 1910.

Let us look at the evidence to be found in the works on the foundations of mathematics. In *The Principles of Mathematics* of 1903 [2], there are already beginning to be signs. We learn there, for instance, that "although any symbolic treatment must work largely with class-concepts and intension, classes and extension are logically more fundamental for the principles of mathematics" [3]. There we do not find the axiom of reducibility and we do not find incomplete symbols, but we do find the theory of types [4]. But on the other hand, we do find that classes as things-in-themselves cannot be defined away. We learn that "though a term may cease to exist, it cannot cease to be; it is still an entity, which can be counted as *one*, and concerning which some propositions are true and others false" [5]. This is metaphysical realism. Epistemological realism is affirmed in the discussion of matter: "Complexity... is real in the sense that it has no dependence on the mind, but only upon the nature of the object. Where the mind can distinguish elements, there must *be* different elements to distinguish" [6]. Again, "whatever can be thought of has being, and its being is a precondition, not a result, of its being thought of" [7]. And the two: metaphysical

---

[1] *A Critical Exposition of the Philosophy of Leibniz* (Londen 1937, Allen and Unwin), p. 4.

[2] For the most part "written in 1900" – Introduction to the Second Edition (London 1937, Allen & Unwin), p. v.

[3] Chap. VI, 79.

[4] Appendix A, Sec. 492, and Appendix B *passim*.

[5] Chap. LIV, Sec. 443.

[6] *Principles of Mathematics*, Chap. LIII, Sec. 439.

[7] *Ibid.*, Chap. LI, Sec. 427.

and epistemological realism, come together in the distinction
between being and existence, where existence is asserted to
apply to only some beings [1]. Indeed, "the whole denial of the
reality of relations" is "rejected by the logic advocated in the
present work" [2]. This position is affirmed again at the end of the
book where Russell is warring with Mach for holding knowledge
down to what exists, to the exclusion of what may exist [3].

Somewhere between 1903 and 1910 logical atomism was added
to realism; what were its origins? It may well be that the atomism
was due to Leibniz and can be traced perhaps to the monads.
The logical part was learned from Frege.

Russell's full length study of Leibniz, published in 1910 [4],
shows the strength of influence which that thinker could have
exerted upon him. He must have spent considerable time
pondering the simple substances which were the monads. These
were units of force, a sensitivity and a dynamism imparted to
Democritus' atoms.

The influence of Frege dates at least from the acknowledgment
in the Lowell Lectures, already mentioned [5]. There he credits
Frege with "the first complete example" of "the logical-ana-
lytical method in philosophy", a sweeping claim. The acknowledgment to Frege had already been made earlier, in much the same
terms, in the Preface to the *Principia Mathematica:* "In all
questions of logical analysis, our chief debt is to Frege".

The philosophy of logical atomism endeavored to put together
Moore's consideration of language – perhaps it would be better
to say the implications of the *use* to which he put language –
Frege's logical analysis, and Leibniz' monads. Thus we arrive at
the elements of a system of philosophy. The system was never
constructed; what was set forth was more like the program for
its construction. A construction was not attempted until Wittgenstein undertook it in the *Tractatus,* and there in something
less than completely systematic fashion. What the program for
logical atomism suggested was to start by assuming a world of
atomic facts, and by naming these and combining the names to

---

[1] *Op. cit., loc. cit.*
[2] *Ibid.,* Chap. XIX, Sec. 157.
[3] *Ibid.,* Chap. LVIII, Sec. 469.
[4] *Philosophy of Leibniz,* Second Edition (London 1937, Allen & Unwin).
[5] *Our Knowledge of the External World,* Preface.

construct a logically perfect language which would adequately describe what exists without in any way, linguistic or otherwise, going beyond it.

But we are somewhat ahead of our story.

There were at least three publications of Russell's during the period of which we are speaking which commit him to realism of both the epistemological and metaphysical varieties. These are: *The Principles of Mathematics* (1903), lectures on "The Philosophy of Logical Atomism" delivered in 1918 and published in *The Monist* for 1918 and 1919, and an article entitled "Logical Atomism" published in *Contemporary British Philosophy*, First Series, ed. J. H. Muirhead (London 1925, Allen & Unwin).

The realism of the first of these titles is obvious and unqualified. Russell makes it plain in that work that he owes his realism to the German philosopher, Meinong. In the second and third titles mentioned, however, the situation is somewhat different. For now it becomes clear that Russell supposes he has got rid of realism and, for that matter, of all metaphysical considerations. In its place he has substituted fact and logic only: fact as the undeniable product of sense observation, and logic to deal with the fact.

We shall see that the situation is not so simple as he supposed. Indeed, it is not too much to assert that the subsequent difficulties encountered by his followers are due to the double and incompatible heritage which he left to them (and which, it might be added, he himself encountered along with them, since a later and different Russell became one of his own disciples and one of the heirs and interpreters of the Russell of this period). These incompatible elements were: first, an empirical turn, to which was added logic, and secondly, a metaphysical realism ostensibly disavowed but implicitly readmitted. Russell was too much of a mathematician and too much an admirer of experimental science to suppose that empiricism could be treated without mathematics. But mathematics took him further than that. Peano and Frege showed him that the logistic thesis was sound, that mathematics was an extension of logic. And so as a philosopher he was compelled to go back and admit logic. And by admitting a logic which seemed in a sense to be independent of fact, he admitted also its own metaphysical presuppositions, and these, oddly enough, proved to be those of realism.

For the most part, the metaphysical realism inherent in Russell's position has been neglected by his disciples. Wittgenstein seems not to have acknowledged it, and the disciples of Wittgenstein have gone far beyond him in the ferocity of their attack upon all metaphysics, in which metaphysical realism would of course be included. However, Russell exerted a strong influence also on his collaborator in the *Principia Mathematica* and may even have been responsible for turning him toward metaphysics. Whitehead, the mathematician, became after the collaboration, Whitehead the realistic metaphysician. His other disciples have taken no notice of this development and have by their silence disavowed it. Yet it exists all the same, a strong phenomenon demanding an accounting.

In the *Monist* articles of 1918 and 1919, Russell himself made a passing reference to the situation in which "a certain kind of logical doctrine" served as the basis for "a certain kind of metaphysics" [1]. And a little farther along in the same lecture he asserted that to think something true "is as near to truth as we seem able to get", a reference which at least implicitly admits the independent being – if not the ultimate knowability – of truth itself, a wholly metaphysical statement, and a realistic one, at that.

In the same lecture Russell credited Wittgenstein with making him aware that, while words could name facts, propositions were not names; for corresponding to every fact there were two propositions, one true and one false, and both propositions could not be names. In thus admitting that propositions, though they consist in the combination of terms which are names, are not themselves the names for anything but are governed by other considerations, such as the law of contradiction, Russell has admitted the being of two worlds: the world of fact and the world of propositions, the former detected by means of sensory observation and the latter by the rules of logic.

Russell's philosophy is and always has been founded upon an acceptance of the reality and objective independence of fact. Russell had devoted a considerable amount of time to the philosophy of Leibniz, and he no doubt saw a remarkable parallelism between the monads of Leibniz and the event-particles of

---

[1] Lecture I.

modern physics. To cope with the facts so conceived, a principle of abstraction of a special nature was needed.

Russell's principle of abstraction (also called "the principle which dispenses with abstraction"), runs as follows. "When a group of objects have that kind of similarity which we are inclined to attribute to possession of a common quality, the principle in question shows that membership of the group will serve all the purposes of the supposed common quality, and that therefore, unless some common quality is actually known, the group or class of similar objects may be used to replace the common quality, which need not be assumed to exist" [1].

It would be possible to argue that much hangs upon the phrase, "unless some common quality is actually known"; for if some quality is so known, then what is the case? And, further, how would that differ from the case of the attribution of a common quality where, say, the attribution either could prove successful or even did prove so? Would we be then any further from the obviously nominalistic goal of dispensing with classes to concentrate on its members, keeping them together, so to speak, without ever admitting the ground upon which this was being done?

Russell began the essay entitled "Logical Atomism" [2] by admitting that his philosophy is a species of realism, and then insisting that his realism is not inconsistent with such nominalistic doctrines as the principle which dispenses with abstraction [3].

It is true of course that in settling for the term "facts" and for the simplicity of the assertion that "the world contains facts", Russell overlooked many grave difficulties which have passed on to his followers and which have occasioned many ambiguities and weaknesses in their way of seeing the world. But it is equally true that he pointed to the importance of the statement that "facts belong to the objective world" [4], a statement which might have obviated a few of the confusions which have

---

[1] Bertrand Russell, *Our Knowledge of the External World* (New York 1929, Norton), pp. 44–5.
[2] In *Contemporary British Philosophy*, ed. by J. H. Muirhead (London 1924, Allen and Unwin).
[3] *Loc. cit.*, p. 363.
[4] *Op. cit.*

arisen in the work of Schlick and Carnap, for instance, as well as
Reichenbach and the others of the Vienna Circle, who have
never been sure whether, in their efforts to be as empirical as
possible, they were talking about the subjective effects of
experience or about the objective data revealed by experience.
Russell at the beginning of the game made it plain where his own
sympathies stood; but the Viennese positivists, being of the
German subjective variety after all, interpreted empiricism
subjectively, that is, after the manner of the philosophical
empirical theorists rather han the scientific empirical activists,
which is to say, after those who *interpreted* science rather than
those who *did* science. For it is a curious historical anomaly that
while the philosophers of the seventeenth and eighteenth centuries were interpreting scientific empiricism subjectively in
their theories, the scientists of the same period interpreted
scientific empiricism objectively in their practice.

As for the "propositions" of which Russell also spoke, there
will be some necessity for discussing them here. The topic will
come up again and at greater length in the exposition of the
philosophy of Wittgenstein. Wittgenstein was more cavalier
with regard to facts than his master, Russell, but he investigated
the logical properties of propositions more thoroughly, and lay
bare, even if he did not explicitly acknowledge, their metaphysical implications.

Several points, however, are interesting in themselves, and
the first perhaps is significant. In discussing the proposition as a
symbol Russell issued a warning. "Unless you are fairly aware
of the relation of the symbol to what it symbolizes, you will find
yourself attributing to the thing properties which only belong
to the symbol. That, of course, is especially likely in very abstract studies such as philosophical logic" [1]. So far, so good.
What we have here, clearly, is a nominalistic warning akin to
Occam's Razor. In the case of abstractions, the properties belong
to the symbol, i.e., to the language, and there seems to be no
abstract "thing" for them to belong to. But the curious situation
arises that before the sentence was finished Russell had reversed
himself. He went on "because the subject-matter that you are
supposed to be thinking of is so exceedingly difficult and elusive

[1] Lecture I.

that any person who has ever tried to think about it knows you
do not think about it except perhaps once in six months for
half a minute. The rest of the time you think about the symbols,
because they are tangible but the thing you are supposed to be
thinking about is fearfully difficult and one does not often
manage to think about it" [1]. This part of the passage is a realistic
warning, and reminds us that there are abstract objects corresponding to the abstract language which we use to refer to them,
and that we must not attribute to the language what belongs to
the objects. In the first part, in short, Russell said, do not
attribute to the objects what belongs to the language, as you are
prone to do in the case of abstractions; and in the second part he
added, do not attribute to the language what belongs to the
objects, as you are also prone to do in the case of abstractions.
His followers, except Whitehead, slipped into the habit of
heeding the first warning but not the second, and they do not
seem even aware that the situation described in the second
could possibly exist. For the second warning assumes that an
independent order of abstract objects exists, and this they cannot
admit even when in treating of logical propositions they behave
as though it did.

Russell himself gave them aid and comfort in the same
paragraph when he attacked the notions of "existence" and
"reality" which, he seems to have suggested, can be reduced to
the symbolism whereby they are expressed; they are, in other
words, nothing, for a symbol that does not refer to anything
except itself is not behaving as a symbol should. Here, too,
Russell set the pattern. Having himself in his earlier years been
influenced by Bradley, he cannot help later on thinking of
metaphysics in Bradley's fashion and of course through Bradley
in Hegel's, since Bradley was little more than an English gentle-
man's version of Hegel, as though there were no metaphysics
except the particular variety propounded by Hegel and Bradley.
Hence for Russell the reality of metaphysics means the reality
of discussions about the whole of reality, as though there were
no metaphysics in which the parts of reality were equally real.
Metaphysics, in other words, is by this stricture identified with
idealistic metaphysics, and accordingly disavowed, as it would

[1] *Op. cit.*

perforce have to be in any philosophy which adopted as its method the method of analysis. That there are metaphysical structures which provide for analysis, and indeed need it, has hardly been considered by Russell in this connection and certainly not by the members of his school, again of course excepting Whitehead. It is precisely a metaphysics like Whitehead's that Russell and his followers do not seem able to countenance. And the polite and perhaps scornful silence which the logical positivists and linguistic analysts maintain toward Whitehead speaks – literally – worlds.

The deeper we go into Russell's explanation of facts and propositions the more confused do we become. In his second lecture, for instance [1], we learn that a particular, such as the word, Piccadilly, as in the sentence, "Piccadilly is a pleasant street", can be reduced to a series of classes, no less so, evidently, because these classes are classes of material entities consisting in the things that occupy that particular street, and Russell then asserts that he "believes that series and classes are of the nature of logical fiction". But if the classes are logical fictions and particulars can be reduced to series or classes, then what is it that prevents fiction from being an all-inclusive term? How does it come about then that everything is not fiction? For evidently particulars can be analyzed into propositions and propositions being combinations of classes are simply combinations of fictions.

The answer to this puzzle is given us by Russell in his account of the nature of fact. A particular by itself is not a fact. "Socrates" the man is not a fact, for "Socrates" can be analyzed into a series of his experiences. "Socrates", we learn, is not a particular but a complicated system of classes or series. "However you may explain away the meaning of the word 'Socrates', you will still be left with the truth that the proposition 'Socrates is mortal' expresses a fact". A fact, then, is "that sort of thing that makes a proposition true or false", and a proposition, as we learned earlier, is a complex symbol expressing a fact and is either true or false about it. We have the distinct sensation that we are being taken round and round.

"The simplest imaginable facts are those which consist in the possession of a quality by some particular thing". A fact is not a

[1] Lecture II.

particular, then, but a relation between a quality and a particular, which is very complex. We cannot go below facts because their specificity under analysis dissolves either into generals or into complex situations. In philosophy, the particular is a *general* particular; that is to say, we can speak of particulars, but only in general. "We are not interested in particular particulars but only in general particulars". Particulars possess that self-subsistence that we formerly attributed to substance. The simplest facts, in the sense described above, are represented by what Russell called atomic propositions. Atomic facts, then, are the base-line, and when we talk about particulars we are dipping below it. "It is one of the tests of a logical proposition that you need not know anything whatsoever about the real world in order to understand it". Logic is not dependent on fact; but if it is not dependent, then it is independent; we shall need to remember this shortly.

When we take "an inventory of the world", we have to include particulars and positive facts. You would not have to include negative facts, and – strangely enough – you would not have to include propositions. That there are no negative facts [1] to render negative propositions true, is one more argument for the *logical* rather than the *factual* status of that which is referred to in some propositions, and hence for the independence of the logical status. Propositions must have a status independent of fact, and be real in the sense of being independent. Let us, however, listen to Russell himself on this theme. "If you were making an inventory of the world, propositions would not come in. Facts would, beliefs, wishes, wills, would, but propositions would not. They do not have being independently". Shade of Meinong, shade of Frege!

In the next lecture it becomes clear enough what Russell was trying to do. He was trying to save epistemological realism while dispensing with metaphysical realism. We learn there that facts are real items in the world, and are independent of us and of all our perceptions, but the natural world consists in only one storey. Admitting the reality of propositions and of the world of logic which they inhabit would mean admitting the reality of a two-storeyed natural world. The latter was what Meinong and

[1] Lecture III.

Frege advised and what Russell had accepted for a while and what he now wished to deny.

We shall see that he has already made such a denial impossible for himself, and that he continued to do so. Can metaphysical nominalism be combined with epistemological realism in Russell's way? Only by founding the system on particulars. But we have seen already that Russell did not wish to do this; he wished instead to found it on facts. This might have done very well had it not been for the definition, or at least the explanation, of fact: what Russell meant by a fact, you will remember, is "that sort of thing that makes a proposition true or false", for a proposition is a complex symbol expressing a fact and is either true or false about it. Propositions, then, are not real, only facts are real, and yet facts depend on propositions. Clearly, an inventory of the world which included facts in Russell's sense would also have to include propositions.

There were times in the course of giving the same lectures when Russell himself seemed to think so. Although he proclaimed that "in accordance with the sort of realistic bias that I should put into all study of metaphysics, I should always wish to be engaged in the investigation of some actual fact or sets of facts" [1], he managed to reverse himself very neatly, at least by implication, in the very next sentence: "In logic you are concerned with the forms of facts, with getting hold of the different sorts of facts, different *logical* sorts of facts, that there are in the world". That puts another face on it. There is no objection, except a terminological one, perhaps, for supposing that there are at least two sorts of facts in the world: facts, and logical facts. And clearly the logical sort of facts is not dependent upon the factual sort of facts, since we have already heard Russell say that "it is one of the tests of a logical proposition that you need not know anything whatsoever about the real world in order to understand it". And if the logical sort of facts, i.e. propositions, is not dependent upon the factual sort of facts, and, moreover, if we want so talk only about facts, then why do we – and this includes Russell chiefly, of course – why do we talk about propositions at all? If propositions are fictions and not elements of the real world, then for what reason are they brought up in the

[1] Lecture IV.

conversation? If otherwise we could not converse about fact, that ought to tell us something; it ought to tell us more than it seems consistently to have told Russell. And we could agree to call propositions logical facts were it not that Russell has already ruled propositions out of the world of real beings. Often, however, he seems not to want to; and so we cannot say where this leaves him. One thing is clear, and that is his confusion. He never deserts the cause of epistemological realism, but in the case of metaphysical realism he blows both hot and cold.

The desertion of metaphysical realism occasioned many difficulties, and Russell does not seem to have been aware of their source. If he has to fit everything into one natural world, the world of substance, or as he has agreed to call it in its new version, the world of fact, then there are some items which simply refuse to be fitted. It seems to be this sort of world that he was describing when he endeavored to describe "reality". He said that he meant by it "everything you would have to mention in a complete description of the world" [1]. Immediately, then, he raised the question of the status of a false proposition. In view of his earlier statement that a proposition was not a world-constituent, it is not surprising now to find him asserting that a false proposition is not one, either. Of course, we might under the correspondence theory assign a little more legitimacy to a true than to a false proposition, on the assumption that a true proposition did correspond to something in reality in his sense. He is correct, however, in assuming that the situation is somewhat more complicated than that, for what is a true proposition one day may be a false one the next: "Today is Tuesday" is such a proposition.

Then what are we to do with the status of propositions? We might apply Peirce's criterion of reality to them. Peirce meant by real whatever was external to him, offered some resistance to his will, and had an effect upon the real world. Propositions, including false propositions, are of such a nature. We cannot will them to be other than they are, and they do affect our actions. Moreover, they answer to their own laws, which we have come to recognize as the laws of logic. Therefore perhaps we should say that they are real. And if real, then where in reality do they

[1] Lecture IV, Sec. 2.

belong? Once again Russell is right in not wishing to suppose that this was a world in which false propositions went floating about along with other real things long acknowledged to be real, along with tables and chairs and metals and planets and people. Another kind of natural world is needed in order to house propositions, and we have a sort of second-storeyed natural world provided for them in the world of logic which always is but is not anywhere, a sort of Platonic world of forms, more inclusive than Plato's in containing also the forms of hair, mud and dirt which he excluded, and yet more restricted than his in being a world in which forms have to validate their presence by corresponding to something in the world of sense or else by being a non-contradictory tautology and thus belonging *in se* to the world of logic. False propositions correspond to something in the world of logic, as we shall see later when we come to examine the early work of Wittgenstein.

Russell ran into trouble on the very next page after his definition of reality when he attempted to deal with the reality of error. For error proved to be, like the false proposition, a homeless something which was not in the world yet which had to be dealt with in the world. "Every theory of error sooner or later wrecks itself by assuming the existence of the non-existent". But is it non-existent? An error may be believed, and if it is believed it most certainly is capable of having an effect, possibly even a disastrous one. The difficulty resides right there: in Russell's failure to recognize that belief is psychological rather than logical. The logic of the psychological does exist but its laws are empirical. We cannot make a sufficient examination of belief merely by the use of the "proper logical apparatus", as Russell calls on us to do [1]. Belief is the psychological holding of a proposition as true, and this would include false propositions as easily – and as firmly – as true ones. The study of the degrees of firmness in the holding of a proposition as true belongs to the science of psychology, or, like so much allegedly in psychology, to the science of neurophysiology. It does not belong to philosophy and certainly not to logic. The assumption that it does is a hold-over from the nineteenth century when logic was deemed part of psychology and logical laws part of the "laws of thought".

[1] Lecture IV, Sec. 3.

It is now known that philosophy, including logic, is no closer to – and no further from – psychology than any other science.

General propositions, propositions, that is to say, which can be true or false, do not involve existence. This much Russell saw [1], and he criticized Leibniz for having so much respect for Aristotle that he failed to see it. But Russell himself did not take the next step, which is to see that particular propositions when they occur as the conclusion of a syllogism, such as the syllogism in Darapti cited by Russell, need not involve existence, either.

> All chimeras are animals,
> And all chimeras breathe flame;
> Therefore some animals breathe flame,

does not leave us committed to the truth of the existential proposition, some animals breathe flame, so that we have as a result to believe that the existence of flame-breathing animals has been established. Just as we do not necessarily have to believe that all chimeras are animals, or that all chimeras breathe flame (although this second contention no doubt is true even if the first is false); so we do not have to believe, either, that some animals breathe flame; all that we do have to accept as the result of this proposition is a single hypothetical statement whose components are the three propositions: *if* all chimeras are animals, and *if* all chimeras breathe flame, *then* some animals breathe flame. The conclusion is true just in case the antecedents are true; and, even so, all that we mean by "truth" in this connection is class-inclusion and not class-membership. Those who challenge, as well as those who defend, the validity of the syllogism, have confused the relation of inclusion with that of membership. If the class of chimeras is included in the class of animals, and if the class of chimeras is included in the class of flame-breathers, then it must be that some members of the class of animals are also members of the class of flame-breathers. We do not have to assert the existence of members of a class any more than we do the class. The use of "some" rather than "all" does not have to involve us in substance, for we are in the one case as much as in the other manipulating terms in logic according to the rules of logic. A logical

[1] Lecture V.

particular is not necessarily an existential particular, although it
may be. But the point is that it does not *have* to be.

Aristotle, Leibniz and Russell are together in making that
mistake. But it is Russell with whom we are chiefly concerned,
because it was Russell who influenced Wittgenstein and their
followers. Russell said that "a proposition is nothing" [1], and he
continued to emphasize and insist on this contention, adding
also that "a propositional function is nothing" [2]. If this is the
case, one might ask, then how does it happen, as Russell said
earlier, that "the objective complexity of the world is mirrored
by the complexity of propositions"? If a proposition is nothing,
then it is a curious species of nothing, a species which mirrors
the world in some sense, which is capable of being either true or
false, and which, in Russell's own words, "like most of the things
one wants to talk about in logic, does not lose its importance
through that fact" [3]; in short, a very important kind of nothing!

Russell's dilemma here is clear: he wished to divide everything
between fact and logic or fact and propositions. Logic and
propositions are not facts, and there is nothing but fact; therefore they are nothing. He would have eliminated all his difficulties
and those of many of his followers if he had done what Whitehead
subsequently did, namely, assign a sort of status to logic akin to
that which Plato assigned to the forms. There is no such recourse
once you have adopted the principle that you will limit reality
to the facts of existence. You will stick to the principle, but you
will have qualms, especially when you see that you have interpreted reality too narrowly.

In the effort to discover "what there is in the world", which
Russell agreed is the task of philosophy, it is as much of a
mistake to interpret too narrowly as it is to interpret too broadly.
In the former case you omit so much that the search becomes if
not impossible at least hedged about with difficulties, and in the
latter case, you include so much that the search itself becomes
meaningless. Two instances of the narrowness, and of Russell's
encounter with it once he has set it up, occur. The first of these is
contained in the statement (it would have been better, perhaps,

[1] Lecture IV, Sec. 4.
[2] Lecture V.
[3] Lecture V.

if instead of "statement" we could have put "cry"), "there is no reason to suppose that the mental and the physical exhaust the whole universe" [1]. No, of course not; not, that is, provided the logical with its real propositions, including the false ones, is also admitted. The second of our two instances is a case in which Russell himself seems inclined to admit them, for he distinguished between falsehood and nonsense. "You can consider the proposition 'Unicorns exist' and can see that it is false. It is not nonsense".

Just when you think you have Russell safely categorized, just when you think he is a traditional nominalist in philosophy, he escapes from the category, and you have to begin again to find the proper place in which to fit him. He has been accused of changing his place with fitful frequency, but this is not the case. He has given a good account of the changes himself. He began in philosophy as an objective idealist, then he shifted under the influence of Meinong to realism. Then where did he go in 1918–19 with these *Monist* lectures, and where has he been since?

Not in conventional nominalism, certainly. It is possible to count no man a conventional nominalist who argues against crude physicalism, and speaks of "the belief in the physical world" as establishing "a sort of reign of terror", and of the physical world itself as "a sort of governing aristocracy, which has somehow managed to cause everything else to be treated with disrespect. That sort of attitude is unworthy of a philosopher" [2]. But if not conventional nominalism, what then? "I am inclined", he said, "to think that there are things that are not in time". And he gave as examples "an object like a function or a number, something which plainly does not have the property of being in time at all" [3]. The things which are not in time are mathematical things, logical things. Symbols, in that case, are not nothing; you talk about other things by means of symbols when you are using symbols *as* symbols, but you can also talk about the symbols themselves, and you could not do this if they were nothing [4].

And so it is also with propositions. We have learned earlier,

[1] Lecture IV, Sec. 4.
[2] Lecture VII.
[3] *Op. cit.*
[4] Lecture VI.

and we have been told repeatedly, that propositions are nothing. Propositions are combinations of symbols. But then they are not quite nothing, as it turns out. For "logical propositions might be interpreted as being about forms" [1]. At last, there we are! "Everything that is a proposition of logic has got to be in some sense or other like a tautology" [2]. Tautologies and the laws of logic are no less facts for being facts of another kind than the facts revealed to us by our sense experience; they are facts revealed to us by our abstract thoughts, and in both cases equally independent facts. Logical propositions are combinations of classes, and "the idea of forms is more fundamental than the idea of class"; moreover, "the form is a constituent, that propositions of a certain form are always true", and, Russell added, "that *may* be the right analysis, though I very much doubt whether it is". He managed to assuage his own doubts in the next lecture, however, for he observed that "you cannot have a constituent of a proposition which is nothing at all. Every constituent has got to be there as one of the things in the world" [3].

Russell in these lectures had a favorite term of endorsement, and it was "fact". We began, you remember, with atomic facts, but even with many sorts of atomic facts it soon developed that these were not enough of a set of boxes to make an inventory of the world. Russell drew a distinction, perhaps following Frege, between falsehood and nonsense. "Unicorns exist" *is* false, we are told, but it is not nonsense [4]. Another, and more significant difficulty showed up. In the effort to make an inventory of the world on the basis of facts, Russell ran into a difficulty with induction. It is possible to make a finite number of inductions until all the facts have been enumerated, but then you need at least one general proposition to the effect that these are all the facts that there are. You can say, "Socrates is mortal", "John is mortal", "Harry is mortal", and so on, until you have enumerated all the men there are, but even so you will not ever reach the proposition, "all men are mortal". Russell here ran into the rule that no number of particulars will add up to a universal,

[1] Lecture V.
[2] *Op. cit.*
[3] Lecture VI.
[4] Lecture V.

only this time stated in terms of facts and propositions. Thus at least one general proposition is needed to make a total or perfect induction, a proposition beginning with the term, "all"; and so we have one more piece of evidence for the reality of propositions, for if one is real others may be.

What we have learned in addition to the reality of at least one proposition is that empiricism rests on doubtful empirical grounds. In addition to asking questions about propositions, Russell has succeeded also in raising doubts about facts as a result of the point about cumulative inductions. Facts, as we learned earlier, are not particulars but the attribution of properties to particulars. But the particulars by themselves have no standing, and the properties of universals have none, either.

The last difficulty is one which Russell endeavored to resolve by establishing the existence of something he wished to call general facts [1]. We learn that "'x is a man' implies 'x is a mortal' is always true" is a fact [2]. At what point does it become plain that so-called general facts are merely general propositions which have been tested and seem true? There are general propositions other than logical tautologies. Tautological propositions are true because they can be reduced to identities; they are true, we say, by definition. Empirical propositions if sufficiently general are true until proven otherwise. It will continue to be accepted that "all men are mortal", say, until some man proves to be immortal. It is not a tautology, it is a general proposition well enough, but one whose truth rests simply on the fact that thus far no exception to it has been found. Thus there are in the world of logic a number of kinds of propositions, for all propositions belong in a sense to logic provided they are sufficiently general. Tautologies are general propositions whose truth is a matter of coherence, since it rests upon the consistency of the propositions. Empirical propositions are general propositions whose truth is a matter of correspondence, since it rests upon the agreement with fact. And it is empirical propositions which Russell has elected to call general facts.

In the assertion of the legitimacy of propositions, we see Russell's metaphysical realism reasserting itself. (His episte-

[1] Lecture V.
[2] Op. cit.

mological realism has never deserted him.) In the effort to get
the two natural orders of facts and propositions established,
Russell had to overstate his case somewhat. This is how he came
to assert that propositions are nothing, when he meant them to
be tautologies, and how he came to assert that existence is not a
property of things but only of definite descriptions [1]. We have
seen logic assume for Russell a reality beyond atomic fact, even
with his effort to divide it between tautology and general fact.
Our name for such a construction could perhaps be "logical
nominalism", and we could agree to so describe Russell's "logical
atomism", were it not that metaphysical realism keeps creeping
in. •

We see evidence for this, first off, in the distinction between
what he called "ambiguous description" and "definite description". "Ambiguous description" in his account got short shrift;
the emphasis was on the explanation of "definite description".
An "ambiguous description" by his example is "a man, a dog,
a pig, a Cabinet Minister" [2]. An "ambiguous description", then,
is a particular under a universal. A "definite description" is an
atomic fact. It is also an example of what he called later in the
lecture an "incomplete symbol". Incomplete symbols, like atomic
facts, do not stand for anything at all, "and that is the characteristic of incomplete symbols" [3]. The recognition of the ambiguity
of ambiguous descriptions involves a tacit acceptance of a sort of
excluded middle for particulars and universals. Call them atomic
facts and tautological propositions instead of particulars and
universals if you will, and it is still true that there is no middle
ground. In this direction, too, was the first application in these
lectures of the theory of types, where Russell asserted that
particulars and universals could not be the same in type [4].

Russell's theory of types was another, and more successful,
attempt to get rid of the middle ground. The paradox of the
class of all those classes that are not members of themselves,
disappears when we recognize that once again there is a confusion of class – membership with class – inclusion. That these are
both primitive and yet that neither is reducible to the other, has

[1] Lecture VI.
[2] Lecture VI.
[3] *Op. cit.*
[4] Lecture VII.

not been given sufficient attention. When you make a class a member of itself, you are considering a class to be a member of a class, whereas only particulars can be "members" of classes; classes cannot be "members" of other classes but classes can "include" other classes, which is an altogether different kind of relationship. The theory of types says, in effect, that particulars are of one type and the classes of which they are members are of another. We will call these first-order classes and consider them second types. Then we can have classes of second order, which include classes of first order. But second-order classes are of the same type as first-order classes in being classes. They are of a different order but not of a different type. Thus there are many orders which are orders of classes; but there are only two types: particulars and classes, and the distinction between them is drawn very strictly.

It is not hard to see now that we have been talking about old friends and considering two ontological levels; and this is no less so because we have decided to call them particulars and classes than if we had preferred the terms, particulars and universals, or facts and propositions, or facts and classes, or whatever. There is no doubt that while Russell dispensed with metaphysical realism he assumed it. For the reality of the two ontological levels, the level of facts (or of particulars), and the level of propositions (or of classes), and the inability to reduce the one to the other, while epistemologically considering both to be independent of our knowledge of them, is all that we mean by metaphysical realism. That he would have denied the subscription to metaphysical realism in 1919 as much as he probably would now, and that he would then have probably insisted upon the belief in logical nominalism, is not to the point. For it is as true of philosophers as of less professional folk that they do not know what philosophy they hold, only what philosophy they avow. And the two are not always the same.

It is no use that Russell in the summatory lecture of the series devoted to the exposition of logical atomism insisted still that classes were logical fictions [1]. For in the very next paragraph he admits to the existence of three kinds of ultimate simples: particulars, qualities and relations. If your inventory of the

[1] Lecture VIII.

world contains these three as elements, then you can see at once that you have a two-storeyed natural world: one level containing particulars, which answer to sense experience and resist action, and another which corresponds to feelings and thoughts. The particulars are brief-lived but stubborn, while the two kinds of universals (for that is what they are) are ephemeral yet indefinitely recurrent things. Corresponding to thoughts, feelings and actions, then, (but quite independent of them) there are: relations qualities and particulars, respectively. These are, if you like, classes of metaphysical entities, for that is what ultimate simples mean. The problem of deciding about this is "an extremely difficult one", for they are not empirically given in any simple sense. "By metaphysical entities I mean those things which are supposed to be part of the ultimate constituents of the world, but not to be the kind of thing that is ever empirically given", Russell wrote. Of course particulars and qualities and relations are empirically given, but what is not empirically given is that these are the ultimate simples or the metaphysical entities.

At the very end of his course of lectures, Russell pointed out that when problems are solved we call them science and while they remain unsolved we call them philosophy. This would seem to promise a very uncertain future for philosophy. In this Russell foresaw that as science augmented, philosophy would be diminished. However much the first part of his thesis is true, it does not support the truth of the second part; that is to say, turning over to science the solved problems will not diminish philosophy, and this is so for two reasons.

The first reason is that the problems are indefinitely many, perhaps infinite. If they are infinite, then removing some will not leave less and eventually none. If they are not infinite, at least the number is so very large that there can be little fear of running out of philosophical problems in the near future.

The second reason is that science removes some specific problems from philosophy but hands over to it many others. Science makes assumptions, it has a formal method, and it arrives at conclusions. Analyzing and abstracting the assumptions of science is one of the problems of philosophy, and it is a complex assignment indeed. Equally absorbing and difficult is the task of examining the logical structure of the method. The assumption and the method are the scientific invariants; the conclusions are changed from time to time, and so the task of interpreting the conclusions is an ever-pressing one. And no matter how large or how strong science grows, these tasks, and particularly the latter, must remain. This is an oversimplified picture of the relations between science and philosophy but at least it makes the point that philosophy has nothing to fear from science provided it does not surrender utterly to science and become itself paralyzed in the process. For if it does it will shirk its other obligations. Not all of philosophy is philosophy of science, not all knowledge is scientific knowledge. The arts, to name but one group, will never become sciences, and philosophy has a heavy obligation to them.

Russell gave up realism, but he did not forget it [1]. Meinong, who had influenced him toward realism in his earlier years, was now made responsible for a position which Russell found it necessary to combat. We might sympathize with him when he attacks Meinong's defense of self-evidence [2], but he also attacked him for making realistic distinctions, in particular, that between the thought, its content and the object [3]. Elements of realism, as a matter of fact, are still around in his thinking, and he has continued to combat it [4]. But even in the works in which he chooses to argue against realism he is still involved in it, and this is what in the main has saved him from becoming like his most abject followers or, worse, like the followers of his followers, an uncompromising though wholly unintentional subjectivist. For Russell at least has remained aware of the problem, and has fairly conceded to it what he felt must be done. For instance, he has admitted that he can get rid of any universal except similarity, which "cannot be explained away, like 'or' or 'not', as belonging only to speech" [5]. It appears, then, that, for Russell at least, "In a logical language... there will be *some* distinctions

---

[1] *The Philosophy of Bertrand Russell*, ed. P. A. Schilpp (Evanston, Ill., 1944, Northwestern University), II, 4.

[2] *The Analysis of Mind* (London 1951, Allen & Unwin), p. 262. The book was first published in 1921.

[3] *Ibid.*, pp. 16 and 164.

[4] *An Inquiry into Meaning and Truth* (New York 1940, Norton), p. 14; *Human Knowledge* (New York 1948, Simon & Schuster), p. 197.

[5] *An Inquiry into Meaning and Truth*, p. 434.

of parts of speech which correspond to objective distinctions" [1].

The refutations of all those arguments against realism which Russell has made from a logical standpoint are tempered by the fact that he himself has always left the door open. No conclusive argument against universals can be sustained so long as the reality of a universal as basic as similarity is admitted, for instance. When the later Russell argues against a position held by the earlier Russell, it is always possible to side with the younger man. Since the arguments on this score have been given elsewhere, they will not be repeated here [2]. But there is at least one other argument which ought to be considered, since it had seemed to Russell important for so many years. We find it stated in its first form in a book published in 1921. Behavioristic psychology, we are told, seems to support materialism, while the new physics seems to deny it [3]. The behaviorists "make psychology increasingly dependent on physiology and external observation, and tend to think of matter as something much more solid and indubitable than mind" [4]. As for the physicists, they have been making 'matter' less and less material. Their world consists of 'events', from which 'matter' is derived by a logical construction" [5].

Let us consider this contention for a moment. What is matter if not the static state of that which in the dynamic state we call events? Inversely, events are matter considered dynamically. The physicists in discovering the event-property of the stuff with which they are dealing – and it should be emphasized that they have made no serious alterations in the structure of their method which is still that of science, namely, the method of proceeding from "external observations" – are still materialists, for they continually assign static names to the entities whose processes are the events. We learn about protons, electrons, neutrons, positrons, and so on. These are entities, and hence materials, just as much as their tracks or their disintegrations can be called processes and hence events.

What the physicists make philosophically of their physics is

[1] Op. cit., loc. cit.
[2] Cf. The Philosophy of Bertrand Russell, ed. Schilpp, II, 4.
[3] The Analysis of Mind (London 1921, Allen & Unwin), p. 5.
[4] Op. cit., loc. cit.
[5] Op. cit., loc. cit.

philosophy and not physics, and has no more standing because it is the physicists who make it. They are as inept in philosophy as philosophers would be in physics. But this has already been pointed out by others [1].

A more subtle form of the same argument was advanced again by Russell in a work published in 1940. Nineteen years later, it is not behavioristic psychology, with its naive realism represented by materialism, which is contradicted by modern physics, but naive realism itself [2]. Russell's argument that naive realism leads to physics and that physics shows naive realism to be false, has been reduced to the following: historically, naive realism is the ancestor of physics, while logically physics implies the falsity of naive realism, from whose propositions taken as premises nothing at all follows [3].

Although as anxious as his followers are to take up a position in opposition to that of metaphysical realism, Russell has at least one advantage over them, for he considers his earlier philosophy more seriously than they do. Russell has had at least four positions. Starting with a brief venture into German idealism he became a metaphysical realist. This was exchanged for the logical nominalism he called logical atomism, and that has been modified by linguistic analysis, to exactly what extent, however, is not clear. His modern followers, the logical positivists, have chosen – mistakenly – his logical atomism.

If you wish to be a great philosopher, it is evidently necessary either to have one consistent position which is so ambiguously expressed that it lends itself to varying and diverse interpretations, or to have many positions which are successively expressed. In the latter case, those who follow an earlier position, like the realists in Russell's case, will say that the master once had hold of the truth but deserted it, that he flowered early and early declined; while those who follow a later position, like the logical positivists in Russell's case, will say that he made early mistakes but later corrected them and finally arrived at the truth. The realists will cite the Russell of *The Principles of Mathematics* of

[1] See especially C. E. M. Joad, *Philosophical Aspects of Modern Sciences* (New York 1932, Macmillan).

[2] *An Inquiry into Meaning and Truth*, p. 14.

[3] "Has Russell Proved Naive Realism Self-Contradictory?" by Hiram J. McLendon in *The Journal of Philosophy*, Vol. LIII (1956), p. 289.

1903, while the logical positivists cite – mistakenly – the lectures on logical atomism of 1918–1919. The question becomes, then, not 'who is validly to claim Russell?' but 'which philosophy is nearer the truth?' This issue will not be settled in this place. Suffice to say here only that the revolt against the realism of the early Russell, led by the later Russell and his followers, Wittgenstein and Wittgenstein's own followers (who can number among those who have fallen under their influence in turn, no less a one than Russell himself), has failed.

CHAPTER II

INFIDELITY TO REALISM

The decision to reprint *The Principles of Mathematics* after thirty-four years was a most fortunate one. The work has had a tremendous influence and should be available to all interested students of the subject. Here is a landmark in the history of thought which many persons have heard about but never seen, and now the new edition will place it before the public again. The importance of *The Principles* rests to some extent upon two of its points: it is the first comprehensive treatise on symbolic logic to be written in English; and it gives to that system of logic a realistic interpretation. It is with the second point chiefly that these remarks shall be concerned. Symbolic logic as a discipline is here to stay, whatever its philosophical interpretation; but the interpretation itself is still a doubtful question. Of course, the metaphysical interpretation of symbolic logic is not strictly a problem of logic, but lies on the borderline between logic and metaphysics. In all probability, it belongs to metaphysics, more particularly to the metaphysics of logic. But it is a most important topic for all that, and moreover constitutes a field in which much yet remains to be done.

Are the foundations of symbolic logic realistic or nominalistic? A reading of *The Principles* should be sufficient to convince any sceptical person of the explanatory usefulness of the realistic philosophy. The assumption that relations are real and non-mental, if not true, has at least a pragmatic value; and since the criterion of truth cannot be anything except self-consistency and range of applicability, realism must to a large extent be true. That must have been also Russell's opinion when he wrote *The Principles*. Since then he has altered his position sharply; for now in the new Introduction he challenges the validity of the philosophy underlying the work. He says, "Broadly speaking, I still think this book is in the right where it disagrees with what had been previously held, but where it agrees with older theories it is apt to be wrong. The changes in philosophy which seem to me to be called for are partly due to the technical advances of mathematical logic.... Broadly, the result is an outlook which is less Platonic, or less realist in the mediaeval sense of the word. How far it is possible to go in the direction of nominalism remains, to my mind, an unsolved question...." [1]. The present work takes issue with Russell on his new thesis, and is thus in the position of making out a case for an old book in order to defend it against the new rejection by its own author. In other words, the old Russell is to be defended against the new Russell.

Perhaps the simplest method of accomplishing this purpose would be to set forth all the arguments which have ever been advanced by anyone in favor of the truth of realism, and to refute all the arguments which have ever been used against it. But to attempt to defend realism in such a fashion would mean to become embroiled in a controversy which is most likely endless. There is another alternative. Russell puts forward certain specific and clear-cut objections to the validity of his former position. The simplest way would seem to be to show that these objections are groundless arguments, to demonstrate that his present reasons for acceding to the invalidity of his old work are themselves invalid. This will be the method adopted; and we shall take the arguments one by one in the order in which they are introduced.

The first attack upon realism consists in questioning the existence of logical constants. Russell asks, "Are there logical constants?" By logical constants are meant such expressions as "or", "and", "if-then", "1", "2", and so on. Russell says that "when we analyse the propositions in the written expression of which such symbols occur, we find that they have no constituents corresponding to the expressions in question" [2]. One way in which the refutation of an opponent's arguments can be made to seem the most effective is first to overstate his position for him. This way, his position appears to be self-evidently untenable and is ripe for ridicule. Where possible, Russell has done this for

---

[1] Bertrand Russell, *The Principles of Mathematics*, 2nd ed. (1938), p. xiv. All references, unless otherwise stated, will be to this work.
[2] P. ix.

himself by describing realism in a manner in which it is certain
he himself never accepted it, even when as realist he wrote down
The Principles. Selecting as typical of the logical constants the
term "or", he says, "not even the most ardent Platonist would
suppose that the perfect 'or' is laid up in heaven, and that the
'or's' here on earth are imperfect copies of the celestial arch-
type" [1]. Do there exist any longer realists who would be willing
to accept such a description of their belief? To confine the
realistic position to such an extreme version would be equivalent
to asserting of all nominalists that they are admitted solipsists,
which is very far from being the case. Even Russell has asserted
that the question of how far it is possible to go in the direction of
nominalism is as yet an unsolved one. Much the same defense
might be given for realism.

We can accept a modified realism without asserting the
existence of a realm of essence, or heaven, in which the perfect
actual things are stored in order to cast the shadows which we
mistake for them. Certainly there is no perfect "or" laid up
in heaven, but this does not establish nominalism or deny a
modified realism. From the position of modified realism, the
logical constant "or" is *logical* because it can neither be successfully contradicted nor shown to involve self-contradiction, and
is *a constant* because it involves a constant relationship. The
relation "or" is that of alternativity, which is a logical possibility,
an unchanging relationship which actual things *may* have (but
do not have to have) and which has being (since it *can* exist)
regardless of whether it exists at any special place and date or
not. Thus the reply to Russell on this point must be as follows.
The logical constant "or" is a symbol which occurs in some
propositions. When it occurs in true propositions and sometimes
when it occurs in partly true propositions, "or" has an objective
constituent, the constituent corresponding to the expression in
question being the relation of alternativity.

Russell next argues that the theory of descriptions, as it is
called in symbolic logic, dispenses with the actual particulars
which do service as the constituents of some logical terms. For
instance, he says that in "Scott is the author of *Waverley*" there
is no constituent corresponding to "the author of *Waverley*".

[1] P. ix.

The argument consists in an analysis of the proposition; and the analysis reduces the proposition to the following. "The propositional function 'x wrote *Waverley* is equivalent to *x is Scott*' is true for all values of x" [1]. Russell is correct in his assertion that this does away with the realm of Being of Meinong, in which the golden mountain and the round square have a place. The theory of descriptions does "avoid this and other difficulties", but does it refute realism? The evidence here would seem to be quite to the contrary. The task performed by the theory of descriptions is the elimination of all *specified* actual particulars as the constituents of terms in propositions, and the substitution of propositional functions. Now propositional functions are relations, possibilities which can be specified by actual particulars. These relations or possibilities certainly exist. The relation between the x who wrote *Waverley* and the x who is Scott – one of equivalence – is "true for all values of x", which is to say can be assigned constituents by assigning specific values for x, but holds whether or not specific values be assigned for x.

The theory of descriptions not only refutes the realm of essence but also happily points out the enormously wide gulf which yawns between realm-of-essence realism and modified realism, a gulf as wide as that between realism and nominalism. We do not have any actual golden mountains and round squares; hence the assertion of Meinong that they must exist in a realm of being is equivalent to the assertion not of realism but of crypto-materialism, which is a form of nominalism. Nothing exists really except actual physical particulars, or so asserts nominalism. But golden mountains and round squares *are* actual physical particulars: they are remote actual physical particulars, or so asserts crypto-materialism. The refutation of such contentions, accomplished logically by the theory of descriptions, argues for, rather than against, a modified realism, since it asserts that real existence means possibility of actualization, expressed in propositional functions.

Much the same argument as that employed above can be used to refute Russell's reasons for the abolition of classes. The cardinal numbers, Russell would persuade us, can be made to disappear in a cloud of propositional functions, and he accord-

[1] P. x.

ingly performs the trick [1]. The numbers 1 and 2 are resolved
into invariant relations holding between other invariant relations. The question is, have the numbers "entirely disappeared"?
As numbers they have, because numbers are not and never were
anything more than relations. Russell in his analysis has revealed
their true nature; but he has not caused the relations which
they essentially represent to disappear, nor has he given one
argument in refutation of realism thereby. Any argument to
show that specified things are not independent things but rather
things dependent upon invariant relations which they exemplify
can hardly be said to be an argument against realism. What are
invariant relations, what are propositional functions, if not
possibilities susceptible of actualization but never necessarily
demanding it in order to show their being?

The fact is that Russell has not "dissolved" any numbers nor
made them "disappear". He has merely shown them to be
invariant relations between variables. This is very far from
having disposed of their realistic character. Russell often talks
about logic and mathematics as though he had never heard
of any realism except the extreme realism which supposes that
the Platonic Ideas are laid up forever in a heavenly realm of
essence. Even Plato did not always believe this but sometimes
argued for a status of possibility for unactualized as well as for
actualized universals. Invariant relations, then, are what *can
happen* to variables, and numbers are real possibilities as are all
invariant relations which are non-contradictory.

Russell continues his argument against logical constants by
carrying it over to cover "points of space, instants of time, and
particles of matter, substituting for them logical constructions
composed of events" [2]. The substitution was made following
Professor Whitehead's suggestion. Russell is appearing to
present many arguments, whereas he is only presenting one.
This one is the repeated assertion that, since logical constants
prove to be relations, they are not fixed in the sense we once
thought they were. They are not fixed because they have no
constant reference; hence realism is untenable. The argument
is no more valid in the case of physical relations than it was in

[1] P. x.
[2] P. xi.

the strictly logical field. Space, time, and matter have been resolved into relations varying from frame of reference to frame of reference, but invariant given the frame. The important point to bear in mind is that they are relations instead of actual things, relations which can be exemplified by the actual things to which they refer but not requiring actual things or any specific reference in order to be. This is an argument in favor of realism, and decidedly not one against it.

Russell is taking for granted throughout his argument concerning the disappearance of logical constants a confusion between two distinct meanings of "reference". There is (1) the reference of a symbol to its logical possibility, and there is (2) the reference of a logical possibility to its actual exemplification. Russell refers to them both by the same expression, "having a constituent", which is a source of unutterable confusion. In order to show what we mean let us give an example. (1) The letters a-u-t-o-m-o-b-i-l-e form a symbol, namely "automobile", which may refer to the possibility of constructing a horseless carriage propelled by an internal combustion engine, assuming that there already were or were not any, in the sentence, "Let us build an automobile". (2) The letters a-u-t-o-m-o-b-i-l-e form a symbol, namely "automobile", which may refer to an actual physical object, assuming that there was at least one, as in the sentence, "This automobile runs well". The unfounded assumption that the refutation of the validity of meaning (2) also does away with the validity of meaning (1) accounts for most of the error responsible for Russell's change of viewpoint.

But perhaps there is more hidden beneath the surface of Russell's argument than we have been able thus far to grasp. A further quotation proves this to be the case. Russell goes on to say that "none of the raw material of the world has smooth logical properties, but whatever appears to have such properties is constructed artificially in order to have them". [1] This is only another way of saying that whenever there appears to be a one-to-one correspondence between logic and actuality it must have been faked. The argument runs that, since logic is ideal and actuality is not, logic cannot refer to anything actual. There is an assumption here which will not bear examination. Why

[1] P. xi.

cannot the part refer to the whole, the limited to the unlimited, the example to its exemplar, the actual to the ideal? Let us suppose that the fastest airplane would be one which could fly an infinite number of miles in zero seconds, yet we have to admit that, although no airplane flies that fast and probably none ever will, the airplane which flies four hundred miles per hour is nearer to the ideal than one which flies only one hundred and fifty miles per hour. The equivalence to four of two and two is tautological because that is what we mean by two and that is what we mean by four; yet this knowledge helps us to manipulate everything from apples to madonnas.

None of the raw material of the world needs to have smooth logical properties in order to be referred to by logic, so long as it is admissible for a cat to look at a king. Russell's charge that logic is an artificial construction, since nothing actual is ideal, also assumes the confusion which we have pointed out above in the example of the automobile, the confusion between two distinct levels of reference. Because Whitehead has persuaded Russell to substitute "logical constructions composed of events" for particles of space, time, and matter, Russell feels compelled to the further conclusion that logic is linguistic. This is the nominalistic view; the realist would say that language is logical. But then realism depends upon a careful segregation of the two levels of reference. Smooth logical properties are characteristic both of the tautologies of logic in language and thought, and of the possibilities to which they refer. Actuality exemplifies partially this logical possibility. For the raw material of the world to have smooth logical properties, there would have to be an identity between actuality and possibility, and this would be a signal that everything had happened that could happen. Until then, it is as much a requirement of actuality as it is of logic that the ideal contain more than the actual world.

It would appear that we have wandered a long way from our original point, but such is not the case. Having changed over from "points of space, instants of time, and particles of matter" to "logical constructions composed of events", Russell holds Whitehead responsible for his change from the realistic to the nominalistic interpretation of symbolic logic. But a careful inspection of Whitehead's own subsequent writings shows that

what Whitehead was endeavoring to do was to change Russell
over from a "substance" to a "relations" philosophy. In *Process
and Reality* Whitehead himself still finds "eternal objects" (i.e.
universals) consistent with the adoption of events. Whitehead's
"events" upon analysis reveal themselves to consist of invariant
relations, even the Platonic *receptacle* of simple spatio-temporal
location having gone by the board.

The statement, "Time consists of instants", is shown by
Russell to be false by means of an interpretation of time in
terms of comparatively contemporary events. But the argument
about the time statement is much the same as that we have given
above concerning the cardinal numbers (p. 35). To demonstrate
that an entity is analyzable into a process in terms of propositional functions does not invalidate its logically constant
nature as an entity. A logical constant should only be expected
to be *logically* constant, *not* actually constant as well. Time is
actually composed of instants, as anyone who has actually tried
to live by the clock can testify. Yet these instants resolve
themselves, like all other actual things, into logical events,
entities consisting of relations.

Russell's aversion to the view that realism is a valid metaphysical basis for symbolic logic rests chiefly upon the interpretation of the status of logical constants. Logical constants seem
to Russell to disappear between actual things (the reference of
language) on the one hand, and the formal properties of language
itself on the other [1]. Thus by arbitrary definition of terms he has
managed to argue himself out of realism. For language itself is
merely a shorthand method of formulating and communicating
the apprehension of ideas, and not anything in itself. It is safe
to assert that everything in language refers beyond itself. Russell
himself maintains that "it seems rash to hold that any word is
meaningless" [2]. Russell's error is the same one that we have
pointed out above (p. 36), and consists in assuming that there is
only one level of reference, a situation which automatically
precludes realism. The seeds of this confusion were already

---

[1] P. xi. The first sentence of the last paragraph reads, "Logical constants, if we
are able to say anything definite about them, must be treated as part of the language,
not as part of what the language speaks about".

[2] P. 71.

contained in *The Principles,*where Russell assigned the distinction between intension and extension to psychology [1].

Language has two kinds of reference: tautological propositions refer to possible things, whereas propositions about matters of fact refer to actual things. There is a third classification, and one that contains the greatest number of propositions: hypotheses, of which we do not know the exact reference, if any. Hypothetical propositions may be false, and therefore not existential propositions at all, or they may belong to tautologies or matters of fact. Thus the distinction between hypotheses and the other two kinds of propositions is a matter of ignorance (which is psychological and hence subjective), but the difference between tautologies and matters of fact, or between intension and extension, is a genuine objective difference. Now, Russell's error lies in the supposition that tautological propositions are exhausted by the language in which they are expressed and do not refer to anything objective. Thus he disproves realism by first assuming its denial. Logical constants, like all other logical terms, are part of what language expresses, expressed as part of the language. So long as tautological propositions are valid and have a reference, logical constants are emphatically *not* confined to the choice between referring to actual things and being merely verbal (i.e. having no reference at all).

"No proposition of logic", Russell goes on to say, "can mention any particular object". And he proceeds to show that the well known syllogism involving the mortality of Socrates is a special case of a wider and more abstract formulation. The point taken here seems to be quite correct: logic is ideal, and if actual things could be mentioned in ideal propositions, it would imply that actual things were ideal. There are, however, two dangerous fallacies lying in wait upon the outskirts of this argument. One is the conclusion that if logic is ideal and actuality is not, logic can have no reference to actuality at all. This would make of logic a kind of harmless but useless exercise or game, having no application to the real world. The point is that the Socrates syllogism is an *application* of logic. Logic, like mathematics, is ideal and does not refer to any specific actual thing, but it may be applied to any and all actual things. $2 + 2 = 4$ as a propo-

[1] P. 69.

sition in mathematics does not refer to shoes or ship or sealing wax, cabbages or kings, but it may be applied to any one of them. The fact is that the abstract syllogism does apply to Socrates, but the form of the argument expressed in the syllogism does not have to be a valid syllogism. The mortality of Socrates is contingent upon the agreement of the mortality of all men with established fact. When taken as so applying, the syllogism is an actual proposition and not a tautological one.

What Russell seems to be arguing against in this passage is the absoluteness of ideal possibles occurring as such in actuality. The dilemma is this. If actual things are made ideal, then logic does not seem to be a discipline akin to mathematics and independent of actuality. But if actual things have nothing logical about them, then ideal disciplines such as logic and mathematics belong to a remote realm of essence and bestow their reality only upon a world superior to our actual world. Thus, in protecting realism from the errors of extreme realism, Russell falls into the opposite extreme of nominalism. Logic in the form of "if-then" propositions is not stating anything about logical constants (by which Russell sometimes seems to mean ideal actuals). Neither Socrates nor mortality is asserted in the Socrates syllogism, but (granted the postulates) merely an invariant relation between them.

The question of contradictions is the final argument which Russell launches against his old position [1]. These are chiefly three: the mathematical, the logical, and the linguistic, and Russell offers an example of each [2]. It will be necessary, therefore, to confine our remarks to a few words about each of these specific contradictions as they are set forth in the Introduction.

Burali-Forti's contradiction rests on the assumption that N is the greatest of ordinals. But the number of all ordinals from 0 to N is N + 1, which is greater than N. Does the solution of this contradiction lie in the simple fact that 0 is not an ordinal number at all? Zero may be a cardinal but not an ordinal number. A symbol defined by "nothing" is perhaps required for the ordinal, corresponding to the cardinal, zero. For zero is not nothing; it represents the absence of *some*thing, namely, the

[1] P. xii.
[2] P. xiiif.

cardinal number before one. Zero enumerates but does not order.

The second contradiction may be stated in Russell's words: "We know from elementary arithmetic that the number of combinations of n things any number at a time is 2^n, i.e., that a class of n terms has 2^n sub-classes. We can prove that this proposition remains true when n is infinite. And Cantor proved that 2^n is always greater than n. Hence there can be no greater cardinal. Yet one would have supposed that the class containing everything would have the greatest possible number of terms. Since, however, the number of classes of things exceeds the number of things, clearly classes of things are not things" [1]. The key to this contradiction lies in the theory of sub-classes. Russell's proof that "classes of things are not things" rests on the argument that the last and most inclusive class is not a thing. But if there are sub-classes there may be sub-classes of sub-classes and so on, so that classes form a hierarchical series of inclusiveness, and everything may be a class to the things below and a thing only to the classes above. This would make every class a thing to the classes above (except the last class which would have no classes above it to make it a thing), and would make every thing a class to the things below (except the first thing, i.e. the actual unique thing, which would have no things below it to make it a class). Then there would be first (i.e. actual unique) things that were not a class, and there would be a last class that was not a thing. But all other classes of things would be things.

The third contradiction is linguistic, and, as Russell himself suggests, following Ramsey, linguistic contradictions can be solved by broad linguistic considerations, and lead to the so-called theory of types. The theory of types is a more detailed formula for which de Morgan's "universe of discourse" had already warned us we should have need. But even the theory of types must be applied judiciously. For instance, Russell wants to apply it to show that classes of things are not things. What should be asserted is that classes are not things in their relation to things but are things in their relation to more inclusive classes. He is correct, however, in asserting that the relations of

[1] P. xiii.

a thing are not the relations of the class of which that thing is a member.

The fundamental realism of Russell hardly needs to be insisted upon at the last. Russell, as his own remarks betray, is a realist. However, it may be illuminating to show by chapter and verse what a profound realist he was, and perhaps still is. Let us run through *The Principles* for examples of realism. We shall not take the main categories of the work as evidence (although many of them are), but rather be on the lookout for more subtle remarks, on the grounds that the presence of realism in the assumptions will betray itself more clearly in observations and turns of thought, which could only have been implied by an unacknowledged though none the less real and effective fundamentally realistic viewpoint, than it would in more candid expressions.

The symbolic representativeness of words is the first indication we come across in our search. Russell said, *"Words* all have meaning, in the simple sense that they are symbols which stand for something other than themselves" [1]. Surely, Russell does not mean here that words always refer to *actual* objects. The inference clearly is that the reference of *some* words, at least, is to possible objects. Another instance is the wholly realistic "distinction between a class containing only one member, and the one member which it contains" [2]. The necessity for the viability of such a distinction is highly indicative of a fundamental position. In the same direction is the warning to beware of the extremely narrow limits of the doctrine that that analysis is falsification. The whole may be more than its parts, he pointed out, but they are real parts. And, although analysis cannot give us the whole truth, it can give us truth [3]. "Where the mind can distinguish elements, there must *be* different elements to distinguish; though, alas! there are often different elements which the mind does not distinguish" [4]. But just as analytic elements are real, so are the synthetic wholes, or complexities. "All complexity is .... real in the sense that it has no dependence upon the mind, but only upon the nature of the object" [5]. Since

[1] P. 47.
[2] P. 130.
[3] P. 141.
[4] P. 466.
[5] *Ibid.*

the "complexities" referred to are not only meant to be those of actual objects, possible organizations alone can be intended. "... the whole denial of the ultimate reality of relations" is "rejected by the logic advocated by the present work" [1]. These are plain words; and the feeling is unavoidable that Russell meant them. Order is reducible neither to psychology nor to Omnipotence itself [2]. Relations, and not terms, are necessary to order [3]. In a brilliant anticipation of modern macroscopic physics, Russell even went so far as to indicate the relational analysis of matter. Since "the only relevant function of a material point is to establish a correlation between all moments of time and some points of space" [4], it follows that "we may replace a material point by a many-one relation" [5]. The coupling of such a denial of actuality with the rejection of psychology already mentioned leaves nothing but the reality of a realm of possibility to be intended. This interpretation is confirmed by the assertion that "though a term may cease to exist, it cannot cease to be; it is still an entity, which can be counted as *one*, and concerning which some propositions are true and others false" [6].

As if in support of such a realistic thesis, Russell goes even farther than this in *The Principles*, in a definition of being. He says, "Being is that which belongs to every conceivable term, to every possible object of thought – in short to everything that can possibly occur in any proposition, true or false, and to all such propositions themselves. Being belongs to whatever can be counted.... Numbers, the Homeric gods, relations, chimeras and four-dimensional spaces all have being, for if they were not entities of a kind, we could make no propositions about them. Thus being is a general attribute of everything, and to mention anything is to show that it is" [7]. The entities of mathematics have being and truth, since "mathematics is throughout indifferent to the question whether its entities exist" [8], and "what

---

[1] P. 166.
[2] P. 242.
[3] *Ibid.*
[4] P. 468.
[5] *Ibid.*
[6] P. 471.
[7] P. 449.
[8] P. 458.

can be mathematically demonstrated is true" [1]. Furthermore, propositions that are true are immutably true: "there seems to be no true proposition of which there is any sense in saying that it might have been false. One might as well say that redness might have been a taste and not a colour. What is true, is true; what is false, is false; and concerning fundamentals, there is nothing more to be said" [2]. But a true proposition is one which makes an assertion about that to which it refers. There is no difference between a true proposition and an asserted proposition [3]. Thus mathematically demonstrated propositions are likewise assertions. But pure mathematics, such as geometry, is likewise "indifferent to the question whether there exists (in the strict sense) such entities as its premises define" [4]. What else could such non-existential propositions, as those of geometry, assert, except a realm of possibility, of potential being? Since mathematics is "merely a complication" of logic, the primitive ideas of mathematics being those of logic [5], logic must share the non-existential reference which has been asserted by mathematics.

As a realist (and there can be little doubt that Russell was a realist when he wrote *The Principles*) he was opposed to the earlier positivists, particularly to Mach and Lotze. In the course of his opposition, it is clearly revealed that some of the doctrines of these modern nominalists, the logical positivists, are alien to his position in *The Principles*, since positivism in certain respects remains what it was.

For instance, against Mach's argument of the actual world being only what we find it, "any argument that the rotation of the earth could be inferred *if* there were no heavenly bodies is futile. This argument contains the very essence of empiricism, in a sense in which empiricism is radically opposed to the philosophy advocated in the present work" [6]. The philosophy advocated is "in all its chief features" derived from G. E. Moore [7], and the G. E. Moore of 1902 was certainly a realist. Russell did in fact see quite clearly what the issue was. "The

[1] P. 338.
[2] P. 454.
[3] P. 504.
[4] P. 372.
[5] P. 429.
[6] P. 492.
[7] P. xviii.

logical basis of the argument [i.e., the one stated above concerning the rotation of the earth] is that all propositions are
essentially concerned with actual existents, not with entities
which may or may not exist" [1]. And on this argument, Russell
had already stated his own position definitively, as we have seen.

The fate of Lotze in Russell's work is no better than that of
Mach. Mach had confined reality to actuality; Lotze, so far as
Russell was concerned, repeated the same error in other terms,
for, after Leibniz, he had defined being as activity [2]. Russell
refutes this definition by showing that if activity alone were real,
only valid propositions would have being, since these and these
alone would refer to active objects. But since false propositions
which have no reference still have being, "being belongs to valid
and invalid propositions alike" [3]. Again, the Kantianism of
supposing that propositions which are true are so because the
mind cannot help but believe them, is an error due to the failure
to make the "fundamental distinction between an idea and its
objects" [4]. "Whatever can be thought of has being, and its
being is a pre-condition, not a result, of its being thought of" [5].
Thus Russell has, in his refutation of Lotze, rejected nominalism
on two scores. He has rejected that objective form of nominalism
which consists in holding that actuality alone is real, and he has
rejected that subjective form which consists in holding that what
the mind knows is real in virtue of being known.

Even now, although he has gone a little way with the logical
positivists, he finds himself unable to go the whole way [6]. He
is unable, for example, to accept the wholly linguistic interpretation of logic as that doctrine is advanced by Carnap. In
rejecting Carnap's two logical languages as being too arbitrary,
Russell says that "all propositions which are true in virtue of
their form ought to be included in any adequate logic" [7]. Indeed,
the premises of the realism which we have just succeeded in
tracing in a number of passages from *The Principles* are in
direct contradiction with the whole set of basic tenets set forth

[1] P. 493.
[2] P. 450.
[3] *Ibid.*
[4] *Ibid.*
[5] P. 451.
[6] P. xii, second paragraph.
[7] P. xii.

by the modern school of logical positivists. For instance, against
the notion that complexity as well as analytical elements are
real [1], Carnap maintains that the question of reality concerns
the parts of a system that cannot concern the system itself [2].
Carnap admits for the logical positivists a following of empiricism[3],
that same brand of empiricism which Russell has explicitly
rejected [4]. As for Bridgman, he seems guilty of an extreme case
of the same error which afflicted Lotze, and thus would have to
fall under the same ban of the Russell who wrote *The Principles*.
Lotze made being into activity [5]; Bridgman narrows activity
down to a matter of only a certain kind of activity, namely,
operations [6]. Lotze's second point: the Kantian view that those
propositions are true which the mind cannot help but believe [7],
seems also to be held by Bridgman, who maintains that "our
thinking mechanism essentially colours any picture that we can
form of nature" [8]. And finally, the Russell who derived his
philosophy "in all its chief features" from the metaphysical
realism of the early G. E. Moore [9] could hardly agree with the
view of Wittgenstein that "philosophical matters are not false
but senseless" [10], or with Carnap that metaphysics is expressive
but not assertive [11], and that metaphysics is equivalent only to
mud [12]. It is questionable whether any mind who had understood
realism so deeply and embraced it so wholeheartedly could ever
change his position, no matter how much he wanted to. Despite
Russell's rejection of realism and avowal of nominalism, he is not
a nominalist but a realist, and it is the apparently insuperable
logical difficulties standing in the path of a realistic interpretation of symbolic logic which shake his faith. In other words, he
has not changed his early philosophy; he has merely become
uncertain about the prospects of defending it.

[1] P. 42, above.
[2] Rudolf Carnap, *Philosophy and Logical Syntax* (London 1935, Kegan Paul), p. 20.
[3] Rudolf Carnap, *The Unity of Science* (London 1934, Kegan Paul), pp. 27–28.
[4] P. 44, above.
[5] P. 45, above.
[6] P. W. Bridgman, *The Logic of Modern Physics* (New York 1928, Macmillan), p. 5.
[7] P. 45, above.
[8] P. W. Bridgman, *The Logic of Modern Physics*, p. xi.
[9] P. 44, above.
[10] Ludwig Wittgenstein, *Tractatus Logico-Philosophicus* (London 1933, Kegan Paul)
4.003.
[11] Rudolf Carnap, *Philosophy and Logical Syntax*, p. 29.
[12] Rudolf Carnap, *Philosophy and Logical Syntax*, p. 96.

This situation presents quite another kind of problem. We do not have any longer to pursue specifically logical answers to paradoxes; we have merely to convince Russell that there are some difficulties with *any* metaphysical interpretation of symbolic logic. Whether these difficulties can be ironed out by an appeal to symbolic logic itself, as Russell suggests [1], is debatable. It is not easy to see how an empirical fact can conclusively choose its own metaphysical interpretation. Relativity theory in physics seems to demonstrate for the materialists that all is material; it seems to the realists to show that all is resolvable into relations; and it seems to be an argument that the subjectivists can advance in favor of their own mentalism; and so on. Metaphysics is assuredly a world situation, and, although not arbitrary, it is at least broader than any limited empirical situation and thus not determinable in terms of the limited situation. If a metaphysical interpretation had no necessary implications to situations other than the one whose metaphysical nature was being investigated, it is likely that each situation would suggest its own. But metaphysics represents a system of universal implications in which non-contradiction is one of the essential features. Hence, where one empirical fact "seems to suggest" one broad interpretation and another another, we must conclude that at least one of the empirical facts is giving misleading suggestions.

Russell finds himself, before he has done, driven back to an immutable if as yet unknown truth. He is unwilling to accept the veiled subjectivism of the logical positivists' linguistic interpretation of logical truth. Axioms are not arbitrary, as Carnap would have them; they "either do, or do not, have the characteristics of formal truth...." [2]. To discover whether they do or do not have these characteristics may be a difficult task indefinitely prolonged; but when we have admitted that the question is not arbitrary we have already admitted that there is such a thing as absolute truth, the knowledge of which we seek to approximate in our limited formulations.

[1] P. xiv.
[2] P. xii.

PART TWO

A COMMENTARY TO WITTGENSTEIN'S
TRACTATUS

CHAPTER III

INTRODUCTION TO THE COMMENTARY

This Part has two themes: in the first place it purports to set forth an explanation of Wittgenstein's work to guide those who wish to read it, and, in the second place, it seeks to defend him against his followers, on the plea that never before has a man's work been responded to by such an immediate and enthusiastic set of partial deductions and misrepresentations. His followers adhere to his announced views in a way that in his own writings he did not; they defend him in ways in which he would not wish to be defended; and lastly, and perhaps most damagingly, they claim him in a way in which it is doubtful whether he would wish to be claimed. But whether he would wish to be so claimed or not is, for some purposes, irrelevant; we do not have Wittgenstein with us any more but we do have his work, and the meaning of his work is an open question.

It is clear that the *Tractatus* is a kind of commentary on Whitehead's and Russell's *Principia Mathematica*; both the similarity of the numbering system and the frequent references to Russell – his *Principles of Mathematics* as well as the *Principia* – would indicate this. The range of possible natures of commentaries, however, has to be considered. One could write, for instance, an extreme sort of commentary in which one would attempt to do nothing more than praise a book, and perhaps somewhat extend and elucidate it. At the other extreme one could regard the book as merely a take-off point from which to write a new book, and in this way derive a wholly new set of ideas. If we had to place Wittgenstein's *Tractatus* on this spectrum, we should put it near those commentaries which use the book to be commented on as a take-off point, for Wittgenstein had a new set of ideas – ideas not to be found in the *Principia Mathematica*. His was an original contribution.

How the present work should be classified is another question.

Perhaps it would be possible to say that it is also a new work, since it purports to elicit many ideas from the *Tractatus*, but the elicitations, as his most fervent followers would be the first to insist, are not what he intended, and therefore they are non-Wittgensteinian ideas.

All of this is, of course, debatable. Whether or not it is possible to find in a man's book ideas which he did not pretend to put there, is also debatable. The question is: are they or are they not there, not how did they get there. We must draw here a sharp distinction between a man and his work; he did not build better than he knew if the outcome is not somewhat other than he planned. Wittgenstein would have been the first to insist that words and sentences mean whatever they do mean, and not necessarily what their author intended them to mean; they have a stubbornness, an inflexibility and a meaning of their own which cannot be subverted however much one might try. If Wittgenstein did use the words he did use, and if he did not mean what the words mean, that is not our fault for we have only the words.

The following pages, then, contain one interpretation of Wittgenstein's *Tractatus*. It is made from a definite point of view, and assumes that other points of view are possible. Until it is known which one is correct (if this could ever happen), it will have to be assumed that all are equally legitimate. It differs from the interpretations made by the logical positivists in regard to the admission of metaphysics; this will emerge more clearly in the Conclusions from the Commentary.

We have looked in the first part of this work at some of Russell's writings dating from the period when Wittgenstein was his pupil and when they were, by Russell's own admission, influencing each other [1]. Russell, as we noted, had supposed that he had worked his way out of metaphysical realism, and had employed an epistemological realism to set up a philosophy which he called the philosophy of logical atomism. It is difficult to make a distinct separation between the Wittgenstein and the Russell of this period. Earlier, Russell had been a metaphysical realist, but he had abandoned that position by the time he encountered Wittgenstein. Wittgenstein later became a meta-

[1] See the brief obituary notice by Russell in *Mind*, Vol. LX (1951), pp. 297–8.

physical realist heavily overlaid with the interpretation afforded by linguistic analysis, so he changed, too. But at the time, which was approximately during the second decade of the twentieth century, they were no doubt very close in their views. Russell acknowledged the influence of Wittgenstein in several places in the 1918 lectures on logical atomism. Wittgenstein might not have written the *Tractatus* had Russell not given the lectures on logical atomism, or at least had he not maintained the views there expressed. Certainly it is true in a very large sense that the *Tractatus* may be interpreted as a commentary on the 1918 lectures of Russell. Wittgenstein certainly did not hear them but, as Russell said, the topics were discussed together; and the debt of the *Tractatus* to the views of the contents of the lectures is obvious. Since Wittgenstein was the pupil and Russell the teacher, we may assume, despite the mutual influence, that the greater effect was Russell's.

There is no space in which to go into a thorough analysis of the predecessors of Wittgenstein and of the influences upon him. In addition, there is not sufficient data. One clue, however, we are given. One of his friends has informed us that Wittgenstein "did read and enjoy Plato" and "recognized congenial features" in his philosophical method [1], although, to be sure, Wittgenstein is not said to have been a great reader of philosophy. If, then, we discover in Wittgenstein's work traces of metaphysical realism, this is not so foolish as it may sound to some who are steeped in the nominalism of his followers.

Other influences were no doubt at work. Through Russell must have come the philosophy of Meinong as well as the work of that whole tradition of British realists, from Reid through Cook Wilson to Russell. Also, there was the influence of Gottlob Frege to whom Wittgenstein frequently refers in the *Tractatus*, a logician with realistic metaphysical leanings. G. E. Moore must have exerted considerable influence, though it does not emerge until later. Anyone who was familiar with Moore's method in lectures as well as his writings could hardly fail to see how strongly Wittgenstein was affected by him, especially in the *Philosophical Investigations*. Moore's effect upon Wittgenstein was slow in making itself felt but heavy when it finally arrived.

[1] G. H. von Wright, in the *Philosophical Review*, Vol. LXIV (1955), pp. 543–4.

Wittgenstein's metaphysical realism consists in the following situations: (1) there is logic and it operates in the field of possibilities; (2) there are facts and they exist in the field of actualities; and (3) there is language and this consists of propositions in the logical language which at the same time are derived from facts.

The logic precedes all experience; that is to say, it is *a priori*, epistemologically speaking, and has an independent status, therefore, ontologically speaking, and so, in a way, have the facts: we come upon the facts and we come upon the logic – we discover both, they were always there.

We might have noted from the atomic facts and the logical propositions of Russell's 1918 lectures what to expect in the *Tractatus*, given the influence of Russell on Wittgenstein. The elements as they are employed in the *Tractatus* are: facts and their logic, and the problem is to build a separate world of logic by deriving it from fact by means of language and then relating it to fact, thus providing the explanatory power of a two-storeyed natural world. Thus he undertook a construction allowing himself two items only, two tools with which to work on his representation: first, the empiric world, and, secondly, logic. Working only with fact he proposed to elicit a logic to represent the fact, where by logic is to be understood a logical language, a language containing all and only logic. He proposed that this logical language would represent the world; logic would be shown to exist in a world of logical space and fact in a world of substance; both were to be finite, both were limited, and both considered as being only in the present. Curiously enough, then, the properties of his two worlds, fact and logic, begin to be attributed to each other; that is to say, after we get well into the system of exposition which the *Tractatus* sets forth, we begin to see that what he has set up is a substantial world of logic and a logical world of fact! One problem to be examined then is the following: Can logic completely represent the world?

Wittgenstein's whole structure rests on facts, not on objects. Facts for him are not simple, they are combinations of objects. They are limited in number, limited in themselves, and fixed in a motionless present of space and time: they are finite and here-now. Also, they contain a logic of their own which can be derived from them. When this logic is derived and established on its own ground, we discover that it, too, is limited and flat, a set of elementary propositions to which combinations of the elementary propositions can be reduced. All logical operations are in a sense therefore illusions, they give us nothing new. Thus we find that he is dealing with the relations between facts which are not the ultimate units of the actual world and elementary propositions which are not the ultimate units of the logical world.

One big general point to be understood is that Wittgenstein was endeavoring to follow the scientific method as it is practiced in the experimental sciences; only, where in the experimental sciences the method is complex and the subject-matter, too, Wittgenstein was trying to undercut these by giving a rather primitive version. No one else has ever tried to show a sort of primitive logic and a primitive fact and how they operate as the structure within the experimental method of science. Those who have tried to isolate and abstract the logical structure of the scientific methodology have done so at a somewhat advanced level, but it is the business of philosophy always to become as primitive as possible in order to find out just what is involved.

Wittgenstein's method was to present his philosophy in a series of numbered propositions whose relations are indicated by the numbering. The points he makes do not lie very close together so the reader has to connect them himself, and the connection makes a kind of emotional contact for him. When points are very close together, the transition is simple and the points almost make themselves; but when the points are very far apart, the jump between them involves some emotional effort and the result is dramatic and vivid and the system itself comes alive, much as though electric poles were placed so far apart that the jump of electricity between the poles becomes like a flash of lightning. Thus the *Tractatus* is presented in the form of propositions which lie some distance from each other, and it is in the ambiguity of the interstices that one is able to read one's own Wittgenstein. It is in this sense a *gestalt* or a projective technique.

Wittgenstein's view seems to be a mystical view of logic rather than the usual logical view of mysticism. Affective elements creep in through the very mechanism by means of which they were intended to be excluded − if indeed they were so intended.

Wittgenstein has managed an oracular presentation of a system by means of an imaginative logic.

One last but important point. It is clear from a reading of the entire *Tracatus* that Wittgenstein presupposed in it a metaphysics but he did not say it or allow it to be said (indeed in the *Tractatus* itself metaphysics is explicitly excluded). In this way, perhaps, he has managed to avoid the double postulate problem and the infinite regress, for every metaphysics which is explicitly stated has a set of presuppositions amounting to an anterior metaphysics, and if the anterior metaphysics also has a set of presuppositions then this opens up the prospect of an infinite regress of metaphysical presuppositions. Wittgenstein has at least given the appearance of avoiding this difficulty by a rather subtle though perhaps unintentional method of ruling out all explicit metaphysics. His metaphysics, then, is that of logical empiricism.

With these preliminaries, then, we shall proceed to comment on the propositions of the *Tractatus* themselves. The comments will be given the same numbers as the propositions. In the following comments on the propositions of the *Tractatus*, Wittgenstein's propositions have not been repeated; therefore, to read the comments properly, it will be necessary to have a copy of the *Tractatus* at hand. The suggested procedure is to read the propositions of the *Tractatus* first and afterwards the comments.

CHAPTER IV

A COMMENTARY TO THE *TRACTATUS LOGICO-PHILOSOPHICUS*

[1]   A statement of nominalism. We are going to be talking about the factual, the actual, and perhaps even the barely physical world. The world includes also the *recital* of what is the case. The *Tractatus* does not express an old-fashioned nominalism but a nominalism plus logic; without logic no nominalism could be said, but it is still a nominalism because the sole reality is one of physical particulars which already contains its logic.

[1.1]   This is a heavily loaded ship and Wittgenstein wishes to get it off the ground as fast as possible, so the world which is the case is not to be a world of things but of facts, and facts are about the world. We shall shortly see how.

[1.11]   The world is finite and consists in a discrete number of facts, thus the facts are finite in number also. This is another version of Russell's point that in addition to the inductive enumeration of instances we should need at least one general proposition to the effect that these are all the instances.

[1.12]   We have now logic added to fact, and we have it added in a peculiarly traditional way. Compare Spinoza's second definition "that thing is called finite in its own kind which can be limited by another thing of the same nature". Compare also H. M. Sheffer's stroke function: neither x nor y. We now have both fact and logic. The world of fact already contains logic.

[1.13]   Then there is logical space as well as world-space, a space for logical elements as well as the usual one for facts. Much in what follows will hang on this. And where are facts? In the world or in logical space? In world-space; but what we say about them is in logical space.

[1.2]   Discreteness theorem.

There are levels below facts: there are things, particulars. But not for the world so far as we are concerned. Our world will begin at facts. This is arbitrary, and a strict following of Russell. Philosophy never is allowed to get down to particulars, it starts well above the surface at facts, and that is its world.

[1.21]   The facts of the world are discrete and they can be arranged, combined and recombined, without disturbing anything except those under a combination. It is a world of movable pieces with space between them, so that the movement of one, or the exchange of two, does not disturb the others. The road which Wittgenstein proposed to examine is constructed in such a way that logic can deal with it and logic alone is adequate to deal with it.

[2.01]   Here is the promised definition of a fact: it is to be called atomic fact, and consists in a *combination* of objects and we have given to us as synonyms also objects, entities, things. It is clear now that we are not going to talk *about* particular objects but only say that there *are* particular objects.

The reason why we need a combination of objects in an atomic fact is that when we go to name an atomic fact we discover that our names are classes, for we cannot name an individual in any logical system of language if we name only individuals; we need to name also the similarities between individuals, which is how we obtain classes, and for this we need two objects in order to discover their similarity and to name it.

Here, perhaps, is the crux of all significance in the philosophy of logical atomism. What is an atomic fact? It is not a thing but a combination of things, we are told. In Russell's 1918 lectures he shows (a) that combinations of things are classes, and (b) that there are more classes than things. If this is so, and that it is so is reinforced by the discovery that we can never describe a particular except in general, we can only name it and then only in its presence. Then in philosophy we never do get right down to the world which is everything that is the case, we are always suspended by the limitations of our language at some distance above it, and as a result always in some doubt about the degree of correspondence between our language and the world.

[2.011]   It is clear now that in adding logic to fact we are not adding anything that is not already in fact; in other words, our justification for setting up the second world of logic is given to us in the first world of fact, that is why what we said before is true – namely, that facts have logical characteristics and we shall see later that logic has factual characteristics.

[2.012]   Nothing can "happen" in logic that is accidental, then nothing can happen in fact that is accidental – at least not for logical purposes, and in this account of logical atomism we always have both a logical and an empirical purpose. Since we are dealing with fact only in terms of logic, and we are not going to guard ourselves and move about the facts as a primarily logical purpose, we have justified saying a factual as well as a logical purpose *because* we have derived our logic from our facts.

[2.0121]   All references to possibility henceforth will be entirely in terms of logical possibility. Remember that metaphysics by fiat is ruled out and so are manipulations of fact except in logical terms.

But what are the relations of fact? If they are not logical relations, then all our logic will be limited to relations even though these are the relations of fact.

[2.0122]   Things are independent, but since we are going to be talking only about fact, the independence of things manifests itself in their dependence on atomic fact. Thus we are given the facts when we have derived the logic from them and set up a system of logical coherence.

[2.0123]   An event is an atomic fact and its description as an atomic fact is a logical unfolding.

Perhaps an illustration here will help, for it is the same method which is used throughout the *Tractatus*: I know what it means, say, if someone asks me how I would arrive at a number for the population of New Orleans. I would have to count every person in it as one and then make a simple addition. I know what this means even though I could not do it, for at any moment the population of New Orleans is changing – people are leaving, people are arriving on every train and airplane, people are dying and people are being born. Thus even while I was doing it, the sum would be falsified by the facts; so I could not do it. But even though I could not do it, I know what I would have to do to get it done. Here is the difference, then, between conceivable possibility and factual possibility. In the *Tractatus* we are not going to "do" anything, but we are going to talk about how it would be done. The structure of the object is an element of the object.

It is obvious that every logical possibility exists in the fact — in the atomic facts — considering what in logic we are going to mean by facts; thus there shall be no surprises except to the extent to which we have not completely analyzed in logic the atomic fact.

[2.01231]   For "qualities" here we shall have to read "relations". The bridge between them might have been made easier by regarding them as having as a common ancestor, "properties". Wittgenstein is here answering F. H. Bradley for Russell (since it was Russell much earlier, and not Wittgenstein, who felt compelled to get over Bradleyian idealism). Not all relations are internal, for not all parts are merely parts of the whole. With regard to any object, it has internal as well as external relations. From the point of view of its external relations, it is a part of The Whole; but from the point of view of its internal relations, it is itself a whole. In the philosophy of logical atomism we must regard every object as a legitimate whole, knowable as such through its internal qualities.

[2.0124]   The combination of objects into atomic facts (and two objects or more are always involved in any atomic fact), means that all possible atomic facts are accounted for.

[2.013]   Logic exists in logical space and the space precedes the elements in it. This is purely Platonic: there is a world of logic, a sort of second-storey to the world of fact, and its being does not depend upon its being inhabited by elements known or exemplified in fact.

[2.0131]   The visual field is closed under color, but color is a relation not a quality. In logical atomism there shall be no qualities, no values; logical atomic facts are the building stones.

[2.014]   It is the peculiar property of logical systems to be completely analyzable into their parts without remainder, and these parts are relations.

We were not going to dip below facts to their constituents,

but now we are. If objects contain the possibilities of all states of affairs, then how can it be explained that being part of an atomic fact is essential to a thing? (2.011; we know from 2.01 that an object and a thing are the same.)

[2.0141]   The answer to the last question is undertaken here. It is not objects which are combined in atomic facts but the *forms* of objects.

[2.02]   We have misunderstood objects when we have connected them with particulars. Objects are only forms, else they could not be simple, for we know they have forms and if they had anything else beside forms – matter, say – then they would not be simple, and they are simple.

[2.0201]   Our theme is concerned with ultimately simple relations or forms, and these are finite. The analysis of wholes yields parts without remainder and without falsification.

[2.021]   Substance is the space in which objects are; the substance is always the same in them but there is no substance without them, thus while there is a logical space without logical elements, there is no substance without substantial elements, i.e. objects.

For "form" read "make up". Objects make up the substances of the world.

[2.0211]   It is because of this situation that we shall be able to manipulate the logical elements in logical space.

Sense depends on reference. There will, as we shall later see, be coherence, too. But the sense of a proposition does not depend on it.

It is clear that Wittgenstein meant to describe a finite real world to be represented in logic by a finite number of elementary propositions.

[2.0212]   We know from this that we are going to be able to form a picture of the world of facts by means of logic.

[2.022]   The constructions of the imagination are like those of logic in being combinatorial. In them, the elements of the "real world" are combined and recombined in ways in which they are not in the real world. (The method of art, then, would be a kind of qualitative combinatorics.)

By "real" world, it is obvious from context that Wittgenstein meant actual world, world of existence, world of space and time. It is consistent with the nominalism of the logical atomism he held with Russell, however, that the world of fact should be the only real world, and the other world, the world of propositions, should be a world of nothing (and therefore if not unreal at least not as real as the other, not enough real to be called real, since propositions are, as Russell said, nothing).

[2.023]   The fixed form that the imagined world has in common with the real world consists of the possibility of occurrence in atomic facts (2.0141).

[2.0231]   Material properties are properties and therefore forms. It is propositions which present forms (i.e. relations), not substances.

If objects and propositions have the same structure, it is because they share a common logic and the propositions have this logic because the logic was abstracted *from* the objects.

[2.0232]   Colors are qualities and logic is quality-less, for in logic the properties are relations. Pay attention, however, to the phrase, "roughly speaking". For logic has its own peculiar color. What cannot be said, what cannot be expressed in language, is not logical.

[2.0233]   We have already noted the negative nature of logic. "Difference" = "what is not the case" (1.12). Difference is a logical property.

[2.02331]   "Difference" explained. Excluded middle is the instrument used here. "The law of excluded middle is really just another form of the requirement that the concept should have a sharp boundary" [1].

[2.024]   Definition of "substance". See 2.021. If "objects form the substance of the world" and "substance is what exists independently of what is the case", then objects exist independently of what is the case, i.e. objects are not what is the case. But "the world is everything that is the case" (1), and so objects are again not what is the case. Obviously not: atomic facts alone are what is the case. Then what happens to the principle of combinatorics, of reduction without remainder, for atomic facts are nothing more than "combinations of objects" (2.01)?

---

[1] *Translations from the Philosophical Writings of Gottlob Frege*, p. 159.

[2.025] "Form and content", note. We do not have any matter; it was ruled out in 2.0231. Content is not material; the form is logical and the substance substantial. Wittgenstein did not want to admit that there is any substance, only the form. Yet, again, there are objects and that is what is meant by substance (2.021) and objects combine into atomic facts (2.01) which, we have just shown to be "everything that is the case".

[2.0251] Color is form in logic. See 2.0232.
"Places, instances, stretches of time, are, logically considered, objects; hence the linguistic designation of a definite place, a definite instance, or a stretch of time is to be regarded as a proper name" [1].

[2.026] Objects are reference-points for relations, and that is what the world means in logic. Objects convey their own form.

[2.027] Now we know what we mean by a thing.

[2.0271] If you thought that substantial things changed, while logic was fixed, you were wrong. Each world – the logical and the substantial – refers us to the other. Logic is the set of ways in which things change, and so there can be exchange in the logic, i.e. of relations.

[2.0272] A combination of objects is a configuration; how else could they be combined? See 2.01. Objects combine only with respect to their form, i.e. configuration.

[2.03] Mutual inclusion; inclusion is a fundamental logical relation.

[2.031] Whitehead's method of "extensive abstraction" presupposes this.

[2.032] Definition of "structure". Structure is always the structure of fact; logic is set in this way by substantial things.

[2.033] To the structure of fact, i.e. to the way in which things are strung together in fact, is as far down as logic can go in analysis.

[2.034] In arithmetic, the whole is no greater than the sum of its parts. The structure of atomic facts is closed under the properties of addition and subtraction.

---

[1] *Translations from the Philosophical Writings of Gottlob* Frege, edited by Geach and Black (Oxford 1952, Blackwell), p. 71.

[2.04]   A sort of nominalism of logic. There is no remainder, hence no indefinite boundaries and no infinite.

[2.05]   What is not the case is just those atomic facts which do not exist. See 1.12.

[2.06]   "Reality" defined. Both faces of atomic facts added together and considered as unrelated, a pair of categories, for a negative fact is also a category.

No realist in metaphysics asks for any more than the recognition of the reality of the non-existence of atomic facts, which Wittgenstein did here.

[2.061]   Discreteness theorem applied to atomic facts. See 1.2 where it was introduced.

If those atomic facts which exist determine those which do not (2.05), then how can they be independent of one another? The answer was given, perhaps, in 2.0122.

[2.062]   This is an important empirical principle. It is possible to get from fact to fact only through logic. For instance, if one premise is particular, the other would have to be universal for the conclusion to be particular. Empiricism can only be handled by means of logic.

But remember that logic is an element of the world. The possibility of combining objects (i.e. into atomic facts) exists in the discreteness of the objects. The combinatorial property is not something which is added to objects but exists in them in virtue of their discreteness.

[2.063]   What are we to do with "total"? Can we allow as a property of the world which consists only of facts the proposition that these are all the facts? That these are all the facts, is that an atomic fact? And if not, then how did we get it?

[2.1]   Logic is the picture of fact.

[2.11]   "The facts in logical space" – that is logic. Non-existence paints existence.

[2.12]   Picture, model – different sorts of representation. Logic has a domain of its own: logical space; but what is done there is to represent atomic facts by means of pictures or models.

[2.13]   For "picture" read "map"; the analogue is what mathematicians call "mapping".

[2.131]   The elements of the proposition are in one-one correspondence with the objects of the fact. This simplification is required by the system, but the situation is usually far more complicated.

[2.14]   We have a correspondence between two kinds of combining: the combining of logical elements in the logical picture, and the combining of objects in the atomic fact; and then we have in addition a correspondence between the two kinds of combining. Another name for this would be "two coherence systems with a correspondence between their elements".

[2.141]   Here we have an empirical proposition about logical space. We shall see that very often the factual world is talked about as though it had logical properties (which it is supposed to have), and the logical space is talked about as though it had empirical properties (which it is not supposed to have). But the world of logic, despite protestations to the contrary, was a solid one for Wittgenstein, and contained almost substantial properties.

[2.15]   Representation is made possible by structure, and enables us to tell a great many things about structure.

[2.151]   At least we rely upon the possibility of the representative nature of pictures because of their logic and the logic of fact. If we have constructed our picture correctly logic will guarantee this possibility.

[2.1511]   Reality reaches up to the picture from atomic fact, the reality of atomic fact reaches up, that is, and reflects itself, and so the picture turns out to be a mirror. Here, without the word, mirror, yet, is the beginning of the hint of the master analogue of the mirror; of logic as the great mirror.

[2.1512]   The representation of the world of atomic fact is also a measure of it. It estimates it.

[2.15121]   Between a picture and that which it depicts is a meet at the limits. Measures are boundary-correspondences.

[2.1513]   That a picture is a picture is a fact that somehow belongs to the picture. A picture is that which shows itself forth as a picture. Good pictures need no labels to tell us what they are.

[2.1514]   Logic would not be logic were it not for representation. This, then, is a very fundamental kind of relation.

[2.1515]   In 2.1511 reality reached up to the picture; here the picture reaches down to reality. Metaphorically speaking, of course, there is an activity touched with reality about all logic. And it would be idle to endeavor to understand Wittgenstein without being able to speak and understand metaphorically. The metaphors are models of abstract structures, just as they are in Plato.

[2.16]   Are all facts depictable? They are to the extent to which they are in themselves logical.

[2.161]   If the forms were not in the facts and also in the picture, if, in other words, the logic of the facts and the logic of the representation were not identical, there could be no representation at all.

[2.17]   That the picture and that which it pictures, i.e. the "reality" of atomic facts, have a "form of representation" in common, marks a delicate distinction; for there is a difference between them even though the difference is not what we wish to emphasize.

[2.171]   "Every reality" here means "on different occasions". What would a spatial picture of space be?

[2.172]   No picture, we have noted, pictures the fact that it *is* a picture, but the sense that it is a picture stands out in the picture, it shows it forth. Compare 2.1513. Similarly, in language there is talk about reality but not talk about the way in which there is talk about reality when there is talk about reality.

[2.173]   The picture is outside what it represents, and so there may be a false picture, i.e. one which purports to but does not correctly represent.

[2.174]   The picture is outside what it represents but not outside the representation.

[2.18]   But there are limits to how false a picture can be and still be a picture although a false picture. For a false picture is a picture; but a picture that it is not a picture is not a false picture, it is not a picture at all.

Ordinarily we would suppose that our language is not as complex as the world, for in the past the world itself in every instance proved itself more complex than any of our information of it, but in Wittgenstein and based on the method of constructionism, the logical propositions must be just as complex as the world from which they are derived and of which they are the pictures and to which they apply – no more complex and no less complex, but of an identical complexity.

[2.181] A logical picture is a picture of the logic contained in the facts, and that is all of the facts that can be pictured in logic.

[2.182] Spatial pictures are also logical pictures but logical pictures are not also spatial. A picture contains at least its logic.

[2.19] The logical picture is the most inclusive kind of picture (as we should expect from the fact that, as we have said, inclusion is the fundamental logical relation).

[2.2] A logical picture is not only logic. It is also a picture; its logic is the representation it has in common with that which is pictured.

[2.201] Logical pictures are pictures of the possibilities of existence, and the possibility means the non-existence as well as the existence of atomic facts.

[2.202] Possible states of affairs, which include non-existence can be represented only in logical space; they can be represented as parts of pictures only.

[2.203] Reality = state of affairs = atomic facts.

[2.21] The picture purports to agree with reality; it constitutes a logical judgment, for logic operates between the picture and reality.

[2.22] Representation, as in the case of the form of the correspondence between the picture and reality, is a brute, irreducible business.

[2.221] The picture *always* represents its sense, and this is unalterable.

Frege is responsible for the distinction between sense and reference. "By means of a sign we express its sense and designate its reference" [1]. The distinction between sense and reference in Frege is the same as that between meaning and truth. Meaning is independent of truth; a proposition may have meaning without our knowing its truth or falsity: "There are craters on the other side of the moon", has meaning, but we do not know its truth or falsity as yet. It is when the

---

[1] *Translations from the Philosophical Writings of Gottlob Frege*, edited by Geach and Black (Oxford 1952, Blackwell), p. 61; see also pp. 56–78.

meaning or sense and the reference coincide that we consider a proposition to be true.

[2.222]   But the sense and the reference do not always correspond. When the sense does not correspond with the reference, we say that the picture is false. For instance, if we say, "There are three people in this room", we know what the sentence *means* and this is its sense, but we do not know whether what it means corresponds to that to which it refers, i.e. whether there are or are not three people in this room. If there are, the sense corresponds to the reference, and we say the statement (or picture) is true. If there are not, then the sense does not correspond to the reference, and we say that the statement (or picture) is false.

The distinction between meaning and truth, or, as Frege had it, between sense and reference, is one which Russell found it hard to accept [1].

[2.223]   We compare the picture, not its sense, with reality.

[2.224]   But we need the sense to discover the truth or falsity.

[2.225]   All pictures need reference for this discovery. Sense does not determine truth.

[3]   "Mind" for Wittgenstein means "holding the picture". A mind of this sort without a subject is what is intended here; merely that a picture is, or could be, held. Compare: Hume's theory of perspectives.

[3.001]   We can suppose how an atomic fact could be; thought is here analyzed as though it were a process of picturing. Peirce described thought as the observation of graphs [2] and said that "it is part of the process of sensible experience to locate its facts in the world of ideas" [3].

[3.01]   The image is one of a correspondence between thoughts and the world, the thoughts comprising a picture. This is not meant to be epistemological and does not include a thinker in the image.

[3.02]   The contents of the thought (not the thinking) and the possibility are the same. The thought does the thinking, not a "mind".

---

[1] See *The Principles of Mathematics*, p. 504.
[2] *Collected Papers*, 5.579.
[3] *Op. cit.*, 3.527.

[3.03]   Logic determines the range of thoughts, and thought cannot extend beyond logic. The imagination, then, or the intuition is not "unlogical". Irrationality is simply falsehood. The feelings would have to be logical, and there would be no false feelings.

[3.031]   Logic is the picture of the world. We do not have an unlogic to picture the unworld. There are logical limits to the imagination, and picturable limits to logic.

[3.032]   Language obeys logic as geometry obeys space.

[3.0321]   Empiricism is not as rigorous as logic (we knew that but we had forgotten it, in this sense, at least). Here logic is treated as though it were more real than existence.

[3.04]   Since possibilities are both of existence and of non-existence, possibility cannot guarantee truth. See also 2.225. The debate as to whether truth was logical or empirical, whether, in other words, we wish to have it be a coherence principle based on consistency or a correspondence principle based on fact – consistency, of course, in both cases, only with different elements – is one that recent philosophy has tried to solve. Kant tried to solve it subjectively; empirical science, experimental science, mathematical experimental science, have calmly proceeded on the basis that it has been solved objectively, but there has been no philosophy which has attempted to do this in any justifiable way. In Wittgenstein the effort was made again, this time objectively and in the terms that science would find congenial. Whether his effort was successful or not is another question, or whether it would be suggestive to those who would try where he had failed is another question also and perhaps a better one. But Wittgenstein at least pointed out the road for others even if he has not successfully traversed it himself.

[3.05]   *A priori* truth is here equated with self-evidence, and this has been abandoned in modern philosophy.

[3.1]   Here begins the change from "picture" and "thought" to "proposition", a synonym. The proposition is expressed in the meaning (i.e. Frege's "sense").

[3.11]   The proposition as exhibited in language, e.g. in a sentence, as a projection from the ground of substance upward, as a possible state of affairs. We say in the proposition how things are and/or how they are not.

The content of thought is the correspondence between propositions and possible state of affairs. This is 2.223 *et seq.* but viewed upward instead of downward, in the same relation.

[3.12]   A proposition is a sign (i.e. a propositional function to which there is attached a reference). A propositional sign or a propositional function cannot be true or false. F(x) is not a proposition but a propositional sign or function; it does not state what is the case and so cannot be compared with reality.

[3.13]   The distinction between meaning and truth again, this time in terms of proposition and its projection (toward the world). Compare 2.222.

There is an important distinction between a proposition and its sense, just as there is between its sense and its reference. Otherwise we could not compare proposition and sense, and we need to if we are to show, apart from reference, what the proposition means.

(We are not speaking, of course, of trivial propositions but only of those of which we can speak of in some significant connection.)

There is a further distinction to be made between the form and the content of the sense. The proposition contains only the form; we need the sense for the content.

There are two directions in the *Tractatus*. The first is constructionism, and it consists in the direction up by means of naming objects and then by combining the names into propositions. The second consists in the direction down from propositions to objects, or facts. The assumption is that the first is the only method employed, but under it falsity would never be possible. If there are false propositions, it is because sense and reference do not always correspond. When propositions are checked against the fact, the expected correspondence does not occur, but on the basis of constructionism alone it would have to be there.

[3.14]   The proposition considered as a sign or propositional function is only a definite sort of combination of words, nothing more. It means only what a sign means when we do not yet know to what it points but only that it *is* a sign.

But its significance is a brute property.

[3.141]   A proposition is not merely a propositional function. It says something, if only that it *is* a sign.

[3.142]   A class of names is not a proposition or even a propositional function. But a proposition is a fact and therefore can express a sense.

[3.143]   The logical distance between a propositional sign or a name and a combination of two signs or names is immense. It stretches all the way from arbitrariness to irreducibility. For a "dog" could just as well be called a "blop" and "black" "grel", but that all blops are grel, like all dogs are black, is either true or false and so an irrefrangible logical fact.

Frege went too far when he failed to recognize the great leap between a name and a "compounded name" or proposition.

[3.1431]   On the correspondence of all words and objects, expressing physical objects in signs, sign-words are impossible, unless we name each individual.

The mutual spatial position of the physical objects has its analogue in the logical distance between a proposition and its sense. Note: not its reference.

[3.1432]   Objects say their logic. We say "rabbits are fond of eating lettuce" but only because rabbits are fond of eating lettuce, and not because of the inverse.

Wittgenstein encountered the same difficulty that Whitehead complained of somewhere in his *Process and Reality*, the difficulty of expressing a new philosophy in an old language in which an old philosophy is imbedded. Modern European languages – English and German alike – are built on the Aristotelian frame, on the substance-attribute philosophy and the subject-predicate logic. Now we have a new logic, the logic of relations, and a new philosophy to go with it; and when we strive to express them in the old language, we encounter the resistance and the confusion resulting from the imbedded old logic and old philosophy.

[3.144]   Names are points; logic enters when the points are connected in propositions.

[3.2]   Exact correspondence between objects and language without remainder, is the aim. It cannot be done, but this was Wittgenstein's assumption following through Russell to Frege who had in mind the "logically perfect language".

When we connect language with objects, what we express is logic. For the connection, the correspondence cannot be ignored. Logic is the theory of signification. It begins where names are given to objects and thus become signs.

[3.201]   Declaration of war: dogmatic assertion that the signs shall represent the objects without remainder. Logic is exhausted by its expression, just as art is.

[3.202]   Definitional. Names point, also they can be connected.

[3.203]   Logically speaking, objects and names are one. But facts were everything that is the case, facts which are combinations of objects. It is essential to objects that they are parts of atomic facts (2.011). Why then would it not be sufficient here to name atomic facts? Despite the adoption of atomic facts as the base-line, Wittgenstein repeatedly dipped below them.

The logical constants are the tools whereby language can be arranged to represent the facts. An empirical derivation for the logical constants is suggested.

[3.21]   See 2.202. The relation between signs in the proposition is the same as the relation of space between objects, so that the proposition is a true picture. See 3.1431.

[3.22]   Again, "object", or atomic fact? Here we seem to go back of the "combination of objects" to show how the object itself is represented in language in the proposition. Arbitrary agreement.

[3.221]   Names are only signs; they identify without further information. That is, names for individual objects; class names do more.

[3.23]   Bridging from signs to sense through names. If a sign is simple, then the sense is determinate; but note that this is a postulate: it is what we start from, not what we can demonstrate.

[3.24]   Meaning or "sense" is what is referred to here, not reference to states of affairs. The analysis of a whole is contained in the statement about the part provided that wholes are completely analyzable into parts. See 2.0201. A proposition refers to a complex when it refers as a whole.

[3.25]   Denotation without connotation. Words must mean exactly what they designate and nothing more, no remainder, because designating is done in terms of logic, not value or quality.

[3.251] Logic is exhaustive, again. Its words fit neatly at the joints and it has a single, clear and distinct meaning. See 3.141.

[3.26] An old difficulty still baffled Wittgenstein. The arbitrary is also brute. See 3.221.

[3.261] The way in which language is put together (and hence also logic). It begins with brute arbitrary simples then moves to signs (i.e. words) defined in terms of them, so that the second group does not rest on the same basis. Signs are logically primitive; they indicate that one can go no further in this direction.

[3.262] Use reveals inherent properties or functions not originally exposed. In this way, logic becomes elaborated and we find out what ramifications are involved in application only.

[3.263] Elucidation means elicitation.

[3.3] The proposition is the least entity; names are only parts of propositions. Signs have no sense, in Frege's use of the term, that is, no meaning which could be compared with the state of affairs. See 3.13.

[3.31] The proposition is everything; it is the logical standard. Names are now expressions or symbols, and so are propositions. Anything declared, is.

[3.311] We now have classes of propositions. The expression is the kind of proposition, e.g. a declarative sentence.
The mapping of the elements of one proposition onto those of another makes possible the construction of a propositional variable. A logical entity carries everything with it that it needs, including its relation to other propositions (and the possibility of those propositions).

[3.312] Once again, a declarative sentence, for instance, *is* one without saying that it is one. We cling to the form of the expression, for this contains its logic. It is the only thing that stands still.

[3.313] The values of the variable are the languages of the logic. The propositional variable is made possible by the similarity of form of the propositions which are its values. When one of the values of the variable is substituted for the variable, we have the limiting case. Every proposition to the extent to which it contains expressions is a propositional variable.

[3.314]   We are dealing here with the notion of proposition and range. What can be asserted within the limits prescribed by a proposition. Exaggerated in the case of a system of propositions, i.e. an entire philosophy. The possibilities never change.

[3.315]   The part of a proposition is arbitrary but the whole ("all") is not. Logic enters when the names are combined into propositions. Language is more complicated than the philologists have supposed – one might say, in ways other than they have supposed. It is complicated to the extent to which it has a logic or *is* a logic.

[3.316]   The range of a proposition considered as a variable is determined. $(\hat{a})$ $(a \supset x \lor a \supset y)$, "the a's such that a includes x or a includes y". There is a well-defined range for every variable.

[3.317]   The relation between a propositional variable and the propositions within its range, has to do only with its sense and not with its reference. If for every proposition there is a range of propositions, we are not yet at the level of sense or of reference but of logical association. See for instance inversion, contraposition, etc. We cannot have well-defined propositional variables until we can in advance write down a table of their values, for a variable without the values is meaningless, and the variable with the values is a variable.

[3.318]   The proposition is a function of its range of meanings. And that is exactly what a function is: the set of its values. A function is nothing more (or less) than the values which can be substituted for it.

[3.32]   The symbol is the sense; the sign is the mark on paper, the sound wave in the air, etc. A symbol is a sign with sense – and sense must always correspond with *material* states of affairs. Here is nominalism admitted and asserted.

[3.321]   Two different symbols, e.g. "there" and "their", have the same sound-sign.

[3.322]   *Schiff*, boat, *batella*, for instance.

[3.323]   Distinction between sign-mark and sign-symbol; the meaning may depend upon syntax.

[3.324]   Especially in the case of the "is" of equality and of existence. We ignore too easily the metaphysical implications of language. Not only a logic but also a metaphysics is imbedded in the language, but silently; it is never heard but has its effect.

[3.325]   In order to avoid these errors, we need what Frege called for: a logically perfect language.

[3.326]   How is the sign used in the sentence? That is how we understand it as a symbol.

[3.327]   Logic occurs when signs are combined. Syntax, then, produces logic; logic occurs in the syntax.

[3.328]   Signs have contextual meaning. Logic is always necessary: deductions always, and induction only in the case of perfect induction. The ambition is to limit the language of representation to logic, i.e. to what is necessary.

[3.33]   The sign can never develop new traits. It is only what it is, and that was established when it was established as a sign.

[3.331]   The theory of types cannot be manipulated unless we can get outside of two levels, to speak in the syntax language about types in the object language.

We must distinguish between those propositions which apply to a class and those which apply to a member of a class. The final question of the theory of types is whether class-membership is an inclusion-relation. Probably it is not, but see more on this below.

[3.332]   The propositional sign says nothing about the propositional sign, but the proposition does because it is higher in type. The whole is always higher in type than its parts.

[3.333]   No proposition asserts its own truth. Russell confused class-membership with class-inclusion. Russell's class of all clasess which are not members of themselves is a member of itself because it is higher in type; hence the apparent paradox. If we step outside the *Tractatus* to look at it from beyond its limits with some detachment, then we can see that a metaphysics is called for as well as an epistemology. We have two independent spaces, each containing objects: one, a space of objects and their combinations, and two, a space in which the objects and their combinations are considered, or in other words logic. Thus we shall have a world of fact and we shall see that we have elicited from it a world of logic. Logic is metafactual. But the world of logic in so far as it is a world is independent of fact. The metafactual world is a world independent and beyond the derivation of the knowledge of it. Manipulations can be conducted in the world of logic, not manipulatable in the world of fact. But the abstraction was objective, and thus we have in addition to an epistemological realism a metaphysical realism.

[3.334]   The rules of syntax are derived from the behavior of signs, not the behavior of signs from the rules of syntax. The rules follow the ways in which signs behave, not the reverse. The rules recognize the behavior of the signs; signs do not obey rules, they have instead existential import.

The signs and their combinations are the primitives and nothing else. Everything follows from these, and the possible combinations of the signs are already contained in the signs, only, we cannot see them by observing the signs. It is not clear, in other words, from the signs just what their possibilities of combinations are until we begin to combine them. Thus when we combine signs we elicit information from them about their properties, and this is how we learn about logic; for logic, as well as language, is contained in the possibilities of the combinations of the signs.

[3.34]   The essential features are the reference, and the accidental and logical possibilities of combination. See 3.12.

[3.341]   The essential feature is the form, and this is a result of the abstraction from objects and atomic facts – from the fact that the proposition has a reference.

What is essential is the form of the proposition.

[3.3411]   If names were not simples, then forms could not comprise them without going beyond them. Distinguish between symbols and names of symbol. Names are arbitrary and simple, not always so with symbols.

[3.342]   Notation is arbitrary: this sign would do as well as that if we defined it in the same way. But what is chosen arbitrarily is fixed by being chosen. Compare relativity physics, in which any frame of reference may be selected by an observer, but where his measurements are fixed given the frame. The choice of frame is arbitrary, but once it is chosen

everything is determined. Implication is in the same case.
[3.3421]   The possibility of every single thing is its logic, and
this can be symbolized.

But what is the status of such a term as "a horse", "a man",
"a planet"? It is not a class nor a particular, exactly. For
instance, "a man" does not name any class ("man" would be
the class name), but neither does it name any man ("John T.
Wittner" would do that). It is a particular under a class;
and what is that?

Possibility is possibility of individuals or of singulars, not
mere vague generality. (Consider a contradiction with the
generality of the form of the proposition which expresses the
possibility.)

The single thing in unimportant, relatively speaking; but
that there are single things – this is all-important.

The distinction between general things and singular things is
both marked and at times very confusing. One separate and
distinct general idea could be an individual one; for instance,
the number "two" is an individual lying within the integral
domain, while the question of whether a certain amount of
water which has been diverted from the course of a river is a
single thing or not, is debatable.

[3.343]   The rules of translation are what different symbolisms
have in common. A language that won't translate reveals an
inadequate language.

[3.344]   The sense and the reference – the total signification –
of a symbol is given by the invariance which appears when
symbols are substituted. Substitution unlimited.

[3.3441]   "Not p" can replace "p" in the symbolism throughout
without harm, without changing the meaning.

What the symbol says on its own is unimportant, or, at the
most, confusing. It is how it is used as a symbol that counts.

[3.3442]   A statement concerning canonical form. See 3.201.

[3.4]   See 3.124, 3.141, 3.144.

The world consists of logic-containing objects, but the objects
and their logic are represented in quite different ways in
language: the objects are represented in language by names,
the logic is represented by the connections between the names.

[3.41]   The logical constants locate a proposition in logical
space; they give its position.

[3.411]   There are two kinds of existence; the reality of the objects and the reality of the propositions.

[3.42]   The universe of discourse is what is referred to here. Logical space is closed under the logical constants and the logical operations.

[3.5]   We substitute signs for thoughts.

[4]   The proposition replaces the thought from here on. See 3.02, 3.1.

[4.001]   A language is a set of propositions.

[4.002]   The ordinary uninstructed man communicates with others of his kind by means of a language without having any knowledge of how the words are put together to mean what he makes them mean; in other words, he knows how to use the language without knowing how such a use of language works. The enormous complexities of colloquial language in the hands of uninstructed, and often illiterate, people is a case in point.

The fact that an uneducated man uses the language correctly, this is the surprising thing. For he knows what he means, and he may say what he means without knowing, without ever understanding, how what he says means what he means. He knows nothing of the subtlety of words or of their effects, or of syntax, either. And yet he often makes the necessary adjustments. Language in this way is comparable to elements of the physiological organism, to the changes in the adrenaline level, for instance, or the rate of the heart beats.

It must have been something of this point that led Wittgenstein to the theme of his posthumous work, the *Philosophical Investigations*.

[4.003]   Many philosophical problems can be dissolved in a confusion in the use of language. When we do understand the logic of our language we find we have problems of a similar sort as those we dissolved only at a more clarified and higher level. The genuine problems of philosophy are those that remain or arise when we have solved those which depend upon the confusion of language.

Frege's distinction between sense and reference enabled Wittgenstein to distinguish between nonsense and falsity, between a false proposition and a nonsensical one. The proposition "Franklin D. Roosevelt was alive in 1955" is obviously a false proposition; the proposition "blue is more two than green", is obviously a nonsensical proposition. The distinction is based on relevance to reality. A true proposition is one which corresponds to the facts; a false proposition is one which could correspond to the facts; a nonsensical proposition is one for which there are no facts to correspond or not, since we do not know what the proposition means. In other words, a false proposition has sense but not reference, while a nonsensical proposition has neither.

It is about here that we can begin to talk about the implications of the *Tractatus* as a system. Metaphysical propositions are senseless, and have no reference. If metaphysical propositions cannot refer to themselves, then there will always be something in the world left out of their account; and so the presumption to total inclusion of reference is vain. If the theory of types is correct, then metaphysics is impossible, for metaphysics is the theory of the whole and any proposition about the whole of being will be left out of its own account, and thus the account will not be an account of the whole of being for it will admit the proposition which asserts this.

Where does that leave the metaphysical problem? Let us restate it more clearly. If there cannot be a metaphysical proposition which is about the whole of metaphysics, then it must lie outside metaphysics and be higher in type. But there is nothing higher in type, metaphysics by definition being of the highest type. If there is any proposition higher in type than metaphysics (and there must be if it is about the whole of metaphysics), then it is a metaphysical proposition. But it cannot be a metaphysical proposition and not be a metaphysical proposition, for it cannot lie within metaphysics and also lie outside it.

The above argument is the one upon which the abolition of metaphysics rests. That there is a contradiction uncovered here is not to be denied. But to abandon an entire topic because a contradiction has been discovered in it is not admissible behavior. For if it were, then after Gödel's discovery of his theorem we should have been prepared to abandon the whole of mathematics, which assuredly has not been done. No, when

we encounter a difficulty in a recognized field, we recognize
it as a sign of limitations.

"A crude metaphysics, implicitly held; this, I believe is the
price every philosophy that explicitly rejects metaphysics
must pay" [1].

[4.0031]   "Mauthner's sense" was psychological. Wittgenstein
meant logical not psychological critique.

Wittgenstein credited Russell with having taught him how to
find out from the analysis of language what a proposition
means, in contradistinction to what it may have seemed to
mean.

It is clear here that Wittgenstein was trying to bring together
into one system and one point of view two traditions which
come together in about his period in British philosophy: one
was the tradition of metaphysical realism from Thomas Reid
through Cook Wilson to the early G. E. Moore and Bertrand
Russell; the other tradition was that of British empiricism
from Locke and Hume to the modern school.

[4.01]   The proposition is a picture of that part of reality we
have selected for treatment. See 1.13.

[4.011]   Language, like musical scores, does not *show* that it is
a picture; but its being a picture does not depend upon its
showing that it is one.

In the pictures we make of language, there is no correspondence between the picture and that which it depicts at first
glance. In order to see it is a picture, we have to understand
what it means to be a language – in particular what it means
to use this language in this way.

Logic makes complex pictures of a complex situation, so helps
to picture reality by combining the names for objects.

[4.012]   If you put the sign of a relation between the relata,
you are drawing a diagram of the relation. Every sign system
is such a diagram, and so a language is a picture.

[4.013]   The irregularities of language, like those of music, only
mean that the logic was not simple nor even simply symmetrical.

[4.014]   Logic extends beyond language. It holds whenever

[1] Gustav Bergmann, *The Metaphysics of Logical Positivism* (Longmans, Green),
p. 64.

there is both a structure elicited from the world, and the world itself.

[4.0141] Logic is the projective relation which makes translation possible in any system.

[4.015] Logic makes all tropes and analogues possible.

[4.016] Abstractions are a kind of hieroglyphic writing.

[4.02] Sign and sense have connections which we recognize, not create. Recognition is discovery, not creation.

[4.021] The sense of a proposition explains the proposition and it makes the proposition clear.

[4.022] If you understand a proposition, then you know its sense. The proposition asserts its own truth, here. But if it prove false, it may still have sense.

[4.023] If a proposition is correctly framed, either its affirmation or its negation is true. Both must exhaust the universe of discourse. The completeness axiom.

Propositions refer to objects in virtue of their external properties. It is not essential to an object that it be described, but it is essential to a proposition that it be a description. The logic of a proposition enables it to refer to reality by means of its structure. That is why it has sufficient reference so that if it is false we can still use it as a description by changing the sign ('true' to 'false'). Until we can hold universals down to facts, until we are able to say in a language no more than the facts permit us to say, we shall not have the language that Wittgenstein wanted.

[4.024] The understanding of a proposition depends upon its sense, not its reference. Hence a false proposition has a meaning.

[4.025] Words are parts of how they are put together; the syntax elicits their possibilities; otherwise dictionaries could not translate them as different parts of speech.

[4.026] The authors of the simple signs have much to learn from the observation of the signs and their combinatorial behavior.

[4.027] Propositions communicate a new *logical* sense.

[4.03] As a picture, the proposition tells us something new about the state of affairs it depicts.

[4.031] Something like Peirce's "ideal experimentation" was

intended here: putting words together in propositions as a way of manipulating states of affairs *in absentia*.

[4.0311]   The words are connected in the proposition just as the objects in the atomic fact.

[4.0312]   Logical constants do not represent, but by means of them reproduction is possible.

[4.032]   The picturing depends upon the logic.

[4.04]   One-one correspondence between picture and state of affairs.

[4.041]   The correspondence cannot be represented.

[4.0411]   There is an essential vagueness to generality, as Peirce asserted. There is a logical principle of indeterminacy. Ways of symbolizing must make possible the representation of every element in the state of affairs; thus much depends upon the choice of symbolism.

[4.0412]   The refutation of subjective idealism.

[4.05]   It is not thought but the real, objective world that is being compared here.

[4.06]   The truth-value of a proposition is determined by the real world.

[4.061]   Frege's sense is independent of the reference. The situation is not so simple as one might be led to suspect from connecting the sign directly with the signification: between them comes the sense, or, as we might say, the meaning of a proposition. It is the sense which is connected with signification rather than the proposition itself.

[4.062]   The logical constants do not assert anything by themselves. But in propositions they help the proposition to assert. It follows, then, that the truth is not determined by signs; the signs swing free independently of it, and the truth may or may not correspond to the sense of the proposition without affecting or interrupting that sense. The logical constants, 'not', 'or', 'and', for instance, are elicited from the connections between signs in propositions and so have no correspondence with reality but they enable the signs to have correspondence with reality when reality is as complex as a whole proposition would indicate.

[4.0621]   "Not" and the "not"-sign do not have a material object corresponding to them, that is true; but it does not rob them of all factual reference. We can say that they function in the sense of a false proposition. We can say also their meaning is fixed once it has been assigned.

It is interesting to compare the ways in which metaphysical realists have dealt with this problem. Non-being meant positive otherness for Plato (*Sophist*), and much the same point was made by Whitehead in his conception of "negative prehension".

[4.063]   To learn something about the world, it is necessary first to know what the symbolism is in terms of which the learning is to be accomplished, and that the symbolism involves a logic.

[4.064]   A proposition capable of sense already has sense, and does not acquire it with the reference, nor with the truth.

[4.0641]   It is impossible not to assert something in a proposition. Any collection of words which does not assert something is not a proposition. Thus a proposition which occupies a logical space asserts something and this is as true of a negative proposition as of a positive one.

[4.1]   A negative proposition presents the non-existence of atomic facts.

[4.11]   By painfully constructing names for objects and propositions to connect names logically, we arrive at the totality of propositions and this is all we mean by a natural science.

[4.111]   Philosophy has no empirical data of its own to match against the data of the empirical sciences. It cannot decide what data can decide, but it can relate decisions concerning data. For instance, the relations between empirical levels or between scientific laws in different sciences are not treated by any science.

Philosophy is not a simple representation of objects; that is left to the sciences. What philosophy means, it shall turn out, has to do both with logic *and* objects, and the connections between them.

[4.112]   In order to make propositions clear, it may be necessary to study how they fit together. Philosophy, then, is the study of the "totality of true propositions". (4.11).

If we clarify our thoughts we shall find more than Descartes found when he called for clear and distinct ideas; we shall find that philosophy is an activity and not merely a static theory. The activity consists in discovering the relations between logic and the world, but this, in turn, of course, is also a theory. In order to make propositions clear we shall have to connect them in a whole, for part of their meaning is their possibility of connection, thus philosophy deals with *all* propositions.

[4.1121]   Philosophy has taken a turn toward logic and away from psychology. Psychology is merely the way in which logic is applied to the analysis of thoughts; they have to be logical to be correct, but logic does not have to be psychological. We have just seen that logic has to do with the way in which propositions picture the world.

Ever since Kant's influence spread and Hegel's added to it, logic was considered to be the laws of thought and logic a branch of psychology. It was in this way that we entered the twentieth century. But the scene has changed; the advent of modern symbolic logic with its metaphysical realistic background, and Whitehead, Russell and Frege, as well as the decline in the influence of the subjectivists of the older variety, has meant that we no longer consider logic to be the laws of thought but the theory of relations or the conditions of abstract structures. Consequently psychology, as Wittgenstein said, is a natural science, and there is no more and no less relation between one or another of the natural sciences and philosophy.

Wittgenstein recognized three kinds of space: psychological space, physical space, and logical space. The aim of the *Tractatus* is to show the relations between the objects in physical space and the propositions in logical space without reference to the psychological. This is not to say that the psychological does not exist; only to show the relations between the other two. And the relations between the other two, it is assumed, are what they are, independently of how the knowledge of them was acquired.

[4.1122]   Philosophy is not a science; no, and neither is any science a philosophy, we can be glad to learn.

We also entered the twentieth century under the banner of Darwinian evolution. Evolutionary theory is here to stay; in fact, it has founded the science of genetics, but it, too, has no more to do with philosophy than any other hypothesis of natural science.

[4.113]   Outside of science, all is philosophy. Logical positivists or empiricists would have trouble accepting this.

[4.114]   Philosophy comes in after fact and logic have been brought up; it brings them up.

[4.115]   Limits ought to be displayed. They are there, but unless they are exhibited we should not know them.

[4.116]   The echo of Descartes' clarity and distinctness applies to propositions and their sense, but not necessarily their truth. Descartes had the two confused, but Frege cleared *this* confusion for Wittgenstein.

[4.12]   More and more often we are told that logical form makes representation possible but that form itself cannot be represented. Not by itself, perhaps, but by something else? There are other things in the world than logic – quality, for instance; and the quality which was ruled out of this system may be the very element to represent it! Is it not after all a qualitative impression of his logical system of representing the world by means of propositions that Wittgenstein has been trying to give?

It is clear here, too, that logic is as wide as the world. Ordinarily we call a world-wide logic by another name: we call it ontology.

[4.121]   The propositions show their logical form by means of language. Applied logic is what is meant, of course, for it is logic being used in language to represent the world.

[4.1211]   The symbolism shows forth the sense.

[4.1212]   The logic of language, which makes it possible to say what we do say, cannot itself be said.

[4.1213]   Logic stems from and is determined by signs.

[4.122]   Both facts and propositions have formal structures. They have internal and external properties. It was Russell who introduced Wittgenstein to the doctrine of internal relations of F. H. Bradley, to which they were both opposed. It is Bradley who is being answered here. Relations are held to be internal to facts; the external relations are the internal ones mirrored in propositions.

[4.1221]   The internal property of a fact is preeminent.

[4.123]   Wherever Wittgenstein against his own rules introduced a psychological criterion, we are obliged to translate it for him. For the term "unthinkable" (*undenkbar*) we might substitute "inadmissible in the system". Also, it would help if for "internal" we put instead "a property of an element which is essential to the description of the element".

[4.124]   The internal property of a state of affairs is expressed by the internal property of the proposition. In each, this is where logic lurks.

[4.1241]   Forms do not have properties; only propositions and states of affairs have properties, and these are forms.

[4.125]   Relations, like properties (4.124), are internal to both states of affairs and propositions. Otherwise, what would they be doing in the proposition?

[4.1251]   If internal, then represented as internal; but otherwise not.

[4.1252]   Number; that is, repetition of operations.

[4.126]   By formal concept is meant a logical concept; by a proper concept is meant an empirical one.

[4.127]   The propositional variable discussed earlier (3.313 ff.) is the sign of a formal concept, i.e. a whole expression.

[4.1271]   And so is every sign.

[4.1272]   There is no widest system; for this would be to look for an empirical reference for a formal concept.
Universality is not, as the mathematicians would have it, a special case of generality. It is instead a property of logic alone, and thus it cannot be asserted of empirical propositions; the language of generality is that of probability, generalities are expressed in probabilities.

[4.12721]   Logic cannot be as primitive as the actual objects, for they already contain their logic. To set up logic as equally primitive would be to count it twice: once as it is in the objects, and again alone.

[4.1273]   What about Peano's postulate for the integral domain? (See 4.1252). Mathematical induction.

[4.1274]   Logic alone does not "exist"; that is to say, there is no logic except as the form taken by propositions which assert existence.

[4.128]   Number is a form, i.e. the form of successive operations;

but forms are not numbered. Thus in ontology no categories come "first" or "second". The nominalism is now complete.

[4.2]   The propositions are therefore strictly accountable to facts; they *are* the facts, merely asserted.

[4.21]   One fact, then one elementary proposition.

[4.211]   Consider, for instance, the false elementary proposition. If our true elementary proposition were to be "this horse is brown", we could oppose the false elementary proposition "this horse is grey", which is, however, not a contradiction. We could not have a contradiction of elementary propositions, for the contradictory of "this horse is brown" would be "it is not the case that this horse is brown", which is not an elementary proposition.

[4.22]   The elementary proposition brings names together to represent an actual relation. For the names do not have to be the names of two objects only but they can be the names respectively of one object and one property, e.g. "this horse is brown".

Here a problem arises: if a relation is named, then is the possession of it by an atomic fact crucial or could it be propositional as well? Are we here making clear in our notation that we are at the level of elementary propositions, or could the language just as well be used to describe atomic fact? That we mean by elementary propositions just those which describe atomic fact does not get rid of the ambiguity, for we are then relying upon those propositions which are about elementary propositions to "show themselves". Put this in another way: we have three types, type 1 is the atomic fact, type 2 the is elementary proposition, and type 3 is the complex proposition. Now, all propositions of type 2 are about type 1, and all propositions of type 3 are about type 2, and propositions about type 3 are also of type 3. There are no propositions of type 1.

[4.221]   No matter how complex the propositions, their constituents must eventually be propositions whose components are elementary propositions.

[4.2211]   Infinity does not exclude discreteness nor a correspondence between propositions and facts or objects. The analogy here is Cantor's definition of the infinite as the one-one correspondence between the elements of a set and those of a proper subset.

[4.23]   No matter how imbedded in complex propositions a given elementary proposition may be, the name occurs only as an ingredient of the elementary proposition.

[4.24]   Notational.

[4.241]   Wittgenstein was striving for mathematical precision in ordinary language, which perforce he could not get. If there is a logically perfect language, even if it were not the *Principa Mathematica* it would not be expressible in ordinary language but would require some sort of new, and completely abstract, notation. As it is, the qualitative aspects of existence which are excluded from partial representation in the system creep back into it as a generalized attribute of the whole system.

[4.242]   All symbolic expressions, in so far as their components represent outside the expressions, are only expedients inside.

[4.243]   It is not the names which are related in the proposition in which they both occur but those things which the names signify.

[4.25]   Truth and falsity in the elementary proposition is determined by the existence or non-existence of the atomic fact. But that a = a is not governed by atomic fact at all.

[4.26]   If we had all of the elementary propositions and knew which of them were true, how then would we know that in this way the world was "completely described"?

[4.27]   There are, in other symbols, 2^nth possibilities. This statement is leading up to the truth-tables.

[4.28]   The number of possible combinations of the elementary propositions equals the number of true and false propositions.

[4.3]   Thus we are talking in the end about atomic facts, but always in relation to their existence. The relation between atomic facts and their existence – or non-existence – if explored would take us into metaphysics. Therefore, it is not explored. Existence for atomic facts, logical space for propositions – these are assumed and even declared but hardly discussed and certainly not explored.

[4.31]   The truth-tables. So much work has been done on these since 1922 that it will hardly be of value to discuss them here.

Comment on any of the following propositions devoted to the truth-tables will be chiefly on other points. The name here for truth-tables is truth-possibilities.

[4.4]   Propositions can be tested by the truth-tables.

[4.41]   The truth of all other propositions depends upon the truth of the elementary propositions.

[4.42]   Notational.

[4.43]   Notational.

[4.431]   Frege's contention that truth and falsity are real objects is independent of what signs we assign to them. If we were to agree that $\sim p$ would mean true and p false, the symbolism would work just as well. Elements of propositions are manipulated by their signs but are not determined by them.

[4.44]   Notational.

[4.441]   That the notation is arbitrary is used again to furnish evidence that "there are no 'logical objects'". But the evidence would be acceptable only if there was a one-one correspondence between the notation and that which it denotes. Wittgenstein here fell into the mistake of identifying that which is signified with the sign, when he assumes that because he has full control over the designation of the sign there is thereby nothing which is signified. Nominalism does wish to get rid of the logical object, but Wittgenstein wished to have and not have his logical object. What is it, for instance, that he wished to consider in logical space?

[4.442]   The theory of types requires that a proposition cannot assert its own truth. Cf. 3.332.

[4.45]   The truth-tables enable us to arrange truth-conditions in a series.

[4.46]   The series extends from tautology to contradiction. Wittgenstein is so struck with the notational agreement of tautologies that he neglects to discriminate among them. Modern logicians and mathematicians discriminate non-trivial from trivial tautologies. Nevertheless, the discovery that logical truth is tautological was immensely important.

[4.4611]   Correct: but how did Wittgenstein distinguish between "not nonsensicial" here and "without sense" in the proposition just above?

[4.462]   Tautology and contradictions are the limits of the world.

[4.463]   The proposition in logical space sets the limits for facts (having been derived from facts) but is itself limited by tautology and contradiction.

The empirical world is limited at the top and the bottom by logic.

[4.464]   Probability lies between the certainty of tautology and the impossibility of contradiction.

[4.465] $a + a = a$. Tautology and contradiction are not "presenting relations".

[4.466]   All truths are specific; there are no universal truths, for if there were they would be logical, and logic corresponds to nothing in reality.

[4.4661]   The signs stand in relation to one another only for logical purposes.

[4.5]   The general form of proposition is a language, the syntax. It is the set of rules whereby propositions can be constructed, together with all the possibilities of the propositions.

[4.51]   The propositions are finite in number and static. Logic is limitation.

[4.52]   "The propositions", as distinct from the elementary propositions, are truth-functions.

[4.53]   And with the variable goes a table of the values, i.e. the elementary propositions.

[5]   Propositions are logical complications of elementary propositions.

It was probably Wittgenstein who convinced Russell and Whitehead that we have to distinguish between the "proposition as a fact", the elementary proposition, and the "proposition as a vehicle of truth or falsehood", the molecular proposition [1].

The relation between truth-functions and their bases is the same as that between a molecular proposition and an elementary proposition. The molecular proposition is true if it follows from a true elementary proposition; otherwise false. And the truth or falsity of a molecular proposition is all we shall be concerned with. This is in sharp contrast to the truth

[1] See *Principia Mathematica*, 2nd Edition, Appendix C, p. 660.

of an elementary proposition which is of a different character since it has a reference to states of affairs [1].

[5.01] The elementary propositions are the lowest in rank of the propositions, which are in levels upward.

[5.02] A proposition is a self-sufficient meaning, in a way in which a name is not.

[5.1] Truth-functions are constructed on the analogy of the natural numbers.

[5.101] The grounds of probability fail. Have the axioms for probability, or for any branch of analysis, e.g. the calculus, ever been worked out?
The truth-grounds are the field of a proposition.
There are a discrete rather than a continuous number of gradations of probability, at least in logic.
Universality is a special case of generality.

[5.11] A proposition is true if it follows from true propositions.

[5.12] Every true propositions implies every other true proposition.

[5.121] If one proposition follows from another it is because of the logic they both contain.

[5.122] And what is true of the agreement of truth must be true also for the sense; else it could not be so of the truth.

[5.123] If a god created a world in which logic prevails then he must obey the laws of logic in the act of creation. God, in other words, is subject to the laws of logic, as in Aquinas. Logic is inherent in objects.

[5.124] Deduction is analysis, as in Kant.

[5.1241] All truths form a system. Of every contradictory pair of propositions, one lies within the system.

[5.13] That is, from the truth-tables.

[5.131] If you have the truth of one proposition, then you have the truth of others.

[5.1311] There are logical relations within symbolism that are not at once apparent and must be brought out by the operations.

[5.132] An attack on the axiomatic method. If the method of constructionism is that of presuppositionless combinatorics, then obviously rules of inference are unnecessary.

---

[1] See Appendix C, pp. 660–661 of the Second Edition of the *Principia Mathematica* of Whitehead and Russell (Cambridge 1925, University Press).

The constructiveness of the *Tractatus* is interesting and significant but Wittgenstein wished to use it to deny the axiomatic method. But the proof that one method is useful would not necessarily mean another was not. Proof by the recognition of tautologies in the matrix method, which was Wittgenstein's, does not necessarily show also that the axiomatic method is invalid, for what is it that we do when we recognize a true deduction? Have we not recognized that the consequent is a necessary proposition, that it says less than the two propositions from which it was derived, and that, in effect, its derivation from them is tautological since they contained the same information it contained and no less? If logic is the method by which propositions describe the world, then it must have some properties; for even a method is something and not nothing. So our question now becomes, what are the properties of the logic which it possesses in virtue of what it is and how it functions? And it functions by constituting a set of enabling invariants; the enabling invariants are what allow propositions to describe the world. As to *what* logic is, we do not know from this analysis and will have to hypothecate something which is consistent with this analysis in order to make it fit.

[5.133]   There is no time in logic, for logic is able to operate by means of the reduction of material to formal implication.

[5.134]   But see 2.062.

[5.135]   But there are no two states of affairs entirely "different"!

[5.136]   But there are similarities.

[5.1361]   Not in all their singularity, no; but what about scientific predictions?

Is gravitation a superstition?

[5.1362]   The denial of causality here reminds one of Hume. The point here is that freedom is an illusion of ignorance, and is bound anyway by the logical limits of the world.

[5.1363]   Anti-psychology. Rejection of self-evidence as a criterion of truth.

Russell has confused belief and assertion in the Introduction to *Principia Mathematica*. See his efforts in the second edition to meet Wittgenstein's charges, Appendix C. See also above, 4.1121.

[5.14]   If q implies p, then q says what p says and what q adds. Kant's analytic conception again. Deductive argumentation is cumulative.

[5.141]   Statement of the bi-conditional.

[5.142]   Cf. 4.461.

[5.143]   Cf. 4.466. Wittgenstein saw logic in its space almost like a spatial structure. For him it is solid, much like Bluck's theory of what Plato meant by the Forms. See R. S. Bluck, *Plato's Phaedo*, Appendix 7.

[5.15]   A proposition guarantees another in proportion to the number which guarantee it.

[5.151]   He now wishes truth to be a probability, but accomplished by maintaining its discreteness in a flat logic. Probability raises special problems for constructionism.

[5.1511]   There is no such thing as the probability of a single instance.

[5.152]   The probability of a pair of propositions.

[5.153]   See 5.1511.

[5.154]   This is what Keynes calls "the total positive analogy"; an instance of perfect induction.

[5.155]   Wittgenstein fell here into regarding probability as a function of ignorance. The relative frequency theory would fit his scheme better.

[5.156]   An incomplete picture of a whole may be a complete picture of a part.
If the probability proposition is an extract, then it can add nothing, no new information; yet it does.

[5.2]   The internal relations of propositions are the logical elements.

[5.21]   The logical elements become prominent in the operations which produce a proposition from other propositions.

[5.22]   The structure of the new proposition and of the old ones from which the new one is derived have their logic in common.

[5.23]   Operation here means logical operation.

[5.231]   Formal property means logical form.

[5.232]   A logical operation also connects the elements of the proposition.

[5.233]   The construction of the proposition contains the possibility of its combination. Just as objects contain the logic by which they can be represented in signs.

[5.234]   Truth-functions, then, are derived propositions.

[5.2341]   The derived proposition is a function of the sense of the proposition from which it was derived.

[5.24]   The values of the variable are different propositions and we see through the variable how we can get from one of them to another.

[5.241]   Operations relate forms by what they have in common.

[5.242]   Exchanging values in a variable employs the identical logical operation.

[5.25]   Operating exchanges senses without reference to sense.

[5.251]   A proposition can be self-derived; that is, we can perform logical operations upon it, which do not change it or give it any other value. E. g. we can negate it if we do so *twice*.

[5.252]   Going upstairs in the hierarchy of logical types by performing logical operations upon a single proposition.

[5.2521]   For instance, the class of all classes, which is not itself a class but the result of operations on classes.

[5.2522]   Formal notation. It has not been subsequently adopted. The fate of his notation is similar to that of Peirce's for the logic of relatives.

[5.2523]   The number of operations may be finite or infinite; we have resolved this distinction if we phrase it in this way.

[5.253]   Operations are symmetrical; they face both ways.

[5.254]   Operations are opposites. Is this true of all of them?

[5.3]   Whitehead and Russell say in their Introduction to the Second Edition of the *Principia Mathematica* p. xv, "Given all true atomic propositions, together with the fact that they are all, every other true proposition can theoretically be deduced by logical methods". Elementary propositions were derived vertically from objects and atomic facts. Other propositions are derived horizontally from the elementary propositions by means of logical operations. (The similarity of Wittgenstein's first and last sentence under this number indicate carelessness, perhaps haste of composition and lack of revision.)

If every proposition is either an elementary proposition or a truth-function of an elementary proposition, then what are the propositions of the *Tractatus* insofar as they are consistent?

[5.31]   The truth-tables work equally for complex propositions.

[5.32]   Repeats 5.3.

[5.4]   Logic consists in operations whose possibilities were already inherent in the propositions, their terms, and even in the objects of which the terms are names. Again the contention that there is no logical thing-in-itself. See 4.441 and comment.

[5.41]   If the two truth-operations on elementary propositions are the same, then their results are identical. A sort of logical analogue of Leibniz's identity of indiscernibles.

[5.42]   Logical symbols indicate operations of a logical sort, and not logical constants, not logical *things*. Is not an operation a thing?

[5.43]   A finite set of axioms can generate an infinite number of theorems, as for instance from Peano's postulates.

[5.44]   Logical operations are not *things*, again. See 5.4 above. There can be no logical constants in the sense of logical substances, if they can be made to disappear, as "$\sim$" does in "$\sim \sim p$".

[5.441]   And the same holds true for the denial of negative particular propositions: they affirm the same as universal affirmative ones.

[5.442]   A proposition already contains all its logical possibilities, just as in Leibniz a subject already contains all its possible predicates.

[5.45]   The logical signs guide us in logical operations. They must be clearly defined.

[5.451]   A logical operation is always the same. Yes; but its status in Wittgenstein's system then has as yet to be explained. He seems to want a Platonic world of propositions, but derived from a nominalistic world of logic-containing material objects in the present.

Frege wrote: "The definition of an object does not, as such, really assert anything about the object, but only lays down the meaning of a symbol" [1].

[5.452]   The stroke function of Sheffer was such an event.

[1] G. Frege, *The Foundations of Arithmetic*, (Oxford 1950, Blackwell), p. 78.

There are no unique situations in logic. Whenever a problem is solved successfully by means of logic, then there must be other occurrences where the same solution can be employed.

[5.453]   But there are successive operations. Number, for Frege, is the name of a concept: it asserts something objective of a concept [1].

[5.454]   This follows if there is no preeminent number. And there is none, remember, because there is no preeminent operation.

[5.4541]   The poetry of logical systems here comes to the surface again. To be consistent, men have always supposed that everything fits somewhere into a system. We must think of the world of logic as an abstract structure.

[5.46]   The logical signs contain all the possibilities of their combinations, which operations elicit. The combinatorial logic of discreteness. A continuous logic is, of course, always possible and would be something else. (Cf. Von Neumann's continuous geometry.)

[5.461]   The brackets have considerable meaning, as Quine has shown. Nothing needed in logic is *un*important.

[5.4611]   And punctuation may be crucial to meaning.

[5.47]   Atomic facts are members of elementary propositions; elementary propositions are *included in* complex propositions. The membership relation may be the crucial one, for in it is given both logic and fact. Much confusion has resulted from supposing that an elementary proposition is a member of a complex proposition.

[5.4711]   This does not mean what it may have been supposed to mean, that there is nothing beyond logic; it means that it is not necessary to go beyond logic because logic properly understood reveals itself to be ontological.

The meaning of Wittgenstein for philosophy, and more particularly for metaphysics, is that ontology must not extend beyond logic without some logical necessity. In other words, philosophy-metaphysics-ontology can now be expressed in logic. The key to the bridge is a notion of system: systematic logic. Philosophy is a field of inquiry and logic is the philosophical method.

[1] *Op. cit.*, pp. 63, 115.

[5.472]   The proposition is the primitive sign of logic, and what it represents is of course fundamental.

[5.473]   Logic leaves everything as it is; it merely tells us how we can combine or uncombine real things; it does nothing to them, therefore what it does can be done again and again.
If the symbolism is handled correctly, i.e., in accordance with its definition, then there can be no mistakes in logic.

[5.4731]   Logic conditions thinking, but we must have the right premises or axioms.

[5.4732]   Whatever sense we give a sign is what the sign means.

[5.47321]   In logical symbolism whatever is not necessary is unnecessary.

[5.4733]   Assigning meanings is arbitrary, but changing meanings is impossible. Sometimes adjectives and nouns of the same name do not have a meaning in common.
One of the chief shortcomings of the *Tractatus* lies in the fact that Wittgenstein gave us no rules of procedure for deciding when an elementary proposition has sense and when it has not. On this hangs perhaps the chief difficulty; on more than one occasion before this, Wittgenstein ruled out self-evidence, yet it would seem that we are to determine whether an elementary proposition has sense only by inspection. To complete the structure of the *Tractatus* would we not need to have decision procedures for use in such a case?

[5.474]   We may have as many signs as we want, but it is better for economical purposes to want no more than we need.

[5.475]   Logic is a system of signs and signs are signals for operations, but there is no limit to the possible number, logically speaking.

[5.476]   This is a rejection again of the axiomatic method in favor of constructionism. The unlimited number of signs and their consequent operations is a function of the constructive method.

[5.5]   Notational.

[5.501]   This is all notational.

[5.502]   More notation.

[5.503]   Proposal to use the notation to construct propositions.

[5.51]   An illustration.

[5.511]   We are talking now about the indefinite extrapolation of complex propositions. Philosophers since Plato have been so busily engaged in defending or attacking the doctrine of the Ideas that no time has been left for investigating them and their conditions. We need now to assume that the doctrine is here to stay, and to begin its investigation. We need, in short, to climb inside the great mirror and have a considerable look about.

[5.512]   The expression of logic is aided by an adequate notation, but logic itself is independent of logical signs.

[5.513]   A notation is simply that which is common to a set of propositions which the notation can express at once. Logic in this way can be said to be a summary of conditions.

One could also add to this statement that logic is independent of logical language. This is Frege's realism and Russell's early realism, but it certainly was not Wittgenstein's second book!

[5.514]   Logical notation mirrors its conditions.

[5.515]   The logical constants, so called, connect propositions and thus indicate the presence of complex propositions.

[5.5151]   This is the sense in which logic is already given with the proposition; for instance, the possibility of the denial of a proposition is given with the proposition. There is, so to speak, a lateral connection in logic as well as a vertical connection of sense and reference.

[5.52]   The negation of a variable and its values, where these are complex propositions, is a negative particular proposition.

[5.521]   The truth-function has to do with the operation of a succession of propositions, not with the sum of them.

[5.522]   The symbolism of generality makes realism urgent. Wittgenstein wished to avoid realism; he assumed it, but he did not want it stated explicitly or admitted to this extent.

[5.523]   Generality is a set of instances. This is the nominalistic postulate for logic again.

[5.524]   *All* does not add anything to our knowledge but makes a claim for it that we may not be able to sustain. Whatever we have in our logical equipment, that is all that we have.

[5.525]   Propositions do not express ontological conditions, such as possibility or impossibility or certainty; they refer to states of affairs or they do not refer to states of affairs. Certainty, possibility, or impossibility refers to propositions.

[5.526]   Wittgenstein was caught between a realistic logic and a nominalistic approach through atomic facts. Either the world cannot be described completely or it contains no unique particulars.

[5.5261]   There are no simple, generalized propositions. But there is a world of symbols, a symbol society, a symbol world.

[5.5262]   Part of the total world is that part which is accounted for by logic (logic faces both ways, the actual world of atomic facts only one).

[5.53]   When we understand logic we understand the different ways in which things are, not different things.

[5.5301]   No two objects are identical.

[5.5302]   Equality won't do for logic though it will for mathematics. But this is true of many signs. In order to get mathematics from logic, we need a logic which differs from mathematics.

Wittgenstein here asserted that the definition of a quality called for by Russell, namely, that every predicative function satisfied by x is also satisfied by y, means $x = y$, is impossible; they cannot have all their properties in common. And this is true: no two objects do have all their properties in common; there is always a difference in space-time location even if there are no other grounds for distinction. (See *Principia Mathematica*, 13.01.)

[5.5303]   No two objects are identical; this is quite correct. It is a distinction between logic and fact that in logic we might have two signs which mean the same thing, though this would be useless and confusing, but in fact we cannot have two objects which are the same objects.

We could have identity in a molecular but not in an atomic proposition. An identity of signs is viable, not an identity of objects.

[5.531]   Wittgenstein substituted repetition for identity; to make things equal, he repeated the operation.

Notational indication of repetition rather than identity.

[5.532]   Functions are solved by alternativity.

The trouble here of course is with identity and singular terms. No two actual individuals are identical, a limitation of general logic in the face of particular fact.

[5.5321]   Further elimination of the identity sign.

And, analogously, for implication.

[5.533]   Wittgenstein supposed that he had got rid of the identity sign, but perhaps the logical situation had not been completely analyzed. What about the analysis of equality as mutual inclusion? Could we get rid of it then? Only as simple, when it is complex.

Cannot the need for any particular sign be circumvented with an appropriate notation? It is necessary to keep the logic which leads to mathematics from falling into the mathematics. The distinction between logic and mathematics is a genuine one.

[5.534]   This merely says that if we have no equal sign, we shall have to find another notation similar to what was done just above to express propositions which express identity.

Thus a = a is not a logical proposition, for in logic we are not prepared to count.

[5.535]   The postulation of an infinite number of propositional functions as in Russell's axiom of infinity is now no longer necessary according to Wittgenstein; for this he substituted the necessity for an infinite number of classes which are required for an infinite number of numbers. He was close here to Cantor's definition of the infinite.

The number of names is not to be specified, and so not asserted to be infinite.

[5.5351]   Identity has been rejected for logic; now, self-identity is to suffer the same fate. Was not Wittgenstein on weaker ground here?

[5.5352]   Question: Is the indication of the non-existence of a particular a particular proposition? Is "There is no such person as Theophilus Q. Smith, the current Treasurer of Tulane University" an existential proposition? Does it describe a unique particular which is acutal?

[5.54]   See Russell's Introduction to the *Tractatus*, pp. 19–21; also *Principia Mathematica*, Introduction to the Second Edition, p. iv (Cambridge 1925, University Press). The proposition is a fact, yes, but only in a logical world, in logical space; and from there its relevance to states of affairs has to be explained.

[5.541]   Psychology does not *add* anything except an irrational constant. Is "I think that 2 and 2 are 4" any more illuminating than that 2 and 2 are 4? Economy is violated by adding to both sides of an equation, e.g. God's world is served by God's good.

The proposition has meaning (i.e. in Frege's "sense"), and it has reference (i.e. to states of affairs), but it does not have belief.

[5.542] From the standpoint of logic, all psychological and epistemological considerations add nothing but identity. "A believes that p" says no more than that "the assertion of p is the assertion of p".

[5.5421] The soul in psychology is the same as an identity symbol in logic which merely repeats.

And the soul does, too, if it is simple. If it is compound, then it is something else unanalyzed, of which a component may be the soul.

[5.5422] Inside logic, everything has at least some logical meaning; outside logic, logic cannot judge.

Psychology does not deal with negation, it is not able to.

[5.5423] In logic, in a whole there are only the parts.

[5.55] Now we have something different. The elementary proposition becomes unanalyzable, and its composition involves axioms.

[5.551] This follows from the way in which logic *is* "the world in symbols".

Constructionism properly carried out must always be able to tell us where we are. What cannot be decided by means of the notation of logic cannot be decided in logic. But we do not always know in advance intuitively just what our notation will tell us on every question.

[5.552] Logic is the set of conditions under which there can be an experience. Experience can tell us nothing about logic that was not already so.

What room is there in a constructionism for an *a priori* logic? Either logic is derived from the objects we are naming and is part of the combinatorics of names, or it is not. An *a priori* logic is an axiomatic logic and this is precisely what Wittgenstein most of the time was trying to avoid. On the other hand, when constructionism is accomplished, one finds that it has run into a logical world in which the conditions for the solution of every problem of a logical nature have been decided in advance; in short, a Platonic world of forms which are independent of our experience of them and independent also of the states of affairs from which they have been abstracted.

[5.5521]   In order to account for logic in the world, it is necessary to suppose that logic was given *with* the world.

[5.553]   No preeminent number because numbers are repeated operations. The only other logical system besides the Hilbertian is the Hegelian, a circular logic; and a circular logic, i.e. a lateral logic, is needed for logic if logic is to produce linear Hilbertian mathematics.

[5.554]   And so there is no preeminent logical form, either.

[5.5541]   There is a special logical world, but in this world not anything about the actual world can be decided in advance. Existential import.

[5.5542]   The answer is: not if the notation has been constructed correctly.

The second question is intelligible in terms of the first.

[5.555]   What is peculiar to logic is the notion of system.

Logic is real, the notation arbitrary. This makes it difficult to know exactly the status of logic, only its structure.

The presupposition of system stands behind any procedure (otherwise it could not be consistent, orderly).

[5.556]   A flat logic.

[5.5561]   A finite world, therefore finite logic; the infinite appears only in the intensity, not in the extensity. There are an infinity of distinctions about the world and its logic, though both are finite.

[5.5562]   What we set up in this way cannot be arbitrary; everybody's logic is the same.

[5.5563]   A foreshadowing of Wittgenstein's later work. Our analysis of what the colloquial language contains tells us all that we can know about the world, and logic shows us how.

On the argument from language to the world before Wittgenstein see Plato, *Cratylus*, and Leibniz in Russell's *History of Philosophy*, Ch. XI.

[5.557]   Logic becomes involved immediately when we talk

about anything in any language; and that indeed is what logic is. And we apply logic when we use this knowledge.

But is eliciting the logic the same as using a logic?

[5.5571] What is *a priori* (i.e. employed as presuppositions) is the method whereby it is agreed that we shall construct all and only those elementary propositions which are possible, given the objects that there are.

[5.6] Don't I symbolize everything that I can? Then this proposition follows from the next above.

My action is limited by fact; my understanding of fact, by logic. I cannot go outside the world – or outside logic. See Russell's Introduction to the *Tractatus*, pp. 17–18.

[5.61] 'My world' is a logical world, and logic is everybody's solipsism.

[5.62] Wittgenstein has got rid of the vexed question of subjectivism by going the whole way with it, and so showing that in this way it contributes nothing. But only in this way can that be shown.

[5.621] To be alive means to that extent to be aware of the world and its logic.

[5.63] I am what I can experience from here, i.e. from me.

[5.631] Has anybody recognized that Hume was not a subjectivist, and so Kant was not, either, although all of his followers have been? Only by getting knowledge away from the object and from the subject can we see that it is not *knowledge* after all with which we are concerned but *system*.

A complex subject would only compound or confuse the knowledge of the world. He has the support of Hume here. The subject is not part of the subject's experience.

[5.632] The subject is not a *thing* any more than a logical constant is. Knowing and the knower are the limits of knowledge (not of the known).

[5.633] The theory of perspectives. An occupant of a perspective is a locus, and not an occupier, not a subject; for when a perspective is not occupied it still exists.

And from the fact that the eye is not part of the visual field, we can understand that to put the subject back into the world of the subject would be logically unallowable.

[5.6331] The field of signs is rather a form like this.

Eye — ⊃

[5.634]   This can only be said by excluding time from logic, and by remembering that we are speaking only in logic.

[5.64]   AT LAST – the metaphysical presuppositions!

J. R. Weinberg in his *An Examination of Logical Positivism* (London 1936, Kegan Paul), p. 68, speaks of "a solipsism without a subject"; he points out on the previous pages that an objective science which was organized without respect to any particular experiencing subject would not be meaningful in Wittgenstein's system since, for him, science is an organization of individual experience. He, therefore, holds that the *Tractatus* is inconsistent with experimental science in this regard as well.

One small point, however, might solve the problem. We have said elsewhere that, according to Wittgenstein, logic is everybody's solipsism (see the comment on 5.61); if the solipsism could be extended to every subject, then we should have a world view which was consistent with that of experimental science.

Epistemological realism, of course. That Wittgenstein's system involves metaphysical realism was shown above.

[5.641]   We talk about the world from the perspective which we occupy and from which it appears to be thus and so.

[6]   The general proposition is a truth-function, i.e. not derived from one-one correspondence with facts but from other (elementary) propositions.

[6.001]   The operation is the negation of all the values of the propositional variable. See 5.501 ff.

[6.002]   Constructing complex propositions from elementary in a way analogous to the repetition of operations to produce numbers.

[6.01]   Notational.

[6.02]   Definitional.

[6.021]   The repetition of operations again repeated for numbers. The *Tractatus* follows the general plan of *Principia Mathematica* to differ with it. (See 4.1252, 4.1273, etc.)

[6.022]   Number as class is, simply, the numbers. High level nominalism.

[6.03] The cardinal is a standard operation on a proposition.

[6.031] We are permitted to enumerate operations but not to collect them by summing them up in a class. The operation of integration would yield a class, would it not?

But what about sets of operations?

[6.1] If the propositions of logic are not tautologies then they are contradictions.

[6.11] They tell us about the meaning of language.

[6.111] We have attributed to language the properties which derive from the world, from actual states of affairs, and Wittgenstein wished to restore them to the world and to call the remainder 'logic'.

Logic says nothing (i.e. nothing empirically).

[6.112] It makes them the ordering operators.

[6.113] Logical truth goes by inspection; factual truth by investigation, if it can be found at all.

Logic does not have to go beyond language, fact does.

[6.12] What we learn *in* logic tells us nothing about the world, only about propositions. But what we learn *about* logic tells us about the world, for logic is part of the world; it is the second storey of a two-storeyed world.

[6.1201] Logic is simply obeying the rules.

[6.1202] Logical propositions can be constructed with the use of contradictions.

[6.1203] The intuitive method in logic. Resembles Whitehead's extensive abstraction.

Tautology by overlapping.

[6.121] Again, a foreshadowing of Wittgenstein's later work. When logic eliminates itself it leaves language representing the real world. Logic is how the process of linguistic representation operates, but logic itself does not represent.

[6.122] There would be no logic as such in a logically perfect language.

[6.1221] One use of notation is to make the logic clear.

[6.1222] Logic is independent of experience, yes, but has constructionism shown this? To confine our manipulations to combination may, but how was combination authorized?

[6.1223] The axiomatic method, answered Wittgenstein, is to be confined to the devising of an adequate notation. We may, in other words, take undefined terms but not primitive propositions.

[6.1224] The logical forms and the combinatoric inference.

[6.123] Logic without presuppositions, without a meta-logic. Simple notational combinatorics. Simple rational intuition all by itself; Brouwer, without the subject.

[6.1231] For instance, the relation of a converted particular affirmative proposition to the original proposition is tautologous without being general.

[6.1232] "Accidental general validity" is where we have a universal proposition whose truth is observed but where the reasons for it remain unknown, e.g. "all men are mortal". See 3.34. The distinction between accidental and essential generality has been recognized traditionally under other names. For accidental generality we would have said empirical generalization, and for essential generality, universal proposition. The former aspires to a condition of the latter in the same way that probabilities assume parameters.

The axiom of reducibility is non-logical because it cannot be proved in logic, i.e. deduced from logical principles. If true, it means that mathematics is not altogether derivable from logic. For every general proposition, there is an elementary proposition to which it may be reduced. True? Assumed by Wittgenstein but, as in the analogous case of the axiom of reducibility in *Principia Mathematica*, not deducible.

[6.1233] Logic is not concerned with the validity of extra-logical principles. The existential import of the *Principia Mathematica* requires that it get rid of real classes. Wittgenstein held that if you do not set them up in the first place then you do not have the obligation to get rid of them, and he did not hold that they need be set up if constructionism be adopted as a logical method rather than axiomatization.

[6.124] Logic constructs a scaffolding by which to make a picture of the world, or more simply a mirror by which to view the world.

Logic teaches us something about the world; namely, that when signs behave in the way that they do, lend themselves to the combinations that they do, it is because the elements of the world contain such possibilities.

The final abstraction from the subject, his knowings and his intendings, is accomplished by this method and *its* meaning. Logic is inherent in symbol systems. Wittgenstein forgot there is more than one of both but only one of each *kind*.

[6.125] If we properly distinguish logical consistency from factual truth and call the former logical truth.

[6.1251] Logic is an unfolding; elicitation may involve novelty of presentation though not surprises.

[6.126] Tautologies provided the base-line of logic. Logical space is defined by the containment of tautologies.

[6.1261] In logic, what we get is what we have already. See 6.1251.

[6.1262] Logic is a method, not a subject-matter. Mathematics must show consistency with axioms; for Wittgenstein, logic must show reduction to tautology.

[6.1263] Proofs of the method of proof are impossible; for by what could one prove them?

[6.1264] If the elements of a proposition have been properly named, then logical connectives used properly constitute all the proof that there is; and in the case of the complex propositions the process is merely repeated.

[6.1265] Logic shows itself forth.

[6.127] A statement of the flat logic. Logic is not itself an axiom system. Important, and maybe crucial, if true. For it would mean that the system from which the axiom systems of mathematics are deduced is not itself an axiom system.

[6.1271] Another attack on the axiomatic method. Self-evidence is not bound up with this method nor any longer admissible in it.

[6.13] Abstractions which are true are facts – facts about the world.

When Wittgenstein had built up from his atomic facts to the final stage of complex propositions, he found that he had encountered a logic that was there all the time. Logic exists in a sort of Platonic second-storey natural world where it was ready to be used in connecting the names into elementary propositions, and the elementary propositions into complex propositions. Wittgenstein wavered between two views: (1) that of a logic which was derived from the objects along with the names for them, and (2) a logic which was already *a priori* in logical space. The former is more consistent with constructionism; the second has to depart from natural conditions of nominalism to admit a second-storey logic which is independent in a sense of the first storey of natural objects and atomic facts.

[6.2]   In order to show that mathematics is a logical method on any structure different from the axiomatic method that mathematics employs, it would be necessary to arrive logically at the starting-point of mathematics, that is to say, at its axioms or at the presuppositions set for the axioms, as their meta-axioms. This Wittgenstein did not accomplish merely by defining numbers as repetitions of operations.

[6.21]   They express logical relations, which are there whether we think them or not; and that is why we can think them. Thoughts, however, do express mathematical propositions.

[6.211]   Applied mathematics does not apply to mathematics but to empirical propositions, to states of affairs.
Logic helps language to tell us about the world.

[6.22]   Mathematics is such that applied mathematics says nothing logically; it only shows forth what the states of affairs are.

[6.23]   Mathematics behaves like logic.

[6.231]   Logical elements contain logical possibilities; mathematical equations, mathematical ones.

[6.232]   It is not the case that two expressions are equal because the sign of equality says so; but the sign of equality can say so because they are equal.

[6.2321]   In mathematics we consider the relations of atomic facts so generalized that they can be abstracted from the facts and their "correctness", i.e. validity, decided from inspection.

[6.2322]   The identity is carried by the meaning, and if it is asserted, then it is present twice, and the repetition adds nothing.

[6.2323]   The equation only says what is already said in the equation, in its two expressions.

[6.233]   The insights are in logic and not contributed to logic.

[6.2331]   Calculation tells us what we want to know, by eliciting the information from logic.

[6.234]   An extension of logic.

[6.2341]   The mathematics that Wittgenstein needed to make out his case is a highly selective version.

[6.24]   The rules of inference include besides unlimited substitution also detachment, *modus ponens*.

[6.241]   Proof in mathematics and logic means merely eliciting the tautological properties.

[6.3]   In logic there is regularity, and we know whether we are in logic or not when we do or do not encounter accident, i.e. irregularity.

[6.31]   Here induction appears as the choice of axioms. It was not needed for Wittgenstein's logical constructionism, which of course for him *is* logic.

[6.32]   Causality, then, is a logical law; it has been exhibited by Whitehead as a nexus. And laws of causality are nexūs.

[6.321]   On Wittgenstein's earlier contentions for probability this would not be the case. Unless tautology can be shown of empirical instances.

[6.3211]   Before Maupertuis, but not much before, it must have become evident that dynamic systems did not change configurations without change in total energy so that the action was held to a minimum. The empirical experiences must have been brought to a logical head. The *a priori* aspect only means that all logical conditions always have prevailed, and only their selection is peculiar to the empirical stage of knowledge at any time.

[6.33]   It is the logical forms of empirical laws and not the laws themselves which are *a priori*. The distinction, however, is inadmissible, if logic is imbedded in objects, as we were led to suppose in the earliest pages of the *Tractatus*.

[6.34]   For every scientific law, then, there is a logical form which means that every scientific law is a set of scientific laws! Do we solve empirical problems logically? Sometimes this is possible, but not always.

[6.341]   The axiom systems of empirical science, the mathematical descriptions, are quite arbitrary. The flat logic is applied to the network in such a way that we are given no criterion for choosing a fine mesh over a coarse one. A crude picture is a legitimate mirror (5.511).

Wittgenstein finally managed to get rid of all mathematics and all natural science, for both commit the error of setting up deductive systems. What portends to be scientific or mathematical must square with the *Tractatus* if it is to survive logically, and no axiom system meets these requirements.

[6.342]   A partial description is as much of a description, so far as it goes, as a complete one. We learn something, then, by comparing meshes.

[6.343]   But the world is not static.

[6.3431]   Empirical science aspires to the condition of logic but for another purpose.

[6.3432]   But the result is to increase the fineness of the network. Thus empiricism contributes to logic, even though aspiring to describe the world. Logic is a set of enabling invariants for the description.

[6.35]   Logic tells us nothing about the world, and all that it says it says logically.

[6.36]   Wittgenstein wanted us to understand the law of causality as the form of all scientific laws.

[6.361]   The laws of science can only be formulated in terms of regularity, for uniformity of nature is regularity of law; but the situation has in recent times been interpreted otherwise: as statistical laws which are not causal.

[6.3611]   Time is not causal, and exists only in a comparison of happenings. The theory of relativity.

[6.36111]   Logical conditions of the world are independent of logical manipulations and of the world as well; for that is just what logic means.

[6.362]   To the extent to which states of affairs lend themselves to logic, they can be described in language, and causality is the language of events.

[6.363]   Induction is construction, not axiomatization. In constructional induction, we have to imagine only names, not axioms, and that is why it is simple.

Wittgenstein could not admit induction in the ordinary way, for induction is the choosing of axioms and thus is tied in to the axiom system; but the method of constructionism is opposed to and is intended to replace the axiomatic method.

[6.3631]   Induction is not logical; see 6.31.

Induction can have no logical foundations. No induction, then no hypotheses; and we are not to have hypotheses in the method of constructionism.

[6.36311] The sunrise tomorrow is a high probability, as Peirce pointed out, not a certainty. Then where is the "causal law"?

[6.37] Causality is logical or it does not hold. It is not empirical. The necessity of the empirical field, of states of affairs, is logical in character.

[6.371] Causality and all laws of nature are laws of logic merely; they do not altogether "explain" the world.

[6.372] The laws of nature are not sacred; they are probabilities merely.

[6.373] Because I will, which is a happening, something in the world corresponding to it does not have to happen as a consequence. See 6.37. The world is not in a logical connection of necessity with my will.

[6.374] Whatever happens, happens objectively.

[6.375] The conditions are logical.

[6.3751] When qualities misbehave, they do so logically. It is possible to have clashing colors, for instance. But logic itself is neutral: it does not do anything; it is what other things do when they do something incorrect.

[6.4] Logically speaking, of course.

What we call the 'flat logic' is in the *Tractatus* intended to replace the logical hierarchy in the *Principia Mathematica*. Constructionism builds up to flat logic; the axiomatic method derives down to a set of theorems of unequal rank depending upon their degree of removal from the axioms.

[6.41] Logic furnishes the conditions for accidental happenings, and so does causal law.

[6.42] In logic there is no value, hence no ethical values.

[6.421] Transcendental, in Kant's meaning, i.e. beyond experience. Ethics and aesthetics are two sides of the same values, looked at up or down.

The contradiction of this proposition with 4.003 is undeniable.

[6.422] Actions, like logical propositions, carry their own meaning and bring about their own consequences. It can be shown only by being done.

[6.423] The will belongs to psychology, not philosophy. It is clear that Wittgenstein had experienced only German subjective and psychological metaphysics and epistemology: Kant, Hegel, Fichte, and the like. But not all metaphysics or even epistemology has to be of the subjective idealistic variety.

[6.43]   The coloring of the subject changes the world of the subject; more properly, gives the subject that aspect of the world, selects in the world for the subject.

[6.431]   For the subject; the solipsism without a subject henceforth can exist after death – but not for the subject.

[6.4311]   Is life always like this sample? Then this is it.

[6.4312]   We think of another world for the soul, and we can think only in this-world terms; but it would be another world that we were thus wrongly describing.

[6.432]   The reason for the world is not to be found in the world. God, like logic, is a world condition.

[6.4321]   The logical conditions and not their carrying out in practice are what sit still.

[6.44]   Being, not mechanism, furnishes the inexplicable. That is why, in philosophy, we start from there, from the logical locus of ontology.

[6.45]   We look at the wholeness of the world from inside, so to speak, where this side of its boundaries are discernible; we see its boundaries as limits, otherwise perhaps we would not see it as a whole. "All determination is negation", said Spinoza. To see it as timeless is to see it as unaffected by time, and this is only as a whole.

Hence the mystical feeling in all of Spinoza's philosophy.

[6.5]   When there is no answer, then there is the wrong question.

[6.51]   Doubt can occur legitimately only where there is sense, and the doubt of the agreement of sense and reference. Doubt in the case of nonsense cannot occur.

[6.52]   There is an extra-scientific area. Wittgenstein called it living problems; it includes the values: good, beautiful and holy.

[6.521]   The living problems vanish in Wittgenstein's system, and then we see them as having been pseudo-problems. Whatever can be asked can be answered; but this we do not know how to ask.

[6.522]   The logical and mystical: that is all there is. And we can ask no questions concerning the mystical, and so receive no answers, for there are no problems since none can be framed.

[6.53]   Philosophy is limited to the natural sciences and to the denial of metaphysics. This proposition is what the logical positivists have followed, but this only and not the others; and, as we have seen, there are others. They would not themselves have resulted from the strict following of this method. Wittgenstein was not himself a logical positivist.

[6.54]   But then this is a system for not following it. It is a viewpoint which corrects an older, metaphysical viewpoint, and like it, must be thrown away. And what results is neither, but a fresh look at the world, a viewpoint without presuppositions.

[7]   We must limit what we say in philosophy to what by fact and logic can be justified.

CHAPTER V

CONCLUSIONS FROM THE COMMENTARY

Since this whole book is not to be given over to the *Tractatus*, we have devoted a disproportionate amount of space to it already, and our conclusions from it will perforce have to be brief. We shall begin, then, with a glance at the background.

The *Tractatus* came out of discussions with Russell when Wittgenstein was or just had finished being Russell's pupil at Cambridge. It is certain that Wittgenstein influenced Russell, but it is equally certain that Russell influenced Wittgenstein. And, what is equally important, Russell was on the scene first.

Russell began with metaphysical realism, and with a new logic by means of which he hoped to defeat it. That he began with such a realism is clear and generally admitted as well as admitted by him [1]. That he did regard realism as fundamental he also admitted [2]. The *Principia Mathematica* contains many attempts to get around the basic Platonism of which such realism consists. The theory of types, incomplete symbols, the axiom of reducibility, all these were devices intended to assist in contriving the elimination of such abstractions as would lend aid and comfort to a metaphysics of the Platonic variety.

That the *Principia* failed in this aim at least was shown by – of all people – one of Russell's own pupils, Wittgenstein. In the *Tractatus* he set for himself two tasks. The first was to show that a realism was built into the very method by which the *Principia* worked, the axiomatic method. If the aim was to get rid of the independence of the abstract entities, and to show that they were reducible to the language by which actual physical objects were named and manipulated, then the *Principia* defeated itself, for it assumed such an independence by starting

---

[1] Bertrand Russell, "Logical Atomism" in *Contemporary British Philosophy*, First Series, ed. J. H. Muirhead (London 1925, Allen and Unwin), p. 359.
[2] *Op. cit., loc. cit.*

its procedures in a realm and with such entities as it already possessed, and by implication assumed the independence in question. For the axioms of an axiomatized system are notoriously independent of that sort of truth which consists in a correspondence with the data disclosed by experience. If you have an axiomatized system, then you have a Platonic realm and Platonic entities, in short you have realism. The only requirements we make of an axiom-set is that its propositions be independent of each other, not inconsistent, complete, and fruitful, the last being the requirement which puts them importantly at the head of a deductive structure in which they play an essential role.

In the final analysis the *Tractatus* suffers from the defects of Russell's *Principia*. In the *Principia* the use of the axiomatic method is confronted with the attempt to use a theory of descriptions and a doctrine of logical constructions. The metaphysics of the former is metaphysically realistic and of the latter nominalistic, and Wittgenstein suffered from these contradictions.

That Wittgenstein tried to show this in the *Tractatus* is evident in every one of its references to the *Principia*. Even the derivation of the natural numbers, which in the *Principia* were deduced in such a fashion as to allow them a Platonic status, were in the *Tractatus* reduced to the repetition of operations, a more nominalistic notion. Whether Wittgenstein succeeded in his first aim is another question, and a more extended and technical one than the present examination permits; for it would be necessary to review the subsequent literature on the criticism of the *Principia*, as well as all subsequent logical developments, before answering.

Wittgenstein's second aim in the *Tractatus* was to succeed where he supposed Russell had failed. He intended to show that by the method of constructionism a logic can be built without any of the assumptions or acts of commission which might imply a realism. In this he most distinctly failed, for, starting with atomic facts, which were, as we have noted already, somewhat above the ground, he allowed these to be named, and then admitted that the connection of names into propositions by means of the logical entities, which he was careful to point out, *had no other status*. The manoeuvre in the end proved to be a cruel one, for if the logical entities had no other status, then they must belong to the logical space of which he found himself compelled to speak, in short, they must be Platonic entities and the logical space a Platonic realism with not only its own entities but its own ground rules as well.

In short, where Russell began explicitly with the assumption of independent axioms and deduced down to theorems capable of application, Wittgenstein began by hoping to assume nothing and built up to the discovery of the logical realm with its independent entities and rules. In both cases, a kind of logical nominalism was attempted (as being the only kind of minimal nominalism logic could legitimately undertake) and in both cases it not only failed but furnished evidence that at the very least a restricted realism was required in order to account for what is present. This, if not a proof of the validity of realism, is certainly a strong argument in its favor.

The realism of Russell's early work spread his influence in two directions. One, and the one to which we have devoted most of our attention, is represented by Wittgenstein and his followers. The other is represented by Whitehead.

Wittgenstein's followers evidently thought that he had succeeded in his efforts to support a logical nominalism, and they continued the work in a spirit of dogmatism which he had never evinced. It will be necessary, then, to follow his efforts a little way in order to show the error in more detail.

The dilemma in which Russell was caught – between metaphysical realism on the one hand and logical nominalism on the other – can be specified with regard to the status of classes. From the metaphysics he could deduce that the class is an object, and from the nominalistic logic he could deduce that the class is a name for a collection of objects (its members). Between classes as real objects and classes as names for collections of real objects there is a genuine contradiction, and it is one which he never resolved. Subsequent inquirers, such as Wittgenstein, who refused to recognize the reality of classes, were caught in the same dilemma. Whitehead escaped it only because he adopted the theory of the reality of classes as well as of the collection of objects of which they are the names; thus Whitehead

was forced into a metaphysical realism which refuses to distinguish between classes and their members on the basis of their
reality, and on this he built a whole realist philosophy, whereas
Russell went on struggling with his dilemma. It must be admitted, however, that the dilemma has been fruitful since it
produced both Whitehead on the one hand and Wittgenstein
and his followers on the other.

The points of similarity between Wittgenstein's second book
and Whitehead's position are often striking. We shall consider
chiefly two.

The first is the similarity of Wittgenstein's method to what
Whitehead called "the fallacy of misplaced concreteness".
Wittgenstein wished to get rid of philosophy because it interferes with our view of the world; Whitehead wished to get rid
of the *wrong* philosophy, for the same reason. Wittgenstein's
position was a more extreme one than Whitehead's for while
Whitehead thought there was a *right* philosophy which would
give us the correct view of the world, Wittgenstein held that a
correct view of the world can only come after we have eliminated
all philosophy.

The second point of similarity is in the tentativeness of the
method. Whitehead subscribed to the doctrine of fallibilism,
though not by that name, and Wittgenstein did too, but he had
no name for it, either. It consisted in a certain tentativeness, a
certain caution, and a certain unwillingness to be more than
half-committed to any positive position. It also consisted in a sort
of probing method, a sort of febrile exploration of the field, with
a delicacy which did not want to disturb anything it examines.

If this book has a moral it must consist in showing that
Whitehead succeeded where Russell's other followers, including
Wittgenstein, had failed. Whitehead's achievement flowed from
the extent to which he tried to solve by means of metaphysical
realism the problems Russell raised for his followers by denying
it. After all, Whitehead wrote the *Principia* with Russell, and
the best part of his life to that point had been devoted to professional mathematics. He saw, evidently, that the implications
of the new logic required working out, but he saw also, as the
others did not, that it required a metaphysical realism. This he
proceeded to develop in a series of books until he had produced

"the philosophy of organism", in which everyone recognizes that what he was proclaiming was a basic Platonism, but one brought up to date by means of the new logic and the revolution in physics. The logical positivists, who are the inheritors of Wittgenstein, on the one hand, and Whitehead on the other, claim to square with science in their philosophies; and more time and thought will be required before it can be determined to everyone's satisfaction which has done so. It is the thesis of this book that the early Russell, the Russell of the period of realism, and the later Whitehead, will prove the most successful.

Philosophy in the Greek period was a free enterprise; it was not bound to any institution. Immediately after Plato and Aristotle, however, it became bound to religion: to the Jewish religion through Philo, to the Greek religion through Plotinus, and to the Christian religion through Augustine's Neo-Platonism. Thereafter it remained bound until after the Renaissance; empiricism set it free, but empiricism came in two distinct forms: objective and subjective. Objective empiricism was never proclaimed, it was only practiced, practiced by the experimental scientists, and in particular the physicists, the chemists and the biologists – the natural scientists. Empiricism was proclaimed as a philosophy by the subjectivists, in particular by the British tradition – Francis Bacon, Locke, Berkeley and Hume – and British subjectivism also infected the Germans who turned philosophy away from metaphysics and into epistemology. Subjectivism comes to an end with the revival of realism. The early Russell was a metaphysical realist. What Wittgenstein tried to do, rather, was to try to bring together metaphysical realism with subjective empiricism. His attempt failed but he did raise the question for us whether a philosophical objective empiricism is not possible. Can we not construct a philosophical empiricism corresponding to what science practices? This is the question he has left us, and his failure to achieve it may be more significant than many another success has been, for it is a suggestive failure and a significant one. The answer could lie in the return to metaphysics, but metaphysics of a chastened variety – a finite metaphysics whose claims are much abated but which, as a structure, is still able to stand; for this reason, in fact, is able to stand more firmly.

We have come a long way since Plato first constructed his theory of Ideas. After the first shock of acceptance of the theory, the flood of theology overcame it. Inquiry into the nature of the Ideas was shut off by making the Ideas thoughts in the mind of God where they were inaccessible to further exploration. This was followed by a reaction to theology in the form of nominalism: a disbelief in the reality of Ideas which also shut off further inquiry into their nature. When science arose, it was not recognized that the exploration of the empirical abstractions was an approach to the theory of Ideas *via* scientific laws. The new logic also gave a key to it which was not recognized.

But now Wittgenstein, in his theory of logical space and of propositions independent of the reality from which they were derived and of which they are the pictures, has again suggested, albeit inadvertently, the exploration of this realm. We now know that another name for the theory of Ideas is the logical realm, the second storey of a two-storeyed natural world [1]. Further exploration is, of course, quite possible and the logicians are moving ahead rapidly both in terms of a modal logic and of the further exploration of what is now in some quarters openly considered to be a Platonic logic. The aim is to keep this realm free of affective elements; we wish to explore it but not to adore it, for to adore it alone is to omit the world from which it was derived and to forget the world to which it applies back. The world of logic is not the whole world of nature but the second storey of a two-storeyed natural world.

The endeavor of the *Tractatus* is clear. It was to substitute the method of constructionism for the axiomatic method. Instead of the assumptions contained in the axioms, we would begin with atomic facts as given, although half assuming that the objects which the atomic facts combine are disclosed or at least disclosable by sense experience. In this way, a presuppositionless technique could be devised, the method of presuppositionless combinatorics.

Wittgenstein seemed to think that he had got rid of deduction, and hence inference, by substituting combinatorics, for in mere

---

[1] A better term, perhaps, might be Whitehead's. He spoke of the "duality of nature" in *An Enquiry Concerning The Principles of Natural Knowledge* (Cambridge 1955, University Press), p. 98.

combinations we do not infer, we only calculate. But knowing when to make a calculation and what sort of calculation to make implies a background of deductive schema in terms of which we are operating. Wittgenstein attacked the whole axiomatic method in detail, that is to say, he tried to avoid setting up axioms, he refused to admit the necessity for rules of inference and he did not wish to have the proofs by means of which we support theorems. But while he attacked the axiomatic method in detail, he did not succeed in getting away from it in the background: it hides behind the assumptions of his structure, for while we increase in generality as we go from atomic facts to elementary propositions to complex propositions, if we turn the system around and look at what we have, we will find that what we have is an axiomatic method, only we have set it up in reverse. The axiomatic method begins with the axioms and reduces down to the theorems and from them to their applications in particular: first, particular propositions and then atomic facts corresponding to these.

It will be helpful to pursue this topic a little longer. Do we get away from the axiom-type of system by burying our definitions and proposed rules of inference among the theorems? How would we have known, for instance, the nature of an elementary proposition or the rules by which it was obtained? The *Tractatus* turns out to contain one more axiom-system, but with its elements so rearranged as to appear not to be one. Constructionism considered as an empirical method is satisfactory, but Wittgenstein has shown two things inadvertently: (1) that it begins not where it seems to begin, namely, in the action of naming objects, but with presuppositions, by taking for granted certain rules of procedure; and (2) that when it is proliferated sufficiently, the only hope for restoring or preserving order is to arrange the propositions in the shape of an axiom-system.

He is guilty, then, of committing the genetic fallacy of assuming that what has been done in one way must *be* that way. He derived his structure constructively while the axiomatic method derives it deductively; but the end result of both methods is the same, for the complex propositions are greater in generality than the atomic facts no matter which way we twist and turn and no matter from which end we start to build our structure. So what counts is what structure we have and what its properties are, and not how we arrived at it in the first place.

If the *Tractatus* did not have its own axioms, we might be more inclined to sympathize with Wittgenstein in the success of his search to avoid them explicitly. For he assumed them implicitly, no doubt of that. His very effort to avoid all assumptions carries with it its own. After going through the system of the *Tractatus* in some detail we can now see what the axioms were.

Thus we might describe his first axiom as follows. A system of philosophy can be constructed on the basis of a presuppositionless combinatorics.

His others follow in quick succession, and emerge from the pages of the *Tractatus* as it were together. Without endeavoring therefore to rank them we will merely list them. Thus they are: a nominalistic logic; metaphysical realism; epistemological realism; constructionism as methodology. Let us say a word in explanation of each of these.

The nominalistic logic means an orthodox nominalism, i.e. the predominant reality of physical particulars, tempered with the reality of a ghostly logic which is able to facilitate representation without itself being anything at all. The logic is an intuitional logic, of the Brouwerian variety, combined with Frege's distinction between sense and reference (i.e. meaning and truth), a motionless, flat logic.

The metaphysical realism of an independent real world of logical propositions and their inter-relations. The worlds of fact and logic are both finite and bounded; there is a timeless solipsism.

The epistemological realism whereby both the world of fact and also the world of logical propositions are as they are, independent of our knowledge of them.

Constructionism has as its method a beginning in atomic facts (which are combinations of objects). From the atomic facts is elicited their logic, and by this logic we can represent the atomic facts by means of elementary propositions. We are now at the second, and last, storey. At the level of this second storey, complex or molecular propositions are constructed by combining elementary propositions.

The axioms set forth above are intriguing, but they lack the first requirement of an axiom-set, that is to say they are not consistent, and their inconsistencies emerge in the contradictions which make themselves so evident in the *Tractatus*.

What is the evidence for such a system, apart from the method by which we took as our primitives only the nature of atomic facts and the language by which they could be named?

In philosophy usually the attempt is made to describe reality or what there is. In the *Tractatus* what is described is the atomic facts and that these are all the facts. But there is no claim that the facts are all there is. The facts, we were told, are combinations of objects; and we are not told what the objects are or whether they are all the objects. Moreover, the facts belong to a timeless world of the present; there is no effort to admit a flux of events or to account for one. In philosophy usually, too, there is an attempt to include the knowing subject and the knowledge process. In the *Tractatus* there are facts in the world and a logic corresponding to the facts and elicited from them, but the knower and his knowings are not part of the world. The evidence of which the *Tractatus* consists is incomplete even if it is admissible.

Wittgenstein's system has a structure after all just as every axiom-system has, it was merely arrived at differently. Constructionism presupposes axioms and neglects to bring them out.

Although the whole system of the *Tractatus* rests upon atomic facts, and hence upon objects, no analysis of fact was ever undertaken in it – fact is one of the givens of Wittgenstein's system. This is a simple way of escaping from a very complicated problem. No one who has ever undertaken the analysis of fact will deny that the problem is extremely complicated. When do we know that what we have is a fact?

In the case of the *Tractatus* the problem of what a fact is becomes even more complicated, for in 2.01 we are told that an atomic fact is a combination of many objects. How many, two? an indefinitely larger number? an infinite number? Much hangs upon the answer which is made to this question and, in general, to the analysis of both atomic facts and objects.

Another difficulty with Wittgenstein is the status he assigns to logic. Weinberg has stated his position well for him: "It amounts to denying that the propositions of logic express anything. They are merely formulae which indicate the admissible transformations within a language" [1]. Logic does nothing but allow transformations in language and the language does nothing but mirror the world; we have a logical space in which the world is mirrored, but the objects in logical space have no other function but the mirroring and yet they require a logic by which they may do this. Logic is obviously not nothing, and operations which it allows are allowed by something.

What he has suggested on the one hand, namely, the second storey of a two-storeyed natural world consists in logic and in the language of logic, or perhaps we should say the logical language, and on the other hand he has denied this in saying that it is nothing. It is only nothing from a nominalistic postulate in which a natural physical object is something, but the actual reality of the intelligible object is required by his system. We may take his first statement as correct, namely, that there is logical space (1.13), except a caution that logic is nothing, and does not express anything, being merely a caution not to go too far in reification. Platonists are always plagued by the tendency and the temptation to reify their abstract objects, to make perfect concrete things of their intelligible things; this is to make two worlds of the same nature, however, and to have not a two-storeyed natural world but a natural world and a supernatural world. One of the postulates of the two-storeyed natural world is that the second world – the world of logical objects in logical space – be different in character from the world of actual physical concrete objects, and we must accept Wittgenstein's strictures as attempts, unclassified, to keep the world in logical space from being a crypto-materialistic world.

Wittgenstein's originality as well as his failure is due, perhaps, to a single curious transformation. Frege had introduced the ideal of a logically perfect language. By this he meant that a language to function most efficiently would have to meet the strict requirements of logic. In Wittgenstein's treatment this somehow was changed to the reduction of logic to language, not a language which expressed a logic but a logic which was a

[1] J. R. Weinberg, *An Examination of Logical Positivism* (London 1936, Kegan Paul), p. 58.

language. It was language and not logic which became the philosophical basis, on the assumption that what we were after was a language-perfect logic. But just as language cannot always be expected to answer to the strict requirements of logic, except, of course, such language as is devoted to logic such as the language of logic, so logic cannot be confined to the language by which it is expressed. The colloquial languages contain more than logic; they may express values, for instance. On the other hand, logic applies to more than languages.

We seem to have, in the end, two contradictory theses: (1) that logic is not affected one way or the other by empiricism, and (2) that it is. In the first half of the *Tractatus* Wittgenstein derived logic from objects in the very process by which they are named and the names combined: logic consists in the possibility of the combination of the names of objects – this is his version of empiricism. Then in the second half of the *Tractatus* he slowly shifted to the view that what happens in logic is unaffected by what happens among objects.

There is a way of reconciling what is apparently a contradiction but Wittgenstein never took it. This would consist in saying that logic always was an independent realm (this is hinted at in its *a priori* nature) but that it is the kind of independent realm which we can learn about through experience. There would be nothing contradictory in this. It would mean that what happens in logic is unaffected by empiricism but that our knowledge of what happens in logic is entirely a matter of empiricism.

It follows, then, that while logic and its tautologies can say nothing about the world, at the same time what we express in logic can. Thus a deductive metaphysics which was properly stated could have the tautological properties of logic and yet contextually would say a great deal about the world. Hence deductive metaphysics is once more restored to favor and the strictures laid against it by Hume and Kant are removed.

That logic says nothing about the world, will not bear examination. It is ordinarily supposed that an elementary proposition, such as "John is in this room", tells us something about the world, and that another, "John is not in this room", does also. Now, we are further informed, if we connect these two elementary propositions with a logical constant, say, "or", then we have a complex logical proposition which tells us nothing about the world. But is this so? The proposition, "John is in this room or John is not in this room", does tell us something about the world. True, it does not tell us perhaps what we wanted to know, namely, whether John is or is not in this room; but it does tell us something else, namely, that he cannot be both in and not in this room at the same time, and that is an item of interest about the world. In fact, it is crucial information of a general nature about the world; and if it is true it may be the instrument for getting rid of a lot of false information, super-stition, etc. Thus tautological propositions of logic do tell us something about the world, and we shall have to distinguish not only between empirical and logical propositions but also between trivial and non-trivial propositions; and of these, those which refer to logic and those which refer to the world. For instance, a proposition which is tautological and therefore logical may be trivial when it is referred to the world and non-trivial when it is referred to some situation in logic. And the converse may also be true: for another proposition which may be of a logical nature may be trivial when referred to logic and non-trivial when referred to the world.

For Wittgenstein the relation between language and the world had to do only with that part of the world we can name here and now. Imaginative constructions, or hypotheses, theories as to the possible names of objects, are not included in Wittgenstein's theory and would not be allowable on the basis of his con-structionism. Thus the picture he makes of the method logically is of science as it exists now, not as it moves forward; we do not have any picture in Wittgenstein, no analogue in Wittgenstein, of the progress of science; and, of course, in science the scientific method is the archetype and progress is its essence. Science which does not progress, which does not make further discoveries, is not a live science but a dead one, and it is a dead science that Wittgenstein is picturing. If the progress of science were to be arrested now, and the relations between its theories and facts shown forth, this would be the *Tractatus* of Wittgenstein.

Wittgenstein went for his empiricism to the place where it was being practiced and not where it was being talked about, and he found it consisted in a kind of an action called scientific method. And he thought that he could abstract this method and present it logically. He did show it – or tried to do so – in the *Tractatus*. He emerged with a system not entirely in keeping with his avowed aims; he arrived at a system, in short, which was consistent with metaphysical realism.

The heart of scientific method is a hypothetical method. We do not investigate observable fact except under the direction of an hypothesis and, according to Wittgenstein's method, no hypothesis could ever be established as such. Thus in this way, too, Wittgenstein's work is inconsistent with that of science.

Experimental science after the choosing of an hypothesis consists of two stages. The first stage is a constructionism in which the observed facts are named and the names combined into propositions; in short, in getting from the observed facts to the empirical propositions, the first stage of science follows a method very much like that set forth in the *Tractatus*.

But the second stage is the mathematical stage, and in this stage the propositions are rearranged to conform with the requirements of an axiom system and the concern is wholly with deduction.

It is this second stage which the *Tractatus* would deny. In confirming the first stage it is felt called upon to deny the second, thus it is half right and half obstructive.

The rejection of metaphysics in the *Tractatus* is very much like the rejection of the second stage of experimental science, for metaphysics is a deductive theory and deductive theories are inadmissible in the *Tractatus*.

The second argument against metaphysics consists in the fact that metaphysics is, in Wittgenstein's version, non-empirical and non-empirical propositions are also inadmissible.

But what about the *Tractatus* itself? It has presuppositions, a method, and a conclusion, and all of these lend themselves to metaphysical interpretations. All of them, so to speak, call for presuppositions of a metaphysical nature, so that where the *Tractatus* does not deal directly with metaphysics itself, it requires a metaphysics in order to put itself in the position where metaphysics is needless. The acceptance of one metaphysics always does render all other metaphysics needless.

Metaphysics operates in such a way that the more you displace it from the center the more you place it upon the periphery. You do not get rid of metaphysics by allowing nothing in your system except objects combined into atomic facts, named and represented then by the combination of names and elementary propositions and by their combination through logic and the logical constants into complex propositions. In all of this it is alleged that metaphysics has played no role: the propositions are empirical propositions and the logical constants which connect them belong to logic. Then where is metaphysics?

We could answer, what else is all this we have been talking about? We could call metaphysics the whole structure in which facts are represented by propositions by means of logic – that is metaphysics.

The elimination of metaphysics, which is one of Wittgenstein's aims and one which the logical positivists and linguistic analysts picked up with such celerity, is based on the assumption that a proposition must either refer to logic or to fact, since there is no third kind of thing to which it could refer. He has forgotten, evidently, that while a metaphysical proposition does not refer to logic or to fact it might refer to the relation between logic and fact and include both logic and fact at both ends of the relation. In other words, it might refer to the structure whose elements are propositions and facts.

The assumption that metaphysics can be denied by merely showing that it is not admitted is a fallacy. We do not need to affirm presuppositions in order for them to exist as such; a presupposition is usually an assumption made inadvertently. In trying to hold his structure down to fact and propositions, Wittgenstein assumes that there is no place in such a scheme for metaphysics; he did not seem to understand that the scheme itself was metaphysical. Metaphysics certainly can be constituted by a scheme which overtly denies metaphysics as such and this is what Wittgenstein, like Kant, has devised.

To what extent are Wittgenstein's followers in agreement with him? This question will have to be sub-divided, since his followers are.

First we shall say a word about the logical positivists, and then about the linguistic analysts. To what extent do the logical positivists agree with him? In Julius Rudolph Weinberg, *An*

Examination of Logical Positivism (London 1936, Kegan Paul), p. 1, Weinberg says "The two most fundamental doctrines of logical positivism are: (1) that propositions of existential import have an exclusively empirical reference, and (2) this empirical reference can be conclusively shown by logical analysis". Both these notions, of course, stem from the *Tractatus*, but they stem narrowly and in a way omit some of the material for which the *Tractatus* is so important. They omit, for instance, the metaphysical import of the construction from which these propositions emerge, construction which consists in a finite world of propositions and of facts and of the relations between them; and they further omit the oracular emotional connotations and overtones which creep back into the *Tractatus*; finally, they omit also many of the conclusions which Wittgenstein arrived at in the *Tractatus* which were not clear to him from the beginning and which certainly were not to be derived from his own self-imposed restrictions; in short, his followers accepted his restrictions but he did not, and the results are correspondingly dissimilar.

It is clear that in some subtle and elusive way the logical positivists have managed to confuse Frege's meaning of 'sense' with Wittgenstein's 'state of affairs'. A meaningful proposition for them is a proposition which has a reference – a true elementary proposition; a meaningful proposition for Wittgenstein is one which has sense. Since a distinction between 'sense' and 'nonsense' is clear upon inspection, then the only requirement of a meaningful proposition is that it have sense in Frege's understanding of the term; in other words, that it could be true and that it is meaningful. But this is quite different from the operationalism of the logical positivists.

The linguistic analysts cannot be discussed until the books which Wittgenstein wrote later in life and which the linguistic analysts are evidently following have all appeared. The first has been issued posthumously, and will be discussed in a later chapter (chapter IX), this is the *Philosophical Investigations*.

One good effect of Wittgenstein was to crack open the hard shell of dogmatism. So novel was his approach that all of the traditional methods seem inconclusive. After going through his system – and throwing it away – the field of inquiry is wide open again, and this is no small gain.

One bad effect of Wittgenstein is that his followers have established and proclaimed a new dogmatism. Logical positivists are apt to be liberals on every topic except metaphysics and philosophy generally. There the dogmatism asserts itself.

What is the appeal of the *Tractatus*? The logical positivists have found in it a simple system. Deny metaphysics, turn all reliable knowledge over to the empirical sciences, assert the subjective nature of the qualities upon which the value topics are based, and there is no more to do. Why study the history of philosophy and the ancient problems, when they have been dissolved? The appeal of the *Tractatus* is the simplicity it suggests. Anyone can be a philosopher, no profound equipment is needed.

PART THREE

THE VIENNESE AND ENGLISH DISCIPLES

CHAPTER VI

VIENNESE POSITIVISM IN THE UNITED STATES

The affirmative pursuit of truth is more profitable than the negative elimination of error, for there is more of the former than we could ever reach and more of the latter than we should hope to avoid. Known truth is scarce, while accepted error is plentiful; and to spend all available time in rejecting one set of falsehoods would merely mean to hand on the torch to the promulgator of new ones. Hence refutation is a form of self-indulgence even though the blows be struck in the interest of truth and blocks on the road to inquiry have to be removed by someone. Nietzsche's maxim, "where you cannot love, there should you – pass by," is good, yet need not preclude all criticism if it be performed in the spirit of condemning the sin rather than the sinner. Logical positivism has a value and has made a contribution; but it is rather the excess and the claim of absoluteness that is to be questioned here [1].

A proper name for what is called 'logical positivism' would have been 'scientific absolutism'. The original theses have been shifted; some of the subjectivism of Carnap's *Logische Aufbau* has been abandoned [2], for instance, while it is clear from Wittgenstein's later work (and the work of the linguistic analysts who have been influenced by it) that his first book did not mean to him what it has to Reichenbach, Carnap, Feigl and Frank, to name but a few of those who have brought logical positivism to the United States.

The Vienna Circle began with the inheritors of Mach and so was thoroughly imbued with the subjectivistic approach to all philosophical matters. It is clear from a history of the Vienna Circle that Wittgenstein was not a member. The members of the

---

[1] See e.g. C. E. M. Joad, *A Critique of Logical Positivism* (Chicago 1950, University Press).

[2] It should never have been begun if, as Carnap thought, he was following Wittgenstein. See the *Tractatus Logico-Philosophicus*, 4.1121.

Vienna Circle followed Wittgenstein. "Many influential suggestions came from Wittgenstein, though the latter was never
personally present" [1]. It was 1928 before its members organized
themselves as a group around Moritz Schlick [2], some said the
following year [3]. It is interesting that Wittgenstein's *Tractatus*
which first appeared in the edition of 1922, swung the members
of the Vienna Circle in another direction, which they have
persistently proclaimed to be their own. The violent psycholo-
gism of Mach's empiricism has been retained, and they have
simply ignored the violent anti-psychologism of the *Tractatus* [4].

The most important difference between Wittgenstein and
the logical positivists is that in the *Tractatus* every effort was
made to be objective, the subject in all his doing being excluded
from the system, time and again; whereas the logical positivists
have certainly been subjective. The subjectivism of Carnap's
Aufbau, for instance, is certainly clear enough, and others have
had the same drift. Kantian phenomenologists, for instance, who
have followed the Second Edition of the *Critique of Pure Reason*,
abandon the transcendental unity of apperception. The phe-
nomenalism thus produced is a close approximation to positivism
in the contemporary sense of the word [5]. A purely subjective
interpretation of Kant – Kant without the *ding-an-sich* – would
prove consistent with the work of Schlick, Carnap and Reichenbach, but would assuredly be just the opposite of the result which
Wittgenstein sought to obtain in the *Tractatus*. Weinberg traced
very successfully the origins of the Vienna Circle; he showed how
close to its leaders and its leading ideas Hume, Leibniz and Kant
have been, and particularly Mach. As Weinberg correctly said,
speaking of Mach, Avenarius and others, "the work of these
thinkers consisted largely in an attempt to relieve physics and
psychology from metaphysics" [6], but there was this difference,
Mach in particular in this way attacked the metaphysical idea
of an objective world. But observe the departure: where Mach
wanted to get rid of the metaphysical idea of an objective world,

---

[1] Victor Kraft, *The Vienna Circle*, (New York 1953, Philosophical Library), Part I,
pp. 3–14.

[2] Weinberg, p. 25.

[3] Victor Kraft, *The Vienna Circle*, pp. 4–5.

[4] See esp. 4.0412; 4.1121; 5.541; 5.542; 5.5421; 5.633; 5.6331; and 5.641.

[5] J. R. Weinberg, *op. cit.*, p. 5.

[6] *Op. cit.*, p. 8.

Wittgenstein wanted to show by setting up an objective world how it would be possible to get rid of metaphysics. This is quite another statement and it leads to altered consequences.

It is usual to assume that Wittgenstein's ideas were revised and extended – "further developed" – by the members of the so-called Vienna Circle. Carnap, Frank, Neurath and others [1]. This is misleading unless it is assumed to mean that the Vienna Circle confined itself to all and only those ideas which Wittgenstein advanced. Now it may be that the articles of faith of the Vienna Circle were selected from those of Wittgenstein, but did not include *all* those of Wittgenstein and moreover there led to narrow results which they did not lead to in his work. This is clear from Wittgenstein's second volume, certainly, if not from the last thiid of the *Tractatus*, but the last third of the *Tractatus* ought to be quite sufficient to make out our case.

It might be better now to call their enterprise Viennese positivism. The influences of Moore and Frege, to which Wittgenstein had been susceptible, were not extended to his followers, while the similarities to be found in some of the work of Peirce is not an atmosphere which they feel congenial. On the whole the Viennese positivists have stood their ground firmly, nodding in the direction of science and shaking their heads against metaphysics. And they have been as certain in the one case as in the other.

The position of the positivists is both theoretical and practical. Since the practical is a matter of exigency and importunity we had better deal with it first, and then, in the second part of this chapter, turn to more theoretical considerations.

I

The practical activities of the Viennese positivists are to an alarming extent polemical; they are intolerant in the extreme, and all-presumptive. The present-day campaign theses of the Viennese positivists could be stripped down, perhaps, to three. These are as follows.

(1) The only valid knowledge is scientific knowledge;

[1] See, for instance, Richard von Mises' *Positivism* (Cambridge 1951, Harvard University Press), p. 361, *et passim*.

(2) The only valid interpretation of scientific knowledge is that offered by the Viennese positivists, and

(3) The interpretation of the positivists is logical meta-science.

Let us examine these separately.

(1) The scientific claims advanced by the Viennese positivists in the name of science exceed anything put forward by the scientists, and indeed may be said to be opposed to what the scientists themselves implicitly assert. It is the attitude of certainty – one might say the German attitude – that is the most objectionable. Certitude in science, it has been pointed out time and again [1], is alien to the spirit of science; if there is one thing that can be said in general of the scientists it is that they are never absolutely sure of their own position. Absoluteness of philosophical foundations is more religious than scientific, and the Viennese positivists are in some danger of making a religion of science. Scientists themselves are much concerned with art, often with religion, and in general they may be said in no way to indicate that they regard scientific knowledge as the only valid form which knowledge takes. Such claims most leave to the self-appointed high priests of science, the Viennese positivists. It is a case again of "we can take care of our enemies, the Lord protect us from our friends".

On logical grounds it would be absurd to suppose that there is any discipline which does not have presuppositions. The scientific method in so far as it is an orderly procedure takes certain propositions for granted, if only that there is such a thing as the scientific method and that there is a world in which it can be applied with significant results. But these are philosophical truths themselves implying metaphysically significant assertions which can only be denied if we are prepared to deny also the reliability of the method which they support. If the Viennese positivists are to have their way, then we shall have to deny the validity of such presuppositions, and we shall have to throw ourselves upon the scientific method by adopting either a program

---

[1] As for instance by Peirce's fallibilism, and by Whitehead. Cf. Peirce, *Col. Pap.*, 1.7; 1.9; 5.451; 1.10; 6.181; 1.137; 6.603; 5.587. Whitehead, quoting Cromwell, *Science and the Modern World*, Ch. I.

of blind faith or else one which limits itself to pragmatic justification. And in both cases we can kick away the ladder once we
have climbed the wall. It is difficult to see how we shall need the
Viennese positivists for these programs. Science certainly did
exist before the Vienna Circle; positivists did not invent it; and
there were, too, those whose approval of science would admit
of no criticism: fanaticism is not new, and not new, either, is the
harm which it does to the cause it would serve.

What the Viennese positivists claim, then, is that what the
scientists cannot produce in the way of reliable knowledge cannot
be produced. The position is chiefly negative. It does not assert
anything for the Viennese positivists themselves, only for the
scientists. What the Viennese positivists can do chiefly is to
claim the preeminence of science. But there are other forms of
knowledge. One example should suffice, and for this purpose we
will choose art. Can it be denied that art does give us knowledge,
even though it be knowledge of a different sort from that of
science? Have we learned nothing from Shakespeare, from
Aeschylus, from Homer, from Dostoyevsky, from Bach or
Cézanne? The point is too obvious to strain. Artistic knowledge
does not conflict with scientific knowledge; they do not explore
the same areas, but both have areas to explore.

The institution of science is not the first nor the only institution for which claims of preeminence and superiority have been
put forward. The story is an old one. It has happened that the
church and the state, among others, have at one time and place
or another maintained authority over all other institutions. The
Church in the Middle Ages, and the state in periods of absolute
monarchy, have held themselves supreme. And now the same
assertion of absolute authority is advanced in the name of
science, only this time with a difference. The claims of other
institutions have been advanced from within, while the claim of
science comes from without; for the Viennese positivists themselves are not scientists. Perhaps by putting forward a claim for
science the Viennese positivists hope to identify themselves with
it and share in its glory. They could hardly have made a poorer
case. The peculiarity of science is that alone among institutions it
has never claimed absoluteness or infallibility. Science is a late
comer in the field of inquiry; its success has been astounding –

astounding for the very reason that it has not regarded its own findings as final. The modesty of its claims, the very thing which marks it off from other institutions, is being abrogated in its name by the Viennese positivists. There is no reason to accept their argument, for they do science an injustice in speaking for it, a service which it ill deserves.

(2) The Viennese positivists are not scientists yet they presume to speak for science. One would think that on such a premise they would have deserted philosophy altogether, including even that philosophy which consists almost entirely in the approval of science, for work in the scientific laboratory; but this they have not done. Thus they have been placed in a position in which they feel keenly their insecurity, and so they seek to bolster themselves in several ways. The first is to make exaggerated claims for science, as we have already noted. The second is to turn to attack philosophy in the traditional sense. Taking off from Wittgenstein [1], the attack begun on metaphysics by, say Carnap, for instance [2], is still being carried on by lesser members of the troupe. Herbert Feigl writes as late as this year, "My positivistic or logical empiricist background, I must admit, may have made me somewhat allergic to the term 'metaphysics' " [3]. Quite apart from the popular and in this case surprising misuse of the term "allergic", in its intolerance it reminds one of nothing so much as of Dietrich Eckart, the Nazi poet who is reported to have said that whenever he heard the word, culture, he reached for his Lueger.

Despite the bad manners of the Viennese positivists, is it not possible that they are after all speaking somewhat more narrowly than we have assumed? For the type of metaphysics they mean when they attack metaphysics in general may well be the only type they know, and this is the German metaphysics of the transcendental and subjective variety. The battle between the Viennese positivists and metaphysicians proves then to be an internecine war between some absolutists in Vienna and one movement in Germany; it does not concern the whole field of metaphysics, since there exist great areas of it of which they seem to remain in ignorance. Some German metaphysicians are guilty

---

[1] See the *Tractatus*, 4.003.

[2] See for instance R. Carnap, *Philosophy and Logical Syntax* (London 1935, Kegan Paul), Ch. I, Sec. 2; *The Unity of Science* (London 1934, Kegan Paul), p. 21 ff.

[3] *Philosophical Studies*, Vol. V (1954), p. 17.

as charged, Hegel and Fichte, for instance; but can we allow them to stand for the whole of the metaphysical enterprise? It is difficult to estimate whether the Viennese positivists have chosen to make transcendental and subjectivistic metaphysics stand for the entire field of metaphysics because they are ignorant of other types or because they wished to put the case for metaphysics as weakly as possible. In either case they seem to be more against what they are against than they are for what they are for.

Often when the Viennese positivists bury their heads in the sand in this first way they seem more prominent than ever. For the attack on metaphysics by nominalists of one stripe or other has been popular for some time, and it is conducted in other quarters also by those who would rather run than read. And in the second way the technique is time-hallowed, for to indulge in the form of argument whereby you choose to make yourself appear big by making your opponent appear small is a familiar one though not favored by those who seek the truth wherever it is to be found. There are other approaches which are more tentative and exploratory and less finalistic, the possibility of metaphysics as programmatic inquiry. Do the Viennese positivists know, for instance, of the kind of metaphysics advanced by Meinong, Husserl and Hartmann in Germany, and by Peirce and Whitehead in this country and England, as well as a host of others, a metaphysics which endeavors to take empiricism into account? This seems unlikely, and in conversations with some of the Viennese positivists it is possible to gather that such a conception is beyond their admission. They are rejecting what they do not know, and condemning a field wholesale when they have only become familiar with one part of it. It is the old-fashioned German metaphysics, and this alone, which they are condemning. Occasionally there is a suspicion that what they are opposing is not a subject-matter but a word. It is 'metaphysics' they wish to get rid of and not Metaphysics, for they undertake some of the same speculations themselves though calling them something else, phenomenological analysis, say.

Speaking as a metaphysician, one is tempted to observe that the insecurity of the Viennese positivists has cost them their philosophic temper, and so it seems obvious that they are much more concerned with what (they assert) we cannot do than with what they can. They only make a profession of pointing with pride to what the scientists do. The scientists do science, the positivists only point with pride. We shall return to this point. Here it is necessary to say that such intolerance not only does not fit the philosophic temper, it is also hardly at home in a democracy. Such German absolutism from Austria (and after all it is not the worst case we know of in which German absolutism has come from Austria) is boring from within in philosophy and threatens to undermine the whole philosophic enterprise. There are actual cases of departments of philosophy in which metaphysicians predominate, where a Viennese positivist has been hired in order to make sure that contemporary schools are adequately represented. Are there any cases where the Viennese positivists having captured a department have hired a metaphysician for the same reason?

The Viennese positivists assert that their interpretation of science is the only valid one; but has not everybody claimed the success of science? Getting on the bandwagon is after all not exactly an exercise invented by the Viennese positivists. Everybody seems to have spoken for science, and claimed its findings for their own. Let us look at one other example.

The absurd claims of the Soviet Union that Russians invented or discovered everything that was ever invented or discovered by scientists is so well known and so often repeated as to need no documentation. It is startling to find such chauvinistic nationalism in a country whose official philosophy is Marxism, the open enemy of nationalism. The Russians (and of course especially the communists) discovered the airplane, the theory of evolution, the atomic bomb, and what not, if we are to believe them. What they do not see, of course, is that by their very claims they have exposed a fatal misunderstanding of the character of science, which belongs to no one people or national state but is an human enterprise in which thus far certainly Western European countries have excelled.

It is difficult not to be sorry for the poor scientists themselves themselves in all this, for they seem the only ones who are unwilling to claim credit for their discoveries. They are more interested in practicing the method than in making claims based on it, and the findings are never allowed by them to stand in the way of further investigations which may always and often do invalidate everything that has gone before, including work which they themselves may have done. The conception of science which is held by the positivists happens to be a very narrow one. If allowed to have their way, they would not encourage science but stop it. The kind of science which consists. in remaining so close to the data that hypotheses of any general character are dismissed and similar findings discouraged, is very much to their liking. But it is not the kind of science which has been responsible for the rapid development of the sciences; it would never have included the work of Newton, of Darwin, of Freud, of Einstein. Now if the positivists do not understand and approve of science in the proper way, then they have a very poor case to make out for themselves indeed, since this is their chief contention and principal area of operation.

The unfortunate thing, then, is that the Viennese positivists may be right in their interpretation of science (we may not think so, of course, but we cannot afford to violate our probity in matching their intolerance) but even if they were, this would not excuse them from being too sure. They lay claim to a sort of absolute truth and in doing so reveal a lack of humility. For the characteristic of philosophy, as established by the Greeks and most violated by the Germans, consists simply in not being sure and in substituting for certainty a tentative probing and a persistent inquiry. The Greeks, if we are to allow Plato and Aristotle to speak for them, did not hold a philosophy but held to philosophy, and raised more questions than they ever attempted to answer in any final way.

(3) And what, after all, have the Viennese positivists ever done? They seem to approve of all activity in logic and mathematics, and in the empirical sciences; but approval alone is not a contribution. Mathematics and the empirical sciences were doing very well by themselves until the Viennese group happened to misunderstand Wittgenstein and so felt called upon to defend mathematics and empirical science against philosophy, a defense they hardly needed, but also to close the doors to inquiry in other directions, always, as Peirce pointed out, a bad thing to do. The interpretation given to science by the Viennese positivists is not science but interpretation, and interpretation of this sort

can hardly be given any name other than philosophy. As many critics have pointed out, it is an interpretation of science which carries with it its own presuppositions which are themselves metaphysical in character. There is, as everyone knows, no such thing as an official philosophy of science; those who undertake to interpret science do so, so to speak, at their own risk, and nobody is exactly in charge of the field. Viennese positivists have as much right to advance an interpretation as anyone else, but also no more right. Science itself cannot be adduced as a proof that the interpretation placed upon it by the Viennese positivists is the correct one.

And what is the basis of the Viennese positivists' interpretation? Less than the usual logical reasons; for it has a sort of *mystique*: it consists in the faith that when better knowledge is built, science will build it. Apart from the harm done to science by such a contention, since science must suffer in reputation from any exaggeration of its claims, the faith that science must preempt the field of valid knowledge is not anything more than a faith – that is to say, it remains unsupported by reasons. And are we to believe that this is philosophy, that faith in a going concern is more than faith and gathers its rationale from the fact that what it approves of is rational? Liking science does not make a man a scientist any more than liking art makes him an artist.

The Viennese positivists' interpretation of science is nothing impressive, either. It consists chiefly, after the promulgation of approval, of stripping away from science any relation of validity to metaphysics. The argument of the Viennese positivists seems to run somewhat as follows. All sense is what is referred to by the sciences, and metaphysics is not a science, therefore metaphysics is nonsense. Consequences are admitted but antecedents never. Science is evidently a bolt from the blue and carries no presuppositions. And the ignorance which we saw when we examined the poor knowledge of metaphysics which the Viennese positivists possess, is equalled here only by their blindness in refusing to admit that they do not wish to see. The attempt to eliminate metaphysical presuppositions by fiat or by proclamation is not one calculated to win the adherence of anyone trained to require evidence for his beliefs. Science is an exploratory activity and nothing so confining as the Viennese positivists would have it.

The Viennese positivists would not have made good scientists; they would have been timid and could not have called upon the requisite imagination; they would not, like the scientists, have had the courage to be wrong more often than they were right.

They do not make good philosophers of science, either, for they have prohibited themselves from using the very tools requisite for work in this field. The abstraction of the presuppositions of science, the analysis of the logical techniques involved in its method, and the interpretation of its findings, are all parts of science which will not lend themselves to observation but instead require a background of metaphysics. Metaphysics drifts so to speak above the empirical disciplines. There is no way in which an experimental inquiry will ever be able to prove or disprove the truth of its own presuppositions. Yet it has them indubitably and no less so for the unwillingness of its self-appointed apologists to own up to the fact.

From such quarreling, it is clear, science stands aloof. Some scientists, it is true, accept the Viennese positivists' interpretation; but it is also true that others have been completely won over by the Marxist version. Science itself consists in an orderly activity designed to investigate nature, though even the method which everyone recognizes as orderly has never been agreed upon by those whose business it is to examine procedures. The fact is that the field of the interpretation of science is itself a speculative field; and until agreement in this field removes it from the area of speculation, it must remain open and free. And those who would shut the doors to such speculations, on the assumption that their own answer is the correct one, must not be allowed to do so. For just as the life of science consists in the practice of its method, so the hope of inquiry into the meaning of that method must consist in investigating what underlies it. The philosophy of science is a speculative field, call it what you will; and so long as we do not have acceptable answers, that long will metaphysicians and Viennese positivists, and all others, for that matter, be free to advance their interpretations and set forth their claims.

Greek philosophy owes its great success partly to the fact that it was an independent study. Later, it became the handmaid of religion, and now the Viennese positivists would make of it a handmaid of science. That there is and indeed ought to be not only a philosophy of religion but also a philosophy of science,is legitimate. But there is no reason to suppose that such apologetics exhausts the entire enterprise of philosophy. It will always look for its justification to its own independent inquiries. Toward this end, the original source of Viennese positivism, Wittgenstein himself, has pointed the way.

II

We turn now to more theoretical considerations. The technical position of Viennese positivism may be set forth in the following three theses.

(1) Logic and mathematics are tautological;

(2) The analysis of language solves all metaphysical problems; and

(3) Whatever is not fact is feeling.

Our task will be to examine each of these.

(1) The thesis advanced here is that while the Viennese positivists claim Wittgenstein as their source, they do lip service to his work without actually following it. They fell so much under the spell of the *Tractatus* [1] that they failed to see what was in it. They did see, however, what they thought was in it. For the fact is that Wittgenstein is not a Viennese positivist. He may have been influenced by Hume but he acknowledged Frege. British metaphysical realism, through the early Russell, G. E. Moore and others, made its mark on his ideas and strongly influenced the *Tractatus*, and British realism asserts the reality of two external worlds, those of logic and of concrete existence. None of the founding fathers of positivism, then, were positivists. What the Viennese positivists and their followers are doing is to take a nominalistic and Comtean reading of Wittgenstein. This is their privilege though it may mislead some into thinking that they are only following and developing Wittgenstein.

Compare, let us say for example, Wittgenstein's rejection of psychology [2] and of Mauthner's criticism of language [3] with Carnap's *Aufbau*. Again, that Wittgenstein has an ontology has

---

[1] Ludwig Wittgenstein, *Tractatus Logico-Philosophicus* (London 1922, Kegan Paul).

[2] *Tractatus* 5.5421; 5.641; 6.423.

[3] *Tractatus* 4.0031.

been noted [1]. Constructionism requires two real external worlds, one of facts and another of logic expressed through language. The tautology of language constitutes a system of logic which is sufficiently independent of the world from which it was originally constructed to mirror it [2]; for this we need of course a non-trivial tautology, an "infinitely fine network" [3]. To know the two worlds does not require a subject in the old sense, only a "metaphysical subject" [4], a perspective on the worlds, which in this sense stands outside them.

The tautologies of language are the machinery whereby we are enabled to watch the evaporation of traditional metaphysics. But Wittgenstein was not endeavoring to get rid of all metaphysics, only of all metaphysics other than his own, and in this, after all, he has the sanctity of tradition from Aristotle on! For is that not what every metaphysician has done? Tautology is not for Wittgenstein something by means of which metaphysics is got rid of; it is rather the touchstone of the correct metaphysics. Transcendental metaphysics must go, and in its place there stands a view of the world which has been revealed by means of the proper understanding of logic.

The entire *Tractatus* is devoted to this achievement. A couple of examples, however, ought to suffice. Language mirrors the world, and it does so by means of logic. Tautology, then, is the last-ditch consistency [5] whereby the language derived by construction from the world can be said to have a world of its own. Metaphysics never appears, either in the world of facts or in that of logic; but it is that by means of which there is a world of facts and another of logic – that there are such worlds. The claim of tautology is fierce and uncompromising; it is not only that which is shared by all propositions which otherwise have nothing to share, it is the propositions themselves [6]. Logic is the ghostly god whose presence in and between all things which are touched by logic makes real every element of the two external worlds. It is how things are and not itself a thing, not something apart.

[1] Gustav Bergmann, *The Metaphysics of Logical Positivism* (New York 1954, Longmans, Green), p. 51.

[2] *Tractatus*, 5.511; 6.341.

[3] *Tractatus*, 5.511.

[4] *Tractatus*, 5.641.

[5] *Tractatus*, 5.143.

[6] *Tractatus*, 6.1.

Now contrast these views with those of the Viennese positivists. By a rather subtle subjectification of the elementary propositions which refer to facts, Carnap in two books [1] has assumed that the primitive sentences are referable to experience. In his followers we have qualia (Goodman) [2] and the "principle of acquaintance" [3]. The existential interpretation of symbolic logic [4] goes the rest of the way for them, offset only by the modal logic of Lewis and Langford and of Lukasiewicz. Quine and Goodman wish to get rid of the existence of classes, and logic carries Quine in particular along more rigorous roads. But the constructionism of Wittgenstein is not the same as the avowed nominalism of the American followers of the Viennese school.

For nominalism it is, and the term is accepted; it is accepted by Quine [5] and it is accepted by Goodman [6]. If, as Quine says, "to be assumed as an entity is, purely and simply, to be reckoned as the value of a variable" [7], then what is the status of the variable? It is, presumably, not an entity. In other words, if to be is to be the value of a variable, then how is the variable to be? And if it has no being, then what is the relation of its values to it, and, moreover, how, and in what sense, are they its values?

It comes to something like this, that Wittgenstein by constructing his system of logic from the elementary propositions which refer to facts was building a real world of logic in the Frege tradition and not endeavoring to hold the reliable entities down to the facts. The values of a variable are entities partly because of the force of the variable; or, put the other way round, if the variable is dependable, at least as an entity in logic, it is because its values are genuine entities.

The logicians and methodologists who are influenced by the Viennese positivists would have a real world of existence to which logic refers but not a real logic. The real world, and the only real world (apart from that negligible part of it which can be described

---

[1] *Der Logische Aufbau der Welt* (Berlin 1928) and *The Logical Syntax of Language*, trans. A. Smeaton (New York 1937, Harcourt Brace).

[2] Nelson Goodman, *The Structure of Appearance* (Cambridge 1951), p. 144 ff.

[3] C. G. Hempel, "The Concept of Cognitive Significance", *Proc. Am. Acad. of Art and Sciences*, Vol. 80 (1951), p. 61 ff.

[4] See *e.g.* Hans Reichenbach, *Symbolic Logic* (New York 1947, Macmillan).

[5] Willard Van Orman Quine, *From a Logical Point of View* (Cambridge 1953, Harvard University Press), Ch. I.

[6] *Op. cit.*, Ch. II.

[7] *Op. cit.*, p. 13.

in emotive language) is the world of existence, and this is referable to private sense experience (the "protocol language"). And
what, then, has happened to the tautological world of logic as
Wittgenstein has described it?

(2) When Wittgenstein advanced the thesis that the analysis
of language solves all metaphysical problems, he did not mean
that there were no metaphysical problems, only that language
solved them through the logic by which it is related to the world.
Those who have dealt in logic in one connection and in metaphysics (albeit influenced by logic) in another, have never
envisaged such a conception of logic as Wittgenstein's. He simply
wished to pare down metaphysics to the point to which logic was
able to carry it. That logic functions as ontology in Wittgenstein's
system can hardly be doubted [1]. Ontology returns as that which
is expressed by the logically perfect language. Opinions differ as
to what Wittgenstein's metaphysics is. It is possible to hold that a
position not too far from nominalism is what he intended [2], and
that he accomplished this by confining "the undefined descriptive
signs of the ideal language" to "proper names or first-order
predicates, including relational ones" [3]. There are, as we shall
soon see, reasons for rejecting this interpretation, though even by
accepting it we are left with the notion that Wittgenstein had a
metaphysics of a sort.

Wittgenstein, then, rejects transcendental metaphysics only to
accept what, for want of a better term, we shall call logical
metaphysics. And what do his followers of the Viennese school in
the United States do? In a word, they reject the older type of
metaphysics without pretending to replace it [4]. The chief arguments against metaphysics reduce to arguments against the
reality of classes. The rejection of metaphysics therefore must
make the following claims: that modal logic can be reduced to
existential logic; that the categories of being are unnecessary,
since they are not names for anything; and that linguistic
analysis is exhaustive of meaning. It would take too long to enter
into these arguments here; suffice to say for the present purposes

---

[1] *Tractatus*, 5.4711; 6.13; 6.342.
[2] G. Bergmann, *op. cit.*, p. 51 ff.
[3] *Op. cit.*, p. 52.
[4] Rudolf Carnap, *Philosophy and Logical Syntax* (London 1935, Kegan Paul), p.
15 ff.

that the burden of proof rests on the claimants and that the case against metaphysics in these regards has not yet been proved.

It is clear from the attitude of the Viennese positivists that they are expressing their rejection of metaphysics in the emotive language, and if this is the case then we must accord it as little standing in philosophy as they would allow to traditional metaphysics. Two examples may suffice. The first is that which has already been quoted in the first part of this chapter: Feigl's phrase that he is "allergic to metaphysics". The second is an earlier and generally accepted thesis that metaphysics is nonsense, a double-edged proposition based on the Wittgensteinian contention that the business of philosophy is to make propositions clear and not to advance propositions [1], since most of them are senseless [2].

It would be difficult to show that Wittgenstein was a nominalist. The argument would have to prove that he did not mean his constructions of propositions to be real, that is to say, reliable, on the ground that if you build your complex propositions carefully enough out of atomic facts they will owe their reality entirely to the atomic facts, there being no real classes – an argument which, by the way, there is no reason to credit to Wittgenstein. The argument further would have to contend that his later rejection of nominalism [3] was not seriously meant. On the other hand, the Viennese positivists are divided into two groups: those who hold a nominalistic position without wishing to employ the name, on the grounds that since they are against metaphysics they can get rid of it simply by refusing to employ its terminology, as though spades would disappear if we stopped calling a spade a spade; and those, like Quine and Goodman, who unhesitatingly apply the name of nominalism to their own position. In the former case presuppositions are denied, while in the latter case they are avowed; and in both cases, the breach with Wittgenstein is evident.

Berkeley got rid of the knowable external world not too long before Hume got rid of the self. His impressions and ideas, which were all that he bequeathed to Kant, were differently

---

[1] *Tractatus*, 4.112.
[2] *Tractatus*, 4.003.
[3] *Philosophical Investigations*, I, 383.

interpreted by Thomas Reid. The tradition of those who accepted Reid's Wager, namely, that there is nothing to lose and possibly something to gain by beginning in philosophy with faith in an external world which is knowable, led through Cook Wilson to Moore and Russell, and so on to Wittgenstein. British realism, whether of the epistemological variety of G. Dawes Hicks, or of the metaphysical variety of John Laird, or of both, as in the case of A. N. Whitehead, has remained very much alive. It influenced Wittgenstein but evidently failed to touch his followers, the Viennese positivists and their American disciples. Thus they have missed much in metaphysics which is consistent with empiricism. In this instance, too, then, they have claimed Wittgenstein as a source without having followed him.

(3) The values cannot be expressed in language, according to Wittgenstein, for "all propositions are of equal value" [1]. He asserted flatly that "there can be no ethical propositions" [2], hence "ethics cannot be expressed" [3]. Ethics is one with aesthetics and both must lie outside the world disclosed by experience since "ethics is transcendental" [4].

The footprints of British realism are heavy here, though admittedly the position is not the same. That values are ineffable had already been asserted by Moore, who had declared goodness indefinable [5], though he did set up an ethics after clarifying the language and rejecting psychological interpretations [6]. Moore's rejection of psychological interpretations of value, and especially of ethics, closely parallels Wittgenstein's. Other British realists, such as Laird [7] and Whitehead [8], hold to the complete objectivity of values and so also to that of goodness. The metaphysically realistic picture of values in general and of ethical values in particular drawn by these two philosophers would be consistent with the declaration of Wittgenstein's that ethics is transcendental.

Now this is quite different from the Viennese positivists' assertion about values. They say that the values can be expressed

[1] *Tractatus*, 6.4.
[2] *Tractatus*, 6.42.
[3] *Tractatus*, 6.421.
[4] *Tractatus*, 6.421.
[5] G. E. Moore, *Principia Ethica*, I, B, 6.
[6] *Philosophical Studies*, Ch. X.
[7] John Laird, *The Idea of Value* (Cambridge 1929, University Press), Ch. VII.
[8] A. N. Whitehead, *Adventures of Ideas* (New York, 1940 Macmillan), p. 345.

in language and they would go on to distinguish between cognitive meaning and emotive meaning.

Carnap, for instance, evidently supposed that nothing was wrong except the grammatical form of value language, since "a value statement is nothing else than a command in a misleading grammatical form. It may have effects upon the actions of men, and these effects may either be in accordance with our wishes or not; but it is netiher true nor false. It does not assert anything and can neither be proved nor disproved" [1]. Carnap's first statement is of course inconsistent with his second and third. The "misleading grammatical form" can easily be set right, in which case we have translated from a command to a categorical proposition which is clearly true or false and in many cases can be proved or disproved [2].

Among the values, the Viennese positivists and their followers have chiefly singled out ethics for consideration. They say, for instance, that propositions concerning ethical judgments are nothing more than expressions of personal feeling [3]. As stated by one of the first Viennese positivists to direct his attention to ethics, "the moral valuations of modes of behavior and character are nothing but the emotional reaction with which human society responds to the pleasant and sorrowful consequences that, according to the average experience, proceed from those modes of behavior and characters" [4]. Here, said Schlick, is a "fundamental ethical insight" [5]. Action is always in the direction of the strongest impulse [6].

It is not a far remove from Schlick to the American moralists who follow the Viennese positivists. For Stevenson "the central problem of ethical analysis – one might almost say 'the' problem – is one of showing in detail how beliefs and attitudes are related" [7].

---

[1] Carnap, *op. cit.*, p. 24.

[2] "It should be noted that the intelligibility of commands rests upon assumptions that certain states of affairs prevail" – Morris R. Cohen and Ernest Nagel, *An Introduction to Logic and Scientific Method* (New York 1934, Harcourt Brace), p. 28.

[3] See, for instance, Alfred J. Ayer, *Language, Truth and Logic* (New York 1946, Dover), Ch. VI.

[4] Moritz Schlick, *Problems of Ethics*, trans. D. Rynin (New York 1939, Prentice-Hall), p. 78.

[5] *Loc. Cit.*

[6] *Op. cit.*, p. 62.

[7] C. L. Stevenson, *Ethics and Language* (New Haven 1944, Yale University Press), I, 4.

And an attitude is "a disposition to act in certain ways and to experience certain feelings" [1]. Ethics by these definitions is clearly being turned over to the psychologists. There are no objective ethical standards; moral conflicts are the results of differences in belief and so are attitudinal conflicts. If we could by rational persuasion bring them together, then the conflicts would be resolved: they would have the same beliefs and consequently the same attitudes, and the fact that there was nothing corresponding to their beliefs in the external world would presumably not mean that the acts which followed the disposition to act – now happily similar – would not be disappointed by the further fact that there was nothing relevant to act on, nothing, that is, upon which action of a moral nature could make itself felt.

How much in common do the American followers of the Viennese positivists have with them? It is not too far a cry from Schlick's emotional reactions to Stevenson's beliefs and attitudes. The American version is simply a further step in abdication after the Viennese. More difficult, however, would be the task of finding either version in the few ethical comments of Wittgenstein. How different it is indeed to say on the one hand that ethics cannot be expressed in propositions and on the other that it can be expressed quite adequately provided only that the propositions describe empirical conditions discovered and analyzed under psychological headings. Wittgenstein begged the question, but the Viennese positivists do not write as though they had found the question begged; instead, they chose to bury the distinction between ethics and morals – between the study of what the good ought to be and of what it is – very neatly, and proceeded to consider how certain morals get themselves approved or disapproved, this being the only necessity left to them under the theory they adopted, and a wry distinction at best.

We may perhaps sum up the discussion of the positivistic ethics by referring to a passage in Wittgenstein's first posthumous book. He said, we must remember, that ethics cannot be expressed in language. The Viennese positivists and their American followers insist that it can, and that it consists in emotive language, in the expressions of emotional reactions, beliefs and attitudes. Now, it happens that Wittgenstein later proposed that

[1] Op. cit., IV, 3.

there is no problem about the question of words referring to
sensations. "Don't we talk about sensations every day, and give
them names?" [1] Thus if Wittgenstein had thought that ethics
could be reduced to sensations he would not have said that the
former could not be expressed in language and that the latter
could.

It would be wise at this point to hearken back to the first part
of this chapter. We have noted earlier that the Viennese positivists claim the prerogative of speaking for science – of writing,
so to speak, the official philosophy of science. They wish to be
the censors and outriders of science; they would make of science a
dogmatism, and an institution in the restrictive sense; they
would take over science, define its policies and say what it can
and cannot do; they would limit its freedom. But these are not
scientific enterprises in the pure sense; they are only designed to
age science synthetically, to render the institution of science a
prematurely decrepit affair.

In this second part of the chapter we have seen a similar
situation at work. Science is the exclusive domain of the Viennese
positivists, and all philosophical enterprises either do not exist
or belong to the sciences; metaphysics, for instance, does not
exist in any meaningful way, and ethics belongs either to the
science of psychology (Stevenson and Schlick) or to the social
sciences as well (Ayer). In ethics, then, as in the philosophy of
science, the Viennese positivists and their followers are involved
in a nihilistic destruction of all independent philosophical theory:
there is no good or bad, there is only approval or disapproval;
there is no right or wrong, there is only weak or strong belief. We
shall not need philosophy, we are told, when we have the physicists and the positivists. But why could we not argue against
them on their own grounds that we shall not need the positivists
when we have the physicists? The positivists would like to be the
undertakers of philosophy, and they work on the assumption that
undertakers never die. What will they do for an occupation once
they have carried out and buried the body of philosophy? They
will perhaps need to find something else to erode.

---

[1] *Philosophical Investigations*, trans. Anscombe (Oxford 1953, Blackwell), I, 244.

CHAPTER VII

LINGUISTIC ANALYSIS VERSUS METAPHYSICS

I

Philosophers who do not wish to enter into speculations centered on metaphysical questions similar to those which have occupied abstract thinkers for many centuries should at least display the good manners of the recusant. Otherwise, it makes those having nothing to say except that what some other philosophers say is not so, seem like genuine philosophers. Professor Lazerowitz has written a book which makes him appear in this light [1]. And it is a fashionable guise which by now wears the aspect of a well-established tradition. For the logical positivists and the linguistic analysts the attack upon metaphysics is a kind of garden sport, and they do it occasionally just to keep their muscles limber. But while they are only running for their supper, we are running for our lives. When the metaphysician turns and bites back, his teeth do not inject the same venom, for he is only defending himself.

It is no news in the world any longer when a logical positivist criticizes metaphysics. Professor Lazerowitz' onslaught is merely the latest in a long series. However, it is a book-length venture, and its size and pretentiousness makes it worthy of notice. What others have done collectively, *ad nauseam*, he has done singly. Followers are by definition little people, for they do two things their masters never did, namely, follow a master, and exaggerate his mannerisms and claims. A follower is small just in virtue of being a follower, since he is not a leader. The master's method is often tentative and exploratory, that is why he is a master. But the follower is always more sure that the master is right than the master had ever been. Moreover, followers are on the whole perfectly literal in their interpretation, and there is no better way in the world to misunderstand anything.

---

[1] Morris Lazerowitz, *The Structure of Metaphysics* (London 1955, Routledge and Kegan Paul). All page numbers unless otherwise specified are to this work.

To begin with, then, even the title of Professor Lazerowitz'
work is misleading. For anyone who wished to know about
metaphysics might suppose when he came upon a book entitled,
The Structure of Metaphysics, on a shelf or in a bookshop, that
here was a book which would tell him. He would not have any
way in which to know that it was a book that would inform him
only that the structure of metaphysics was made up of a tissue of
illusions and errors; that, in fact, there was no such subject-matter. The book is in this sense somewhat misleading. From the
first page to the last we find nothing but violence done on metaphysics, and, by implication, on the foolishness of those who
engage seriously in it today, or who have done so in the past.

It is a pity to have to attack any secular philosophy, there is so
little of it and it is taken these days with such faint seriousness.
All the more reason to cry shame on those who bore from within,
the men who teach philosophy and at the same time undermine it.
Professor Lazerowitz can have the satisfaction of knowing that he
has devoted an important part of his life not to standing *for*
what he is for but only to being *against* what he is against.

Ludwig Wittgenstein is now the author of two books. The first,
the *Tractatus Logico-Philosophicus*, appeared during his lifetime;
the second, *Philosophical Investigations*, after his death. Those
who base their entire viewpoint on a misunderstanding of the
first book call themselves logical positivists or logical empiricists,
while those who do the same with the second one call themselves
linguistic analysts. For the most part, the logical positivists live
in the United States, and the linguistic analysts in England. It
would seem from Professor Lazerowitz' book that he is an American follower of the English school, an American linguistic analyst.

The bridge between the two is not a vast one, and Professor
Lazerowitz has taken his anti-metaphysical theme from the
logical positivists. A logical positivist is one who does not know
that he has a metaphysics and so supposes that no one else has
one, either, and hence concludes that there is no such thing as
metaphysics. The low point to which philosophy has sunk is
indicated by the fact that it is possible to make a prosperous
career in philosophy by not being a metaphysician.

The positivists have been busy for some time now announcing
to the world the uselessness of metaphysics. Logic, epistemology

and metaphysics have long been the chief branches of philosophy; logic, however, has become a dependent of mathematics, while epistemology has to wait on neurophysiology. What does this do to philosophy? There is no science wishing to take over metaphysics, so the positivists have simply announced it to be nonsense: statements without reference. This leaves them merely the business of liquidators, and the liquidator may be pursuing an honorable profession – no doubt he is – but in any particular instance it is a profession without a future. It is not possible to go on liquidating metaphysics forever. For this reason, the metaphysician who fights back may be doing the liquidator a favor by prolonging his job.

The logical positivists hold the same view of metaphysics that the man in the street does, and it is inherited from the renaissance opinion of what went on among the scholastics: metaphysics is substantially mind-spinning or else a realm corresponding only to the mind; it is a wholly subjective or a wholly remote conception and bears no relation to the real world of actual objects. This is in fact the conception of metaphysics which the logical positivists have made into a career of opposing, and they do not seem to conceive that any other kind of metaphysics is possible. They have, in effect, dug up a straw man from the annals of history for the sole purpose of beating him up again. In order for them to oppose metaphysics in this way, it must continue to remain just what they had supposed it to be, and not lend itself to change or improvement in conception; it must, in short, remain non-empirical.

The age-old question of whether some metaphysics can be eliminated merely by asserting that no metaphysics exists, is still before us, this time in non-metaphysical form. To assume nominalism as a metaphysics, is one thing; but to assume that there is no such thing as metaphysics, and thus no metaphysics like nominalism, is to assume the position which nominalism assumes, and further to assume that to take up such a position is not to assume nominalism or any metaphysics, even though nominalism continues to be to the metaphysician the name for the position which is so assumed.

Like the logical positivists, Professor Lazerowitz has a specific sort of metaphysics in mind when he is engaged in attacking metaphysics. He is thinking of metaphysics of the idealistic variety, and moreover wholesale, without stopping to think that there may be subjective and objective idealists or to remember that there may be strong differences between them. He does not consider the stringencies of metaphysical realism, and he probably does know, but certainly fails to take into account, that nominalism is also metaphysics. Neither realism nor nominalism is guilty of the sort of commitment beyond logic and empiricism – and even against empiricism – of which he so unjustly accuses them. There is no possibility of exculpation when all are condemned because one is guilty. Metaphysics, in order to come under the sweeping gravamen of the positivists' charge, must be all of a piece and uniformly defective; and for that purpose discrimination between various sorts of metaphysical systems must be ruled out.

The differences between metaphysical systems are not serious enough for the opponents of metaphysics to take them into account, but they are nevertheless serious enough to be thought damaging to metaphysics itself. Indeed they are fatal.

"It is not uncommon," Professor Lazerowitz observes, "for philosophers to take scornful attitudes toward each other's views and to dismiss them as ridiculous and an insult to our intelligence" (p. 181). Philosophy, he goes on to point out, despite all proofs and refutations, "stands alone in having no solidly established results". But does it stand alone? Has science any "solidly established results"? The philosophers of science are fond of pointing out that the sustaining part of science is its method of inquiry and not its results, for the results become changed from time to time in a way which indicates that it is not the results which are permanent.

The most serious crime committed by metaphysicians, evidently, and additional evidence, if more were needed, of the fact that metaphysics is a bad road, has been the differences among metaphysicians about metaphysics; that there are, in other words, competing metaphysical systems. If the logical positivists looked about them a little more, they would see that there are competing cultural systems also, and competing religions, and even competing conceptions of art. There are competing sciences, it is true, but this does not mean that all other disciplines would be better off for imitating science in this regard. Is Chinese music wrong and western music right? Is Balinese temple dancing right and western ballet wrong? These questions do not make any sense. Metaphysical systems that conflict do more than merely conflict: each one may be representing a neglected truth, and the fact that implicit metaphysical systems exist in competing cultures, each of which brings something new to the world, is evidence for the fact that there are gains to be had from competing metaphysical systems. The naive search for a single truth on the part of the logical positivists may reveal how poverty-stricken their whole conception really is. We are all of us looking for consistency, but not all at the cost of completeness. The logical positivists do not believe in anything enough to set up a working philosophy, only enough to eliminate the working philosophies of those who do.

Metaphysics, Professor Lazerowitz contends – and it is his main charge – is an illusion consisting of three strata, and he states these as follows: "a linguistically produced illusion that a theory about the world is being announced; a concealed description of an academic and incompletely worked out reediting of language which requires the preservation of ordinary language as a backdrop against which the philosophical sentence produces its dramatic effect; and, finally, one or more unconscious ideas the philosophical statement is made to denote" (p. 230). The first charge is that the language of metaphysics is meaningless but parades as having meaning, the second that this deception is aided by the addition of ordinary language which by itself is presumably meaningful, and the third that the metaphysical language does say something after all and that what it does say is an expression of unconscious thought. We may quickly dispose of these charges and then notice at greater length some of the implications of the side-effects, for these have been responsible for more damage in a popular way.

II

The first and third charges are contradictory provided it is possible for "unconscious ideas" to constitute a true "theory about the world". For the first charge says that the language of metaphysics is meaningless, while the third charge says that it is meaningful, albeit in terms of unconscious ideas. But unconscious ideas are still ideas, and Freud never said that all of the content of the unconscious was false. Some unconsciously held ideas may, and indeed do, refer to the world, even to the extent of constituting a theory about the world. There is a rational unconscious [1], and its content is not entirely meaningless.

The second charge is less serious, being merely supporting evidence that ordinary language, which is meaningful, heightens the dramatic effect of the meaningless metaphysical language which it accompanies. If the metaphysical language is not meaningless, the charge is. The burden of the proof that all metaphysics is meaningless rests on the shoulders of Professor Lazerowitz. And the evidence he adduces that some metaphysics is meaningless – especially when torn out of context – is, as every logician must know, no proof.

Professor Lazerowitz seems often to be confused between the notion that metaphysics is an illusion which has the effect of hoodwinking the metaphysician and the notion that metaphysics is an illusion produced by the metaphysician in order to hoodwink others. When he is feeling kind, he thinks that there is in the metaphysician more innocent self-deception than there is malice engineered with monstrous cleverness. In supposing, as he continually does throughout the book, that metaphysics consists in three different kinds of structured illusion, Professor Lazerowitz pleads that the metaphysician is the most monstrous kind of imposter there ever was. And it is noteworthy that even Professor Lazerowitz is shaken to some extent by the "remarkable and subtly integrated structures" that they are able to produce (p. 230). Judging by the fact that some of the papers in his volume are the results of discussions with students (e.g. Chapter XI), it is clear that Professor Lazerowitz is practicing a profession we may name "un-philosophy". He is, in short, like so many others today, an open enemy within the gates.

A group of mathematicians were once talking about God. One of the number professed himself an atheist. The others pressed him very hard. "Prove", they said, "that there is no God.

---

[1] "The Rational Unconscious", in *The Journal of General Psychology*, 1955, 52, 157–162.

Demonstrate the truth of the following proposition, 'It is the case that no God exists' ''. The atheist tried, but he was no match for his fellow mathematicians, who were convinced that he had taken up a position which could not be defended successfully. Finally, in retreat, he assumed an attitude of mock-piety. Looking at the floor with head bowed, he said quickly, "Gentlemen, there are some things you just have to take on faith". Perhaps those who argue that there is no metaphysics are in the same situation. Professor Lazerowitz' attack on metaphysics would have to be taken on faith, for he has failed to establish it.

Despite the principal attack, which is upon the non-sensicality of metaphysics, Professor Lazerowitz seems to be occasionally inclined toward the notion that, in perpetrating the sort of nonsense he does, the metaphysician is self-hoodwinked. And then we discover that it was not kindness after all. For Professor Lazerowitz follows the lines of the naive argument that was advanced for the first time by Professor John Wisdom in *Philosophy and Psychoanalysis* [1]. Metaphysicians are those who are seriously engaged in attending to nonsense; those who are seriously engaged in attending to nonsense are suffering from a mental disorder; therefore metaphysicians are those who are suffering from a mental disorder (p. 67). Presumably, all men who profess themselves to be metaphysicians ought to be treated for the ailment, and if the treatment fails, hospitalized.

The argument is an appeal to force, for what else can we call the contention that those who disagree with the logical positivists should be physically compelled to give up their argument? Professor Lazerowitz may not like the logical positivists too well but he has adopted their negative thesis as the topic of an entire work. Would not the psychoanalysts, or perhaps even more importantly the psychiatrists, be very much interested in anyone who is chiefly concerned with hostile and negative motives, who devotes himself principally to tearing down what others have constructed without constructing anything of his own? Professor Lazerowitz seems to object to the fact that behind the positivistic charge of nonsense against metaphysics, he notes an emotional attitude of disapproval, and he dislikes it. Yet he himself is able to write a whole book against metaphysics in which it is made

[1] (Oxford 1953, Blackwell), p. 169–181.

obvious that his contempt for metaphysics knows no bounds. He does not want even to allow the logical positivists to castigate metaphysics on their own grounds. Metaphysics, most specifically, must be castigated on *his* grounds.

It is possible of course to give a psychoanalytic explanation of any belief provided that one starts with the assumption that the belief is false. Adherence to it would then have to be explained on grounds other than those of truth, and a psychological mechanism is handy enough and perhaps even suitable; but the falseness of belief is not proven by the fact that the logical positivist does not accept it, or does not accept it, that is to say, merely because it is a belief with a metaphysical content. In refuting Parmenides and Heraclitus on psychoanalytic grounds, Professor Lazerowitz has put the argument on a basis on which it cannot be answered except in kind. Envy and hostility also have psychoanalytic explanations. Criticism is easy when nothing is substituted for it that is new; and Professor Lazerowitz himself, like so many of the logical positivists, may also be the sophist of his passions when he finds comfort in rejection alone, or in aggressions against metaphysical systems which he may lack the power to improve or the imagination to replace.

His arguments on logical grounds are of course specious: that there is real change in the world and real permanence, none who took a detached view would attempt to deny. We are still endeavoring to discover just what the relations between these realities are; and in the meanwhile we do not have the evidence to reject those like Parmenides who say that permanence is superior in reality, or those like Heraclitus who make the same claim for change. In sum, if Professor Lazerowitz is concerned with the psychological motivation which prompts philosophers to undertake the kind of illusion which metaphysics represent, it is always possible also to turn this criticism against Professor Lazerowitz himself, and to wonder what kind of emotional preference prompted him to devote such a very large effort to the elaboration of a negative criticism of metaphysics. Employing his kind of objection, we could say that it must satisfy something in him to join the side of those who hold metaphysics to be nonsense and to expend a great deal more effort in that direction than they ever did.

III

All of a sudden it is fashionable for some philosophers to pretend to themselves that they are at a loss to understand what other philosophers are talking about (p. 85). This is now the common practice among the logical positivists, and that Professor Lazerowitz follows it only shows once more that he is a good and obedient member of a related school. But this kind of group hypocrisy must have some explanation which we do not as yet understand. Twenty years ago the pages of the journals were full of the analysis of epistemological problems. Now they are equally full of voluble confessions by the logical positivists and linguistic analysts that they do not understand what it is that the metaphysicians are disputing among themselves. What will it be twenty years from now? Certainly not the same kind of professed ignorance! It is a misleading thing to keep up with the fashions in philosophy, for there are rapid shifts in it just as there are in other sorts of popular movements – in politics or in women's clothes. If we all sit quite still, the absolute scepticism of the positivists and analysts may pass.

They forget, of course, what the effect of such a controversy must be upon the non-professional public. For a long while now, it has been commonly supposed that philosophy is an unimportant topic, a dead area to be relegated to a Dark Age when such things were taken seriously. Those of us who wish to correct this misapprehension are now faced with a new kind of reaffirmation of it; for now with the spectacles of the logical positivists' onslaught against metaphysics, the public is entitled to say, "You see! What we have been saying is so, for even the philosophers think that philosophy is nonsense, only they differ as to which part is nonsense and which is not: each of them thinks that the other's philosophy is nonsense".

Why should it follow when men disagree about an issue that they have no issue other than the confusion involved in the language they employ? There are true cases of anxiety neurosis, but every case of anxiety is not a case of neurosis. Is it necessary in order to defend metaphysics to defend each and every metaphysical proposition?

This must surely be the state of affairs if Professor Lazerowitz is allowed to consider that he has refuted metaphysics because he has selected a metaphysical proposition at random and showed it to be circular or contradictory. He has reason on his side, of course, when he argues that some metaphysicians both do and do not accept empirical verification, and he has singled out the weakness of one school when he charges the objective idealists with this dual position. In selecting for examination the proposition "everything remains unchanged", Professor Lazerowitz is attacking Parmenides or Bradley. They would deny empirical verification – and at the same time they enunciate a proposition with empirical reference – and then introduce a distinction between appearance and reality in order to escape the refutation of their position which is implied by empirical verification. Objective idealism, however, is only one *kind* of metaphysical position, and in showing it to be untenable we do not reject the entire enterprise of metaphysics. Metaphysics is a genus and objective idealism a species, and we do not throw out the genus by attacking one species with one argument. When a logical positivist attacks metaphysics, he always selects as an example the most untenable of metaphysical positions and then suggests the spurious inference that all metaphysics is of this character.

Professor Lazerowitz employs the technique of exaggeration and hyperbole. The views of an opponent are considered to be refuted when they are absurdly stated or at best naively expressed, Leibniz' monads have with some justice often been compared with atoms; but Leibniz neither said nor could have said that "a chair is made up of minds" (p. 51). The rejection of all metaphysical propositions is assumed to have been accomplished by the rejection of patently false metaphysical propositions, as for instance when Professor Lazerowitz argues that metaphysical theories are non-empirical by refuting the statement that there are no material things (pp. 33–36).

Metaphysics is tenuous at best, and unless some effort is made to understand it, the result is sure to end in failure. It is clear from the efforts of Professor Lazerowitz and his masters that they do not wish to understand metaphysics but insist upon misunderstanding it. Professor Lazerowitz' charge is perhaps the most severe of all; he has followed the English followers of Wittgenstein in saying that metaphysics is a linguistic innovation, the innovation consisting in a special use of the language which renders it meaningless. Now it is highly unlikely that if there were not two different processes – one of learning the correct use of a word and the other of framing an abstract idea (p. 88) – there would be no logicians and probably no philosophers; and perhaps even no scientists or mathematicians. All of these enterprises involve the consideration of words and their meanings far beyond learning the correct use to which they have been put or to which they are customarily in the habit of being put.

Professor Lazerowitz asserts that "it will be clear that knowing the meaning of a word is the same as knowing its proper use" (pp. 89–90). Whenever a philosophical proposition is begun with some such warning as "obviously" or "it will be clear", we know that the proposition which follows it is neither obvious nor clear. If our use of words did not take us often far beyond what we knew to be their meaning, then in literature the literary artist would never build better than he knows, and Lewis Carroll – who was a mathematician as well as an artist in words – would have been wrong in asserting that there is usually more in a good book than the author consciously or deliberately put there. Professor Lazerowitz and his mentor, Professor J. O. Wisdom, would agree with this of course, only, where Carroll means that it is a fortunate extra, the linguistic analysts think that it is time to call in the psychoanalysts (p. 67). What, we might ask, is the correct use of a word? Is the correct use of a word what we mean by the word, or the effect which our use of the word may have on a hearer, or the possible one-one correspondence between the two? And the fact that we have at present no test for finding out just how far beyond our knowledge of the meaning of a word our use has been, does not refute the fact that there may be genuine grounds for such an unintentional excess.

Those who have no feeling for the relations between abstract words and their references can still play the game of philosophy, only they play it in such a way that its terms are non-referential; and so of course an examination of their manipulation reveals no reference. This is a vicious circle. It is clear that Professor Lazerowitz starts from the assumption that the terminology of metaphysics is meaningless, that it has no objective reference. Then he discovers this meaninglessness and exposes it. He found what he was looking for and ended with what he started; he has made no discovery, so far as it is possible to see, except that having started from a given position, he can find himself at the end of his investigation still in the same position. But then what does he prove by these tactics except that for him metaphysics is a meaningless game and not worth playing?

There is no greater nonsense than the nonsense that *all* metaphysics is nonsense. It is interesting but hardly convincing to discover that the kind of metaphysical proposition Professor Lazerowitz singles out for ridicule is the kind which may have been selected by the ignorant or the philistine: "we know the nothing" (p. 181), or "things are but appearances" (p. 199). Such metaphysical propositions, carefully chosen and torn out of context, can quite easily be made to look ridiculous. But where is the feat in that? And what does it prove about all metaphysical systems?

When an inquiry fails, as it does in Hume's case (p. 154), Professor Lazerowitz is quite sure that the culprit is the language, especially since the inquiry itself was not about things but about the language. If only those who think they are following Wittgenstein would go back and read him again, then they would see that the *reason* he investigated language was not the same as *their* reason; and therefore that he did not do it with same emphasis. Wittgenstein thought that by studying language he could find out something about the world, since language had grown up as a description of the world out of the necessity to cope with it. Professor Lazerowitz, with many of the linguistic analysts, seems to think that by studying language we can see that it has no application to the world. This, at least, is what he finds to be true of the metaphysical language. He professes to find a significant analogue for the metaphysicians' attempt to strip away the attributes of substances in order to find out what substance is, in the stripping away of adjectives from nouns in order to find out what a noun is.

When men who suppose that all thoughts refer to words engage in controversy, they do not do so fairly; for they always assume that their words are meaningful while their adversaries' words are meaningless – merely the "linguistic result of juggling with words" (p. 157). The semantic situation is that they are talking sense while their opponents are talking nonsense; and they enter the discussion with this premise and without any justification for the distinction; a case of "heads I win, tails you lose". It is a dangerous game, this business of charging those with whom you do not agree with talking nonsense, as the readers of Professor Lazerowitz' book will discover.

Of course we are told that the aim of the linguistic analysts is a good one: it is all a question of getting our language in order. But when we do get our language in order, what is it that we shall say? When we are in possession of the logically perfect language, presumably we shall wish to speak it. By means of it, one might think we shall be able to find expression for the ideal ontology. In the meanwhile, however, are we forbidden to say anything that is not about the language itself? We are permitted to deal with concrete things by means of language, and the language of experimental science is officially approved. But is this not rather a matter of taking sides in the metaphysical controversy to suppose that the language of science is a concrete language in the first place and that abstract words have no objective reference in the second? We have at the present time, presumably, an approximative language, one with which the linguistic analysts do not agree, and we can express in it an approximative ontology. If we were to be compelled to wait before saying anything until our language was perfect, then we should have nothing to say in the perfect language. We should not in the meantime have brought our ideas up-to-date; for surely the thoughts that we wish to express must keep pace with the development of the language in which we wish to express them.

IV

Whether the statement that universals exist means merely that abstract words have meanings, is left undecided by Professor Lazerowitz (p. 84). The decision to agree or not with his statement depends entirely upon what meaning he assigns to "meanings". If you were to suppose that an abstract word has a meaning which is equally abstract and which is independent of both our knowing it and of its actual exemplifications in matters of fact, then he answer is yes; otherwise, no. After his professed mock-failure to understand what the controversy over universals is about, he finally arrives at one that satisfies him: "It is the controversy over the purported discovery that, in addition to their having an ordinary use, they also stand for entities philosophers have called universals" (p. 87). It is surprising that Professor Lazerowitz is surprised at the distinction between theoretical and practical knowledge, since it employs the same terminology. Surely it is a different thing to say, "bring me that chair" or to think about that chair, than to know that 'chairness' as such is independent of our thinking about chairs, or using of chairs, or even the existence of chairs; he should have known from his logic that a class which has no members is still not meaningless.

The logical positivists are obviously aided in making their point by their implicit refusal to bridge the gap between logic and metaphysics. The notions they reject in metaphysics they will admit and even deal with in logic provided the terms are given logical rather than metaphysical names. This is taking the terminology with a high seriousness indeed. Professor Lazerowitz' argument that there cannot be any universals because there are borderline cases among the members can quite easily be refuted. The example is that if there were a horse which turned into a swan then there would be a point at which it would not be possible to say whether the animal was a horse or a swan and so there was no such clear thing as a membership in the universal "horse" since the members faded off into other animals. But this is like saying that there is neither day nor night because there is also dusk. Professor Lazerowitz seems to think that every universal is surrounded by a clear space in which there is nothing. The universal "horse" does not cease to be a universal because the example comes under either that universal or the universal "swan", and there may even be – provided a hybrid could be arranged – a universal "swan-horse" of which the members were half swan and half horse. How does he suppose that in this way he has got rid of universals?

When a philosopher says that he does not know what a thing is, he fares no better at the hands of Professor Lazerowitz than when he says that he does. When he says that universals are known or knowable, Professor Lazerowitz is very upset; and when he says that he cannot know what a thing is, Professor Lazerowitz seems equally upset (p. 145). He evidently does not want metaphysicians to live in a world in which there are known things or in a world in which there are unknown things. It could only be concluded from this that he does not want the philosophers to live in a world at all. The hypocritical pretension that Professor Lazerowitz and his masters do not know what the philosophers in the past have meant when they have assumed the reality of universals is, in a way, to confess themselves incapable of understanding the history of philosophy. It is a specious kind of pretension and unworthy of them, for to refute a position that you really hold to be untrue, it is not necessary to derogate it or to pursue the *argumentum ad hominem* in the way that Professor Lazerowitz and his masters do. It is not all that difficult to understand Plato and Hegel and Aristotle, to say nothing of the modern metaphysicians such as Whitehead and Peirce and Nicolai Hartmann and Santayana.

If all of these men are such difficult writers as to defeat Professor Lazerowitz' understanding, then perhaps he is in the wrong business, and this, in fact, would appear to be just what he and his masters are saying; they do not want to play at philosophy and, furthermore, they do not want anybody else to play at it either, and before leaving the game, they wish to destroy it altogether. They should remember, perhaps, that it was not the alchemists who destroyed alchemy but the chemists; not the astrologers who destroyed astrology but the astronomers, and in being metaphysicians of a negative sort they have hardly put themselves in the proper way to destroy metaphysics. They had better leave that to some other and more exact study, for they cannot do both – this, of course, all on the assumption that they are correct and that metaphysics is indeed a pseudo-study akin to astrology and alchemy.

By an odd twist of thought, Professor Lazerowitz stands self-condemned; for in considering the existence of universals he maintains that in searching for the meanings of words and pretending to delight in discovering them, philosophers behave as if the words had acquired the meanings without the aid of human beings. To the contrary, he asserts that words only have the meanings which were given to them by someone and which they were always known by someone to have. But if this be the case, his rejection of universals and metaphysics, on the assumption that they are meaningless or illusory, controverts what people have always supposed to be true. For many centuries men have thought that universals and metaphysics were meaningful terms; and now Professor Lazerowitz, along with other members of his school, tells us that they are not, and they pretend that this is a discovery. Paradoxically, they deny on the one hand that the discovery of the meaning of words is impossible, but the discovery of the non-meaning of words is extraordinary and a new illumination in philosophy! (pp. 95–96.)

The attack on metaphysics in general and on universals in particular comes, of course, in the name of science, but the great scientists certainly were stimulated by their metaphysical speculations. "The vast and mysterious gulf between the practice of science and the practice of philosophy" (p. 200) is just what has made possible the right relation between them: they are different, and that is why they can have relations which are both exciting and interesting to the speculative sciences, for it is the very vagueness of philosophy, as Peirce pointed out, which makes it so suggestive. In the science the logical positivists seem to wish for, there would be no speculation – there would only be observation and experiment, but these alone lead to a poverty-stricken kind of science in which there are no bold hypotheses, no imaginative constructions and, hence, no great discoveries. Behind every great scientist, behind every great physicist, as Burtt has shown in his *Metaphysical Foundations of Modern Physical Science*, there has stood a philosopher, or, if not a particular philosopher, then certainly an intense philosophical interest, as even the most recent of the great physicists like Einstein and Planck were quick to admit.

The point is that the prevalence of philosophy has not hindered the development of science in the recent past; what science will be like in the future, if the positivists get their way and metaphysics is banished from the scene, it is hard to imagine. It will be a science of a purely empirical nature which sticks closely to the facts and is too timid to generalize about them. The scientist cannot use philosophy in his speculations about the nature of the physical or biological or chemical world, but a background of philosophy – and in particular of metaphysics – has seemed to provide for him the kind of imaginative facility which he is going to need to develop, and without it he will not be the kind of scientist he once was. And if metaphysics has not held up science in the past, why are the empirical philosophers today so much afraid that it will do so in the present and in the future? Almost every argument that has been used by Professor Lazerowitz against metaphysics could also be used against pure mathematics, and would have been, too, were it not for the importance of applied mathematics in empirical science. For pure mathematics is non-empirical, and its entities are logical and so have no reference.

The logical positivists, no doubt following Hume, seem to be struck with the fact that there is no such thing as an observable metaphysical object. But if this is an argument against metaphysics, then it is an argument against mathematics as well, for there is no observable mathematical object, and yet mathematics wins their approval in a way that metaphysics does not. There has never been a good logical positivistic explanation of this; the explanation, of course, is one they would not care to admit, which is that science uses mathematics so freely and has such respect for it, that since the logical positivists look up to science, they must also look up to mathematics.

This difficulty with mathematics, in fact, leads them to difficulties with substance; for the fact that we do not perceive the subject of attributes does not mean that the attributes are not the attributes of a single subject and therefore that we might mean by the subject of attributes the unity of the attributes, namely, substance; and in this way substance would be there in the same way that the mathematical unit was there but no more observable. No scientist who discovers that his own or someone else's hypothesis was wrong regards it as a "verbal fraud" (p. 149), and when no grounds have been discovered for the proper decision between whether there is or is not a substance or substrata, or for determining what it is, then what is to be gained by such a charge? The logical positivists are no better than other dogmatic philosophers in assuming that they are absolutely right and their opponents absolutely wrong. If they think this is a new attitude in philosophy, they are mistaken; it has been going on for centuries, and perhaps now is the time to change it.

Perhaps we ought to acquire some tolerance of other views than our own when we find that we cannot gain general acceptance for our own. The logical positivists seem as sure of their position as do all other dogmatists; in this they make their position look more like a religion and less like a science; they are absolutely sure of their own position and no scientific proposal was ever made like that.

In his attack on substance, Professor Lazerowitz selects just the definition he wishes to attack, but he forgets, perhaps, that there are many definitions of substance. Substance, to the classical philosophers, is a field of inquiry, not a commonly-agreed upon topic. If the position which Professor Lazerowitz has singled out to attack had been uniformly agreed upon, as his attack would indicate, then this would mean that there were very few differences among philosophers to be reckoned with, except for the differences between those philosophers who believe in metaphysical propositions and those who do not. But, unfortunately for the attack upon metaphysics, there are many metaphysical positions, and to attack one is not to have dismissed them all.

Later Professor Lazerowitz shows that the notion of substance is denied by Hume and accepted by Locke, and he argues that "it is not difficult to see that laboratory science holds out no hope for its solution in the future" (p. 153). But if we are to condemn all metaphysical theories by the fact that science holds no hope of solving them in the laboratory, then how much truth is there in logical positivism, which is not only not held in the laboratory but moves in direct contradiction with laboratory procedures? For the laboratory requires both mathematics and hypotheses aplenty, whereas the logical positivists and linguistic analysts will not endorse – or should not endorse if they are consistent – mathematical theories, and certainly cannot tolerate hypotheses in science when they do not tolerate them in any other field.

It is curious to find Professor Lazerowitz holding Russell up as a bad example in one place (p. 146) and later quoting him in his own defense (p. 147). Substance, it turns out, is something that occurs to philosophers when they transfer to the world what they learned from language; and substance having attributes, it turns out, is the same as a subject having predicates. It is a little difficult to see why "our familiarity with chairs and the like" should prove to us that there is no substance, when "chairs and the like" have in common the fact that they are individuals, and when the individuals are not reducible to anything but universals plus some stubborn property which eludes definition.

V

It is a well known fact that if you wish to have a cruel boss, make a foreman out of someone from the ranks of the unskilled workers. To see a linguistic analyst chide the logical positivists is not without its amusing aspects. Those of us who are to have our throats cut may derive some molecule of comfort from the spectacle of our executioners arguing over whose knives are the sharpest. Professor Lazerowitz has the zeal of a convert. Speaking evidently as a linguistic analyst, he seems to think that the logical positivists are not positive enough, that they do not castigate metaphysics as severely as they could. "Watch me", he seems to be saying, "while I pour it on them".

Oddly enough, there are corners of the philosophical community to which democratic principles of tolerance and liberalism have not yet penetrated. If the logical positivists were really concerned with the welfare of philosophy, they would pursue their own constructive notions and leave the others to their fate, on the assumption that if some philosophers, such as for instance (they would claim) the metaphysicians, are following a bad lead, it will only end in a blind alley and so, like false hypotheses pursued in experimental science, the error will succeed in correcting itself. This, however, the masters of Professor Lazerowitz cannot do from where they sit, for such a program is not theirs but instead only intolerance and outrageous charges. Professor Lazerowitz would be the Robespierre of the logical positivist movement: he would heap the fires higher over the metaphysicians' heads, and does not seem to mind if a few positivists get scorched in the process for that might convince them more than ever of the sincerity of his efforts at condemnation.

Professor Lazerowitz likes to attack metaphysics but he objects when it is done on an emotional basis and seems to prefer an attack in cold blood. "Whatever the facts about metaphysics may be [sic], there can be hardly any doubt that the belief in the

positivistic hypothesis has its main source in the wish to dis-
parage metaphysics" (p. 54). 'I can trust nobody but thee and
me and sometimes I cannot trust thee'. For "some positivists,
after first having condemned the Platonic theory of supra-
sensible universals, are coming back to one or other of its classical
forms, and now accept as perfectly intelligible what for years they
had *seen* to be nonsense" (p. 52).

Professor Lazerowitz is vexed with the evidence of defection in
the ranks of the logical positivists and would call them back to
a strict observance of their negative principles concerning metaphysics. He wishes their opposition to rest on more than an emotional bias (p. 52). The positivists, he thinks, are too weak in
their castigation of metaphysics, for they employ only a negative
criterion, and so (p. 54) he proposes a positive criterion. This is to
the effect that "metaphysical sentences are rejected because of the
kind of propositions they stand for". The rest of his argument
reveals that metaphysics is denied the privilege of speaking its
own language and of referring to what its own entities refer to.
It is hard to see what a logical positivist can do. He is not a
philosopher, because metaphysics is the heart of philosophy and
he rejects metaphysics. He is not a scientist and could not be, for
scientists have to allow themselves many bold, and often mistaken, hypotheses before they discover anything which can be
verified. Professor Lazerowitz has an implicit metaphysics. He
uses terms like "reality" as meaningful, and this in a special sense
which betrays one particular metaphysics to which he unwittingly
subscribes, and, as we have noted earlier it is nominalism (p. 42).

If metaphysics is nonsense, it would be well for the logical
positivists and linguistic analysts to stop berating the professional
philosophers and instead to call this phenomenon to the attention
of those who apply metaphysics to practical affairs, notably the
Soviet Russians and Chinese who are dialectical materialists, the
Roman Catholics who are Thomists, and the Continental followers of the existentialists. Little do they know that what they are
applying is nonsense and their surprise on finding out would be
great indeed. Times of troubles are inevitably characterized by
conflicting developments, and this is no less true of philosophy
than of any other enterprise. In some ways this is the age of the
great metaphysical systems, and we owe much to Whitehead,

Santayana, and Nicolai Hartmann, to name but three of the biggest. But it is also the age of the refutation of metaphysics, as witness the concerted effort of the logical positivists. Professor Lazerowitz' attack is the latest. Any attack on the refutation of metaphysics seems to play into the hands of the wrong people, it suits very well those who have a particular metaphysics which they wish to defend as the absolute truth but do not wish to call by that name. But the positivists are absolutists as well, and in the end all absolutists conduct inquisitions. The rejection of metaphysics *in toto*, and not merely of a particular metaphysics, by men competent to study and understand the history of philosophy, is, in the last analysis, ill advised.

PART FOUR

THE SAVING ELEMENTS

CHAPTER VIII

THE METAPHYSICS OF LOGICAL POSITIVISM

I. THE LIMITED SENSE OF METAPHYSICS

In this chapter as the title suggests, we propose to examine some aspects of logical positivism, or, as it is known more precisely logical empiricism, for the purpose of endeavoring to discover the metaphysics it allows or requires. But before we can undertake even the first step in such a constructive task, we are placed under attack and obliged to defend ourselves. A contradiction confronts us, for, as is well known, logical positivism holds to the doctrine that metaphysics is nonsense.

We shall begin, then, with the metaphysical implications of the statement, "metaphysics is nonsense", and confine our attention to the negative aspects, reserving the more positive ontological and epistemological aspects for the next sections. In this section the argument against the nonsense of metaphysics will have two parts, each of which will be aimed at showing that the position fails to take into account the importance of a certain distinction. We shall argue that logical positivism mistakenly identifies all metaphysics with (a) a transcendental metaphysics, and with (b) an ostensive and explicit metaphysics.

(a) Traditional metaphysics usually has contained large proportions of transcendental elements, and it is those elements which logical positivism holds to be nonsense. The charge is sustained. But in that case is it fair to equate metaphysics with the transcendental elements? To some extent, certainly; for logical positivism can only deal with the metaphysics it knows, and, in general, historical metaphysics is transcendental metaphysics. But, on the other hand, transcendental metaphysics may not be the only possible metaphysics. In order to sustain its position, logical positivism would have to demonstrate that no other type of metaphysics is possible, and this may be difficult if it can be accomplished at all.

The logical positivists who started with the notion that

metaphysics is nonsense are at this point obliged to be more temperate: now they would say that ontology is unnecessary [1]. The positivists attack only one kind of ontology because evidently they can conceive of the existence of only one class of ontologies. This class is the set of ontologies contained under the theory of reality as a part. Under this theory, reality is a subdivision of being, and is opposed by another subdivision called appearance. Some things – change, for instance – are real (or unreal) while other things – such as permanence – are unreal (or real). We are given the impression whenever Carnap speaks of metaphysics or of ontology, that he knows only about this kind [2]. Yet the ontology he accepts implicitly and unconsciously belongs to another set. Carnap wants the position of nominalism without the term, for instance [3]. That is, he wants the anti-metaphysical position implicit in nominalism, but he does not want it to be called nominalism. In this school, ontology is an ugly epithet, to be reserved for each wing to hurl against the other. [4] He recoils with some horror at the prospect that if variables are to be interpreted realistically instead of nominalistically, physics would imply some degree of Platonic philosophy [5], and yet despite the pious approval of Peirce by the logical positivists [6], the fact is overlooked that Peirce believed and said precisely the same thing about physics [7].

In any case, Carnap seems hopelessly confused about metaphysics. Clarification would involve a more extensive comprehension of the topic, including the notion of a set of ontologies contained under the theory of reality as the whole. According to this theory, reality is divided into parts. The parts are the universes: e.g. essence and existence, or possibility and actuality. This kind of ontology is no less ontological for being termed "modality" [8] or "modal logic", as with Carnap. But surely we do

[1] R. Carnap, "Empiricism, Semantics, and Ontology", in the *Revue Internationale de Philosophie* for January 15, 1950.
[2] The range is from his attack on metaphysics in his little book, *Philosophy and Logical Syntax* (London 1935), p. 15 ff. to the essay cited above, p. 31, *et passim*.
[3] "Empiricism, Semantics, and Ontology", p. 33, *init*.
[4] *Op. cit.*, p. 32, n. 2.
[5] *Op. cit.*, p. 32.
[6] Op. cit., p. 39, A. Tarski, *Introduction to Logic* (New York 1946), p. 14.
[7] *Collected Papers* of Charles S. Peirce, (Cambridge, Mass., 1935), 6.361. See also my *Introduction to Peirce's Philosophy* (New York 1946), Ch. 8.
[8] R. Carnap, *Meaning and Necessity* (Chicago 1947), Ch. V.

not learn in this way that metaphysics is impossible but just the opposite; for what we are shown is a disguised metaphysics.

Furthermore, a finite metaphysics may be possible; and if possible would not be susceptible to the strictures laid against metaphysics in general by logical positivism. In short, in asserting that metaphysics is nonsense the logical positivists have identified a transcendental metaphysics with metaphysics, and failed to discern the possibility of a finite metaphysics. We shall see before we are done that logical positivism itself requires just a finite metaphysics.

(b) Logical positivism has identified the metaphysics it labels as nonsense with an ostensive and explicit metaphysics. By metaphysics it means the metaphysics of the profession of philosophy, as set forth in books and in classrooms. But this is a narrow conception of metaphysics, and assumes it to be the exclusive property of the metaphysicians. For if metaphysics is as pervasive as the presuppositions of other orderly fields, and even all other activities, would seem to indicate, then an implicit metaphysics must be more general than the explicit metaphysics could ever hope; and the latter is merely a small abstraction from the former.

It was in the attempt to make the implicit explicit that professional philosophy arose. Instead of confining its efforts to the discovery of abstract structures whose elements have some empirical justification, philosophy followed the fashion of the times and sought to find a place in its systems for the creatures of allegory and symbol; and so from Plotinus to Hegel the field became cluttered up with concrete figures (including those taken from the religious and the subjective worlds). The task of philosophy is not an easy one, and so extreme positions are frequently encountered. It so happens that in empirical science, bold hypotheses have frequently been the means of uncovering certain aspects of the natural world; while appeal to the same method in philosophy has merely led to the making of absurd statements by the metaphysicians, and particularly by those who have supposed that the method of philosophy itself is entirely subjective. Unlike the procedure in science, however, the whole of philosophy is held responsible for the erroneous statements made in some quarters. Science has been identified with the doors

it opens, philosophy with its blind alleys. But we do not need to
confuse metaphysics with the errors of some metaphysicians.
That difficulties have arisen in the efforts to discover the implicit metaphysics is not sufficient grounds for the condemnation
of metaphysics in general, or any justification for identifying it
with its non-empirical aspects.

We see in the above two distinctions, namely that between a
transcendental and a finite metaphysics on the one hand, and
between an explicit and an implicit metaphysics on the other,
that logical positivism has identified the metaphysics it condemns
with the transcendental and the explicit varieties. In dismissing
a metaphysics so constituted, it seems quite properly to have got
rid of the unwanted elements; but the fact is that sufficient
remains to sustain the activity on a basis which logical positivism
can endorse.

A transcendental explicit metaphysics, corresponding to
nothing finite and implicit, seems to be equally the result of
the practice of an unbridled rational dogmatism or else of that
of an uncontrolled empirical scepticism.

These methods lead, strangely enough, to much the same sort
of result. To suppose that reason alone in general, and one's own
reason in particular, is the necessary and sufficient method of
arriving at indubitable knowledge is to commit the error of
rational dogmatism. It may of course lead to any sort of theory.
But then empiricism, too, has its pitfalls. Reliance upon the
senses alone, and upon one's own senses in particular, to the
exclusion of any cross-reference which inference may afford, is
sure to end in the denial of anything objective corresponding to
the senses. That metaphysics is nonsense has not been demonstrated, but only that a transcendental and explicit metaphysics
is nonsense. What has been shown, in other words, is that reason
alone or sense experience alone leads to metaphysical statements
which do not correspond to anything the method of logical
positivism can endorse.

Logical positivism as it stands contains statements of a
metaphysical character [1]. "Metaphysics is nonsense" is metaphysics. There are no revolutions in metaphysics, there are only

---

[1] J. R. Weinberg, *An Examination of Logical Positivism* (New York, 1936), Ch. VI,
esp. p. 175.

cautions. A warning carried too far in this field leads to the commission of the very error against which the warning was directed. The nominalism of considering all metaphysics as nonsense is now painfully familiar. This is a metaphysical position, and no less one for not being openly acknowledged. There does not appear to be anything in sense experience corresponding to the abstract structures of nominalism. If logical positivism is to have a metaphysics, this would hardly appear to be the suitable one for it. For nominalism is the metaphysics which includes a self-denying axiom. The question remains, however, whether a finite and implicit metaphysics does exist which stand in conformity with the rigorous demands of logical positivism. Throughout the following pages this question is answered in the affirmative.

II. THE RAMIFIED THEORY OF LOGICAL POSITIVISM

In this section we propose to set forth the general principles of logical positivism, and then the ramified interpretation of those principles in the light of the position set forth in the preceding section.

The principles of logical positivism fall into three distinct though related groups. The first group concerns the level of logic alone.

(1) *Logic presents the essential features of language.*
(2) *Language is a tautological system.*

The second group concerns the level of empiricism alone.

(3) *The world consists of atomic fact.*
(4) *True propositions are those which refer to atomic fact.*

The third and last group consists of the principles which relate the elements of the first two groups.

(5) *Language resembles the world.*
(6) *Empirical reference can be shown by logical analysis.*

The theses of logical positivism which do not refer specifically to metaphysics are hereby omitted, but they may be mentioned. They include the thesis of unified science, and that of radical physicialism. Since the unification of the sciences is to be brought about by the reduction to physics of all the other sciences, the two principles can be resolved into one, and that one left to the empirical sciences to execute if indeed it is to be done at all.

Before introducing the ramifications formally by means of extended principles corresponding to the above set, we may introduce them informally in commentaries. We may add that in these commentaries the first suggestions are made of a finite and implicit metaphysics which is consistent with, and allowed by, the principles of logical positivism.

(1) *Logic presents the essential features of language.* By "language here is meant system, a language is an abstract symbolic communication-system. Logic is by this theory thus redefined as the theory of abstract systems. The essential feature of systems so far as their internal relations are concerned is their logical nature. Linguistic systems of communication assert nothing in themselves that is not logical, and they are not empowered in themselves to go beyond logic.

(2) *Language is a tautological system.* This principle follows from the first, evidently from the last part of the previous discussion. 'All X is Y' is a formal proposition whose conventional meaning is trivial; whereas when we assign values to X and Y the proposition can have a meaning which is no longer conventional and may be significant. Thus if we substitute 'men' for X and 'mortality' for Y, we have 'all men are mortal', which is a material proposition to be considered for its content; but 'Either all X is Y or there exists at least one X which is not Y' is to be considered purely in virtue of its form; just as $p \lor p . \supset . p$ does.

The subject, the knower, the promulgator, of propositions drops out, leaving only the system of propositions. Thus we have in Weinberg's admirable phrase, "a solipsism without a subject" [1] The entire involvement of subjectivism is here at one stroke removed. For it is truth we are after, and promulgation is unrelated to truth.

But there is more to the story, for by releasing the proposition from its psychological bearings, it is admitted to be independent, and assumes the status of all universals in the theory of metaphysical realism. Indeed the closeness of logical positivism to metaphysical realism is obvious, provided only that logical positivism abandon the absoluteness of its anti-metaphysical

---

[1] J. R. Weinberg, *An Examination of Logical Positivism* (London, 1936), p. 68.

position, and realism abandon its transcendental nature and admit only those universals for which there is some logical or empirical evidence.

(3) *The world consists in atomic fact.* That is, the world is whatever it is, and is not made into anything else by the circumstances surrounding our perception of it. There is a world to be known which is no different for being known. Once again, then, the subject is eliminated, and the relation studied is that between a real world and a real system, not between a knower and a known. The world consists in a set of knowable facts which are eminently capable of isolation and systematic representation.

(4) *True propositions are those which refer to atomic fact.* Only one world exists: the world of atomic fact; but more than one proposition exists for every atomic fact, and presumably more than one logical language for every set of atomic facts. False propositions exist, more false ones than true ones – which are the true ones? The question can only be answered by planned inquiry: the true ones will be those which refer to atomic fact.

(5) *Language resembles the world.* Language grew up in answer to the need to understand the world, to explore it, and to manipulate and control it. It is partly the result of experience with the world, having been revised, corrected and extended in accordance with such experiences. There is some reason to believe, then, that it has a structure, and not merely elements, corresponding to that of the world.

(6) *Empirical reference can be shown by logical analysis.* The self-identical elements can have an extensional meaning without impairment of the tautological property. We have already seen that the substitution of values for the variables in the universal affirmative proposition in (2) did not change the formal properties of the proposition. This would be equally true of the tautological principle, for 'either horse or horse implies horse' has the same tautological meaning as the same proposition stated in terms of the three variables, pp and p.

So much for the principles, now we must turn to the ramified theory, and this is best stated as a set of additional corresponding principles. The ramified theory in this second set of principles purports to extend the original set of principles of logical positivism in the light of the metaphysical commentary and with the addition of a rigid and analytical scientific method whose precision was developed through the extension into controlled experimentation of this same set of principles (plus some others). For the sake of comparison, the second set of principles will be given corresponding numbers.

(i) *Mathematics contains the essential features of systems.*

(ii) *Mathematical systems consist of tautologies.*

(iii) *Existential propositions have a reference in data.*

(iv) *Mathematical equations refer to instrumentally-discovered data.*

(v) *Mathematics and the instrumentally-discovered data are isomorphic.*

(vi) *The data can be interpreted by means of equations.*

(i) *Mathematics contains the essential features of systems.* The development of logic in any topic involves the retreat of psychology. Admittedly, the knowledge of anything depends upon its being known – that is a truism; and the holding of knowledge is a capacity of minds; but that being is independent of knowing is a theory held out by the very existence of internal relations. The more complex a structure is and the more internal relations it has, the more its being is manifestly self-dependent.

Now in a mathematical system we have an advanced logical system, an abstraction whose structure of theorems, definitions and deductions depends only upon postulates whose set-extent and truth-conditions may remain undetermined. Knowledge is here reduced to a minimum, and structure is all-important. We define logic as the theory of systems and mathematics as all deductive systems.

(ii) *Mathematical systems consist of tautologies.* We introduce here the principle of the autonomy of levels. A mathematical system with its elements is closed under its set of operations. The origin of the elements and operations is a matter of indifference to the nature of the system as such, and even to the performance of its operations. Truth by definition is formal truth within the kind of logical system that mathematics preeminently is.

Tautological propositions contain only class names and refer only to logical states of affairs. This situation has occasioned considerable misunderstanding, for it has been assumed that what refers exclusively to logical states of affairs has no reference, on the confused psychological assumption that logical propositions and their references are together exclusively psychological. But the holding of logical propositions is no more – and no less – mental than the holding of empirical propositions whose external and independent world-reference is obvious and clear cut.

(iii) *Existential propositions have a reference in empirical data.* Although all propositions of necessity contain class names, existential propositions contain proper names as well, and are regarded as such because of their reference. We shall return to this point later on [1], meanwhile defining existential propositions as those which have a class containing a member which is unique. Empirical data are objects and events analyzed by means of instruments, e.g. the microscope, the spectroscope. An empirical datum from the point of view of propositions can be specified by dated universals, e.g. blue here-now, circle there-then [2].

(iv) *Mathematical equations refer to instrumentally-discovered data.* We are here at a deeper level of analysis. For propositions we have now substituted mathematical equations, and for atomic fact we have instrumentally-discovered data. What we have stated is a description of science at an advanced state of development. The same is possible in metaphysics, for the same sets of conditions prevail: an empirical field and an abstract structure to account for the field.

(v) *Mathematics and the instrumentally-discovered data are isomorphic.* That is to say, mathematical systems and the relations between the data are similar in form. We make an ontological model for the domain of existence. It is not true that there is only one ontology corresponding to any given domain; but of any two, one must serve the purpose more adequately than the other. The perfect model is yet to be found.

(vi) *The data can be interpreted by means of the equations.* We do not know what the data mean until we have found some abstract formulation that fits them. There are no data, only the indescribable flashes of phenomena, apart from their place as the

---

[1] See Section IV.
[2] Cf. Bertrand Russell, *Human Knowledge* (New York, 1948) p. 84.

elements of some system, for by themselves they are meaningless. Their discovery is governed by logic as well as by the necessity of conforming to the data. The systems are made up of equations and text. Hence logic and fact have their separate lines to metaphysics. In the next two sections we shall see what these are.

III. THE METAPHYSICS OF LOGIC: ONTOLOGY

In this section we consider the metaphysics of logic to be ontology, and in the next section we shall consider the metaphysics of empiricism to be epistemology. Both subdivisions of metalogic, the metaphysics required for logic, will be ordered in accordance with what is allowed and even demanded by logical positivism. For metaphysics by seeking conformity with logic meets the demands of empiricism as well. It obtains the requirements of logic through pure logic and mathematics, and the requirements of empiricism through applied logic and scientific method. Thus metalogic is a proper designation for the metaphysics of logical positivism.

Metaphysics is a field of inquiry and logic is the method employed in that field. Every method must have presuppositions of a metaphysical nature and a field in which to operate. This makes logic and metaphysics circular, for logic depends on metaphysics (for its presuppositions) and metaphysics depends on logic (for its method). We can only escape the difficulty by concentrating on operations. The latter are persistent and progressive: conclusions are always subject to change whereas the method and its presuppositions lend themselves only to amendment. We have no right to hold onto anything more than the method itself, together with its presuppositions, and the existence of a field of its operations. We can hardly escape the consequences of these minimal involvements and at the same time make any sense out of the logical method.

The fact that logic is the method of investigating metaphysics reveals special difficulties. For it seems we can investigate metaphysics only by making special metaphysical assumptions. Here we must be governed by logic: we shall admit a presupposition if and only if we can show that it is required for the specialized inquiry at hand. Thus we see that logic appeals to metaphysics in one way and metaphysics appeals to logic in another. Our only relief is that the appeals are made in different ways.

The result is the curious one arrived at by Wittgenstein. Philosophy – metaphysics – ontology, can now be expressed in logic. The key to the bridge is the theory of systems, systematic logic. Metaphysics is the world from some logical point of view, set forth in a system. Philosophy seeks mathematical precision but uses common sense language, in order to include the sweep of connotation. The result is that every ontology, since it is a logical system presented in the terms of everyday discourse, contains oracular elements: a prophetic notation of rigorous logical laws. Philosophy is so general by nature that the stricter the forms of its expression the vaguer it becomes, but also, we may add, the more suggestive.

The ontology required for logic is the proper ontology. The same logical state of affairs can be expressed in a number of different ways, and this situation reveals ontological assumptions underlying the logic. This is made evident, for instance, in the equivalence of propositions by the method of conversion, obversion and contraposition [1]; in what Wittgenstein has called "the disappearance of the logical constants" [2]. $\sim \sim p$ becoming p; and in the reduction of the truth-functions to joint denial or alternative denial [3].

The meaning of logical positivism, or logical empiricism, is that ontology must not extend beyond logic without some logical necessity. For ontology, there is a kind of Occam's Razor of logic. The obverse principle also applies, however, and ontological entities must be multiplied at least to the extent demanded by logical necessity. The two principles can best be combined in the statement that ontological entities must be multiplied just to the extent demanded by logical necessity. It is logic and nothing else which properly requires that ontology extend beyond logic and which determines how far that extension should go.

The determination begins with the class considered as a sign. Once a sign has been given a meaning, however arbitrary, it

---

[1] E.g. Cohen and Nagel, *Introduction to Logic and Scientific Method* (New York 1934), pp. 57 ff.

[2] *Tractatus Logico-Philosophicus* (London 1933), 5.441.

[3] W. V. Quine, *Mathematical Logic* (Cambridge 1947), p. 48.

leads a life of its own. This is true, irrespective of whether the sign refers to something or some set of things in the actual world, or to a connection between other signs. Factual signs, as we shall term the first group, are recognized in logic as being classes of individuals; classes alone but not individuals alone, except as classes of individuals alone. As to the second group termed logical signs, these have minimal meanings, but meanings they still are; and even grammatical connectives are meaningful.

All signs can be considered in abstraction from the elements in the actual world or from the state of affairs in logic which first suggested the necessity for them. There is an aura of absoluteness about all abstractions. They stand somewhat apart from the fluctuations of time and the distortions of space. The problem is, how to get rid of all transcendental presuppositions in a finite ontology. Clarification is elicitation; to make clear what we are talking about is to draw out details we had not known were involved, and some of the details are of the nature of qualifications. Hence the adoption of such a procedure at this point may exhibit limitations which will save the position. We intend to suggest that ontological import does not have to convey transcendental meaning. It has so often in the past happened this way that the identification is habitually made, and a refuge from the combination is sought in the particular and individual world of singular fact. But logical meaning need not be reduced to factual meaning in order to eliminate the infinite nature of abstractions, for there exists a finite logical meaning as well. Moreover, every such reduction throws out the very subject-matter which is the most in need of explanation and analysis, and is therefore self-defeating. It is the paradoxical custom of radical empiricism to practice a rigid metaphysical economy which begs more than it abandons, and in the end runs invisibly wild.

The position toward which the argument is tending is best illustrated with model interpretations.

Let us take the grammatical connectives 'and', 'or' (or 'either-or'), 'if .... then', and 'not', as a set of logical constants. First of all, these four can be reduced to two. For 'if .... then' we substitute 'and', and for 'or' we substitute the appropriate 'ands' and 'nots'[1]. We are left by this reduction with 'and' and 'not'.

---

[1] See e.g. W. V. Quine, *Elementary Logic* (New York 1941), pp. 14 ff., and 20 ff.

'And' has both a factual and a logical meaning, and these two meanings are distinct. The logical meaning of 'and' is the definition of a collection [1]. For instance, 'a and b and c' is a collection, in which we have nothing but the terms and the grammatical connective. The statement that 'and' defines a collection is logically true. But there is also a factual meaning of 'and'. The factual meaning is defined ostensively by space-time togetherness. That this book and this cigarette box are contiguous considered as an actual state of affairs exemplifies 'and' in factual truth. Now the lesson of scientific method is that when there is a correspondence between logical truth and factual truth, we are in the presence of ontological elements. Here the term, ontology, which has had so bad a history, is shorne of its transcendental and infinite implications and confined to the field which Carnap once so well defined as the systematization of scientific knowledge and so seldom returned to examine [2]. What precisely we mean by "ontological elements" will become clearer as this section develops.

We shall find that the same principles hold in the case of 'not'. The logical meaning of denial determines the truth-falsity function of coherence. A statement and its denial are inconsistent, and consistency is the governing function of coherence within a logical or mathematical system, or of any system which aspires to logical coherence. 'Not' is the notion of falsity, but the use of the tilde before a false statement renders it a true one. 'Ice is hot' is false, but '$\sim$ (ice is hot)' is true. The factual meaning of 'not' denotes absence or positive otherness. Where x is any actual thing, $\sim x$ denotes anything else from the point of view of x. Here, too, as in the case of 'and', we have a correspondence between logical truth and factual truth; and so ontology arises as a description of this state of affairs. In general it could be said that the legitimacy of ontology as a field of inquiry is to provide for just those situations which Russell's Theory of Descriptions fails to take into account.

[1] B. Russell, *Principles of Mathematics* (London 1937), p. 69.

[2] In castigating metaphysics as nonsense, he says, "I do not include in metaphysics those theories – sometimes called metaphysical – whose object is to arrange the most general propositions of the various regions of scientific knowledge in a well-ordered system". R. Carnap, *Philosophy and Logical Syntax* (London 1935), pp. 15–16. The point needs to be clarified for terms before we are ready to treat of the more complex propositions.

The objective correlates of the logical constants, discovered in the relation between the logical and factual references of grammatical connectives, constitute an ostensive definition of the type of elements to be found in the finite ontology. A system of ontology would not be so simple, but it would be a complex constructed of such simples. In order to exemplify this point, let us elaborate the construction of our model interpretation by progressing from a consideration of the grammatical connectives to the elements of Boolean algebra.

The binary operations of the Boolean algebra, indicated by 'meet' and 'join', correspond to our 'and' and 'or' [1]. Then by means of suitable combinations of these functions the calculus of classes can be derived. To see the ontological implications of the Boolean algebra, we have only to read the various types of combinations made in terms of 'meet' and 'join' as similarities and differences. Then with two more steps we are in the midst of an ontology.

The first of these steps is to notice that the similarities tend to persist and the differences to change. This distinction gives to each of the basic relations an altogether separate character. For persistence and change have their own set of properties. We notice that what is persistent is also abstract and general, while what is changing is not. On the other hand, the changing is characterized by a vividity and an immediacy of effect that the persistent does not enjoy. The persistent does not involve any elements of change; whereas change is not possible except from one persistent element or a set of persistent elements, to another element or set of elements.

The second step involves an answer to the question, similarities and differences of what? If we use the broad term, quality, here to cover all types of static and dynamic values, indeed everything that is not covered by the term, logic, then we can say, similarities and differences of qualities. The similarities persist in the recurrence of the qualities, and the differences occur in the context of space and time of the recurrent qualities. In postulating logic as the basis of mathematics, we have learned the lesson of the greater generality of difference.

---

[1] Birkhoff and MacLane, *A Survey of Modern Algebra* (New York 1948), p. 318.

For instance, the tautological Boolean function

$$A \cup A \subset A$$

we have a statement of greater generality than in the algebraic equation

$$A \times A = A^2.$$

It should be noted, however, that while $\cup$ has been said to denote '.—or ....," and $\cap$ to denote "—and ....", this is a similarity rather than an identity; for while in elementary algebra it is true that

$$A + A = 2A,$$

in Boolean algebra

$$A \cap A = A.$$

The reduction of mathematics to its lowest terms in the Boolean algebra teaches us that it is impossible not to assert something in a proposition. If we interpret the proposition as a statement rather than an assertion, the contention can be upheld. For a statement promulgates, even when it does not carry the presumption of truth-value. The minimal ramifications of logic are ontological. Logical positivism has been in the habit of testing the old metaphysics against the new logic and of finding the results unfavorable. And the conclusions have been regarded as final for all metaphysics. We can, however, more suitably have a new metaphysics and test it against the new logic. The results, we shall see, are somewhat different. Metaphysics can be treated like logic or like empirical science. We do not abandon logic when old conceptions appear insupportable, we revise it and emerge with some new conceptions which we think capable of holding water. In physics, we subordinate Newton, provisionally accept Einstein, but keep the method intact and with it the field of its operations. If we admit a logical method, then we can admit also an empirical field proper to logic, and this field is ontology.

IV. THE METAPHYSICS OF EMPIRICISM: EPISTEMOLOGY

The study of epistemology arose as an attempt to satisfy the demand for ontological proof. The first efforts at proof were feeble enough to indicate that something was wanting. Self-evidence, far from being a satisfactory proof, was good grounds for suspicion: when anything is asserted to be true because it appears obvious, watch out. The enormity of the implicit ontological presuppositions underlying the critical philosophy of Kant ought to provide a needed lesson for everybody. Russell points to the fact that self-evidence lurks in the most unsuspecting places, even behind the laws of contradiction [1]. On the other hand, however, he has also shown the inadequacy of extreme empiricism [2]. Somewhere between these limits the truth must lie. There is a baffling factor lurking somewhere here.

It does often seem as though epistemologically the statement that "metaphysics is nonsense" means that we are permitted to make inquiries but not to reach conclusions, or that we are to investigate a subject-matter but not to employ its proper terminology [3]. It is as though a license had been issued for the examination of the knowledge process, on the express condition that it must be a failure. Just how much metaphysics do we need to make empiricism possible? That is the basic question. If there is nothing in the empirical world capable of serving as an endorsement of the principle of empiricism, if, that is to say, empiricism is not self-validating, then its justification must lie in logic and the metaphysics of logic. We shall return to this theme.

In the meanwhile it is worth observing that self-evidence is not the most suspect among the older forms of proof. The positivists like everyone else are at their best in their constructive efforts; however, they do have a case to make out in their opposition to the nonsense of metaphysical proof. The kind of assertion they love to attack is familiar enough [4]. Usually the statement of the assertion is considered sufficient to indicate its nonsensicality, but we may go a little further. Three examples chosen at random should suffice.

Let us begin with Aquinas. Theology is a fertile field for this sort of thing. We open the *Summa Theologica* at random and find

---

[1] *Principles of Mathematics* (London 1937), p. 455.

[2] "Logical Positivism", in the *Revue Internationale de Philosophie* for January 15, 1950.

[3] See e.g. Louis O. Kattsoff, *A Philosophy of Mathematics* (Ames, Iowa 1948), p. 2. Kattsoff divides the philosopher's problems into two groups: metamathematical and epistemological. The typical problem in the former group, whose name is taken from Hilbert, makes it clear that the subject-matter is metaphysical, but that the dread name must be avoided at all costs.

[4] But see Weinberg, *op. cit.*, p. 175.

ourselves in an argument for the goodness of God. God is good because He is the "first effective cause of all things" [1]. But the whole cannot be adduced in support of one of its parts in any unassailable argument. God is good because although not all things desire God, things are good just in proportion to the extent to which they do; and therefore God, the object of this desire by things which are good, is Himself good, "for the very thing which is desirable in it (i.e. the nature of the good) is the participation of its likeness". When the reasoning is inspected closely enough, it turns out that the goodness of God is invoked to prove the goodness of God.

Our second example is taken from Spinoza. In seeking to prove that the universe is a unity, he posits an all-embracing substance then argues that everything that is not substance as such consists in some modification of substance. However, it so happens that the definition of substance and the conception of substance together make up a circular argument. Substance is defined as "conceived through itself" and substance alone has this property: whatever is conceived through itself is substance. If this were not true, then anything that existed besides substance would limit it; so that "conceived through itself" would not apply. So the monism depends upon the definition, and this might be well enough were it not intended to be regarded as a proof consisting of *a priori* reasoning from postulates considered to be self-evident [2].

Our third example is taken from Paul Weiss. Men are not social in essence, he argues, otherwise embryos and infants would not be human [3]. Earlier we have been told that infants are "not social to begin with" and that "man has a nature before he attains the status of a social being" [4]. We could dismiss this argument on the simple basis of empirical evidence to the contrary, for what could possibly be more social than a newly-born infant who is helplessly dependent upon his mother? But this after all may be a matter of difference in definition, for Weiss may mean that a man is not social until his relations with other human beings are deliberate and conscious. He certainly does mean that the human

[1] Q. 6, Art. 2.
[2] See e.g. C. E. M. Joad, *Guide to Philosophy* (New York 1936), pp. 122–125.
[3] *Man's Freedom*, (New Haven, 1950), Recapitualtion 16, p. 310.
[4] *Ibid.*, p. 37.

is the individual. In other words, embryos and infants are human but not social, therefore the predicate "human" does not involve the predicate "social". The *a priori* argument rests upon an imperfect knowledge of what constitutes the "social". Can embryos and infants get along without the aid of adults? It would seem not; not, anyway, and be what we call human. On those rare occasions when human children were raised by other animals, when found they corresponded to nothing we call human, for they had no language. Likewise, Weiss mistakenly assumes that the social is the group: a mere assemblage of persons. He insists that "Everyone retreats from society many times during the day [1]" and it is evident that he means retreats into solitude. But in solitude we are still surrounded by the tools and institutions of culture. A man alone in a room that he did not design or build is leading a cultural and therefore a social life in a sense. The social is the cultural. The abstraction of the social apart from tools and institutions is an *a priori* one, and could not occur by induction from empirical data.

What we are contending here, however, is not that these propositions of the metaphysicians are not true but that they are not proved. The absence of proof does not demonstrate falsity. Metaphysics is a postulate-set, and the truth of postulates cannot be demonstrated inside the system in which they serve as postulates. Theorems can be proved, of course, but it is seldom admitted and quickly forgotten what the proof of a theorem involves. Theorems have the coherence of consistency, but they do not have the truth of correspondence outside the system in which they have been proved merely because they have been proved inside, not, that is, unless the system as a whole has. The postulates, it must be remembered, have not been proved unless self-evidence is accepted as a proper proof; yet the correspondence of the theorems to relevant material outside the system rests upon the assumed principle that what follows from a true proposition is true. Is what follows from a self-evident proposition true, or what follows from one whose truth rests on theological authority or on conventional definition? These kinds of tenuous proof are misleading. But the proofs of metaphysics are precisely of that nature; they seek to prove what is taken as

[1] *Op. cit., loc. cit.*

self-evident, and the proof depends upon the self-evidence of the truth of the definitions, or on some similar invalid method.

The logical positivists have concluded too much from the success of their attack upon bad proofs. They have concluded, in short, that metaphysics has nothing to prove – no subject-matter. It is as though no invalid arguments were ever construc-ted in defense of a valid position, or that a field like metaphysics which presumes too much could not legitimately make any pre-sumptions at all. That metaphysical proofs may be nonsense does not constitute a proof that metaphysics itself is nonsense. The occasion for epistemology has been enough to guarantee its failure. Under the scrutiny of logical positivism, ontology must be held down to what is logically required, to a kind of ramified logic, but epistemology disappears altogether. Its province is taken over by empirical psychology [1] on the one hand and by semantics on the other.

Some logical positivists have misunderstood this latter consequence, and have reintroduced the epistemological subject-matter through the analysis of meaning. Now it so happens that meaning has two parts: a relation between sign and object and another between sign and subject. The first is sufficient for logical and mathematical systems. The second is epistemolo-gical, Wittgenstein has argued; and Carnap has fallen into the error of reintroducing an emphasis upon it. But if, as Wittgen-stein would have it, the picture of reality is a locked logical system, then the subject is not the ego but merely the ability to hold the picture and relate its elements. The relation between sign and object is a form-content relation, that between subject and sign is a sense relation. Signs make impressions on the senses, so that this relation, too, can be treated objectively, if it is to be treated at all in connection with logical positivism. But that is not the way Carnap treats it. He uses the term, pragmatics, to cover the entire reintroduction of the subjectively-oriented epistemology, which is no less a blind-alley in this context than it ever was in any other.

If, then, we admit to semantics all questions relating to the theory of signs, and to empirical psychology all questions relating to the theory of subjects, what becomes of epistemology? Carnap

[1] Wittgenstein, *op. cit.*, 4.1121.

has not provided the answer by taking over from Morris the pragmatics of Peirce, for Carnap does less than James with it. Indeed, after introducing pragmatics in the first of his series of volumes [1] it is hardly ever mentioned in the subsequent ones [2].

Let us return to the original occasion for epistemology which was our starting point. We have said that it arose as an attempt to satisfy the demand for ontological proof. When this fact is recognized, epistemology assumes a position subordinate to ontology; but when it is overlooked, then, epistemology merely expresses an ontology in complicated and disguised language, as in the case of the critical philosophy of Kant. These observations lead us to the contention that there is no such thing as epistemology alone. This contention can be supported by two additional points. In the first place, we do not find in our investigations of the foundations of knowledge anything that we can regard as reliable and ultimate; and in the second place, we do not allow ourselves the means to put together what we do find, when we are arbitrarily limited to epistemology proper. To be forced to the choice between settling for an epistemology which does not allow the development of an ontology, and settling for an ontology which not only allows but requires an epistemology, means to find the latter the more advantageous. Any epistemology which requires that the world of the known depend upon the experience of the knower is of the former type. Any ontology which requires that the world as known be selected by the perspective of the knower but not determined by him is of the latter type.

We have promised to hold our metaphysics down to the requirements of logic. What is the epistemology that logic requires?

We start with facts which are the product of experience. Logic is not directly concerned with the difficulties inherent in the analysis of the nature of experience, but only with the products. Here we encounter a curious obstacle. Every fact of experience is ineluctable. We can have experiences, but we cannot know that we have them except through the medium of language. The existence of non-linguistic knowledge is highly debatable. The subject having experiences can no more tell us about them than

[1] *Introduction to Semantics* (Cambridge 1946), pp. 8 ff.
[2] *Formalization of Logic, Meaning and Necessity.*

he can tell himself. For the experiences that we know we have are those we recognize in ourselves and communicate to others through the medium of language. Some realists [1] as well as the logical positivists [2] have taken cognizance of the necessity of language to the recognition of fact. Russell has expressed the relation from the point of view of the fact, when he says that "whatever implies anything is a proposition" [3], thus indicating the propositional import of all things and events. For logic to be viable there must be real events whose effect upon us is that of real experiences, and a real language system in which those experiences can be more or less adequately expressed.

It will be noted at once that there is a hiatus between language and the event-meaning of the experiences which the language endeavors to express. Put another way, we can say that there is a gap between sense data and system-elements which has never been crossed. It does not at the present time appear possible to cross. A peculiar property of logical systems is that they can be completely analyzed into parts, i.e. relations. We call this in logic the search for simples. The simplest properties are similarity and difference. In logic the part is arbitrary but not the whole: there is no widest system or largest number. The epistemology of logic is the only field in which the structure and its function are so close.

To sum up, far from furnishing ontological proof, epistemology itself requires a minimal ontology. The existence of similarity and difference makes experience, and hence knowledge derived from experience, possible. Epistemologists would have us believe that the process of knowing interferes with the objects known and colors them to such a large extent that a part if not the whole of what we know is our own knowing. But, as Wittgenstein has pointed out, we do not see our eyes but other things through them. He leaves us a minimal epistemology consisting of a perspective from which knowledge readings are taken, and though we may specify the readings by naming the instrument, the readings are taken *from* the instrument, they are not readings *of* it.

Logical positivism holds that questions of fact must be referred

---

[1] "There are no self-contained matters of fact capable of interpretation apart from their place as elements in a system". – A. N. Whitehead.

[2] R. Carnap, *Foundations of Logic and Mathematics* (Chicago 1947), p. 7.

[3] *Principles of Mathematics* (London 1937), p. 16.

to observation, and that questions of logic must be referred to consistency. The metaphysics of logical positivism holds in addition that logical systems can be constructed with the facts that observation endorses. To the development of the implication inherent in this latter statement we shall next turn our attention.

V. THE LOGICAL METHOD

Metaphysics, we have agreed, is an empirical field of inquiry, and logic is the method employed to explore the field. The field contains relations but also other empirical elements – qualities, for instance. Hence metaphysics is not to be limited to logic but to the metaphysics required by logic. Logical positivism is not to be understood as dictating "sovereign principles destructive of philosophy but as precepts of limited jurisdiction within philosophy." [1] In philosophy, whatever is not factual is logical. And logic provides the only method for getting at the facts. Logic and fact overlap: each contains more than the area they have in common. This leads to the quasi-independence of each, and requires the two levels of exploration, the logical and the empirical. It is the ground they do not have in common which makes a problem for their interrelations. Then again, facts do not move outside their autonomous realm, only logic is capable of such a manoeuvre. Scientific experimentation is merely advanced applied logic. Hence the empirical is surrounded by the logical: above, by tautologies, below by contradiction. It is moreover permeated by probabilities.

All this is of course imperfectly understood. The mediating role of abstract structures or logical systems is neglected by those whose implicit nominalism leads them to suppose that we go directly from facts to the action they dictate. Facts suggest or inhibit action, they never call for it directly. Indeed we do not go from facts to action but only from facts to theory and from theory to action. When facts seem to be best accounted for or explained by means of some particular theory, we do not call it a theory but a law; and it is the law which calls for action. The curious thing is, however, that although we act in terms of law and not of fact, we cling to the fact over the law. For when a

[1] W. H. F. Barnes, "Is Philosophy Possible? A Study of Logical Positivism", in *Philosophy*, Vol. XXII (1947), p. 45.

fact and a law conflict, we save the fact. The procedure is correct whatever the reasons for it, but our reasons for it are wrong. Facts are the reliable elements, and laws are valid in so far as they are conformable with fact. The laws together form a closed system We test the facts by observation and the laws by logic.

For the purposes of this inquiry we are not unprepared, and the peculiar nature of our preparation must be taken carefully into account. We do not start our philosophical inquiries from nothing but rather from an implicit system of beliefs. This sytem, however unconscious, is nevertheless framed in language. Language, said Peirce, is a kind of algebra [1] and it is in terms of our implicit system that we calculate the truth of newly-learned propositions. Criticism is always oriented. The first necessity is to know the point of view the criticism takes off from as well as the statements toward which it is directed: criticism *from where* as well as criticism *of what*. Criticism always implies a criterion: an ontological standpoint, if you like, as well as a logical method.

The question arises, how do we examine our own systems apart from venturing to apply them? We speak of metamathematics because we do not set up the presuppositions requisite for a logical, mathematical or ontological system and then construct the system, but rather we construct the system and then seek to discover the presuppositions required in order to have done so. This is procedural, but the result of this inductive method ought to be a set of presuppositions sufficient as well as necessary for the construction of the system.

The logical method, then, starts from a knowledge of logical structures. It cuts back to the discovery of the postulates clothed as presuppositions, then forward to the testing of their consistency, completeness and fruitfulness. Postulates, however, are never applied. Peirce's pragmatic definition of meaning is therefore too wide. It does not apply to every element of a system. Instead of declaring that the meaning of a proposition is its conceivable consequences [2], he should have said that in a system the meaning of a *deduction* is its conceivable consequences. For

---

[1] *Collected Papers*, 3.419.
[2] *Collected Papers*, 5.2, 5.9.

the postulates are only indirectly applicable: the deductions from them alone can be applied.

The pragmatists and the logical positivists have been responsible for a great deal of the confusion between meaning and truth. We must distinguish between what a proposition means and the truth (or falsity) of what it means. It is the truth and not the meaning of a proposition which is determined by its method of verification. On the other hand, before we can determine the truth of a proposition we must first ascertain its meaning. Linguistic analysis can help us to solve the problem of meaning, but this does imply that analysis is merely verbal [1]. Once we know what a proposition means, we are in a position to test its truth. But also before we can test its truth, we must determine the truth-conditions. These are the conditions under which the truth or falsity of a proposition could be decided. Thus there are two prerequisites for the testing of truth: we must have in our possession a knowledge of the meaning and a knowledge of the truth-conditions.

Suppose as an example we take the familiar proposition, 'There are craters on the far side of the moon'. We have to ascertain with some precision what we mean by every word in this sentence and from the syntax what we mean by the sentence as a whole. Then we shall have to agree about the circumstances under which we shall accept a verdict as to the accuracy of this meaning. If we mean that 'the moon' is a proper name and that 'craters' are the funnel-shaped openings which mark the vents of volcanoes, then we mean that there is a singular object possessing these markings.

What, then, are we prepared to accept as evidence that this is so (or not so)? Only too often the answer to this question is settled *ex post facto*, for the principles underlying the weighing of evidence are thus far almost exclusively the property of the mathematicians who study statistical probability. Before we are through we shall have to discover that a great technical preparation is required for every problem in philosophy. The day of the enlightened amateur, as every professional whose equipment consisted in a knowledge of the history of philosophy and a strong belief in the judgment of his common sense must now be considered, is almost over. A dim understanding of the situation

---

[1] Barnes, *op. cit., loc. cit.*

merely allows caution to inhibit judgment. We must learn to proceed with more exactitude and not merely with more timidity.

Our attitude toward postulates at the beginning of the systemic investigations must be that which we have toward any proposition for which at present we can conceive no method of verification: we must not be sceptics but agnostics. When working back up through deductions to postulates, we should remember that it is always easier on matters of policy to deal with the president than with the office boy.

If we redefine reasoning as the combining of elements, then the distinction, hitherto so absolute, between deduction and induction, is softened. Deduction becomes the combining of elements by substitution, and induction the combining of elements by deduction, i.e. by the choosing of postulates for deduction. In this way, although postulates are never truth-tested, they are related to the actual world, and their correspondence to fact is not supported merely by the application of the deductions from them. In this way, too, what is persistent among the elements of empiricism get sucked up into logic, like a ladder drawn up through linguistics. Logic refers to the world, but only in so far as the world possesses logical properties. But it is by means of these logical properties that the world can be grasped.

Some inquiries are like physical machines in that they accomplish much because a certain kind of blindness prevents them from being diverted from their logical course by less relevant side possibilities. The system of ontology is a tautology at the mathematical level based on elements derived from experience, on empirical elements. The world of ontology is a locked logical system, and, as Wittgenstein made clear, not the mind but the system mirrors the world. He forgot to add that the world in this connection also mirrors logic: the world and logic reflect each other systematically; and the reflection is what we mean by ontology.

An ontology is an abstract structure invented to account for the world. In so far as it has internal consistency, it is independent; yet its elements are derived from the world. It is a tautological instrument whose operation requires the repeated substitution of constants for variables. We do not go from ontology to practice but to lesser theory – to ethics or aesthetics, for instance – and from this to practice. There is an implied endorsement in successful application, yet more, much more, is required. Practice often tells us which systems are worthy of further logical scrutiny. The progress of knowledge involves an endless and intensive study of logical and mathematical systems, the ascertainment of fact by means of complex instruments, and their interweaving by means of the scientific method.

CHAPTER IX

REFLECTIONS AFTER WITTGENSTEIN'S
PHILOSOPHICAL INVESTIGATIONS

Every philosophy is like a man speaking a language which he has learned imperfectly. One has to determine just what it is that he wishes to say before one is in a position to decide whether he is right or wrong. In the following pages some lessons are drawn from Wittgenstein's *Philosophical Investigations* which it must be clear he himself would not have approved.[1] It is too late for there to be any danger of subverting his influence. Each of his two books has already given rise to schools; logical positivism has come out of the first and linguistic analysis out of the second. It may be that Wittgenstein himself was not a member of either school. We could at least entertain the hypothesis that *Philosophical Investigations* is an outcome of the *Tractatus Logico-Philosophicus* and not opposed to it. In his second book he has shown a way of getting at the proposals advanced in the first, where 'getting at' means literally 'getting out of'. *Philosophical Investigations* continues the proposition next before the last in the *Tractatus*.

Wittgenstein's *Tractatus* is a systematic ambiguity whose elements are problems. One might say that Wittgenstein began his work by picturing a world in logic, only it is such a world as logic requires. For it soon becomes plain that by logic he means the logical language, that is to say, the logically perfect language; and by the world, only those features of it which can be depicted in logic. Thus we get the logical aspects of the concrete world and a kind of substantive view of abstractions. The world pitches us up to its representations in logic, while the logical picture not only reflects the world but indicates downward, so to speak, that it does so. In addition to the convention of existential import (which refers only to factual meanings), there is also a logical import to facts. And even so he soon gets away from the world

---

[1] (Oxford 1953, Blackwell). All page numbers refer to this work.

in quest of what Frege called a logically perfect language. The logic of the language carries that part of the world which it refers to around with it.

Having reached to logic by climbing up on fact, fact is next hauled up, so that we have been prepared for a second book in which the logic of language, and not the world, is the theme. But let us pursue the implications to fact here a little further. The logical import of actual things is as important as (though perhaps no more important than) the existential import of propositions. It is not at all a question of setting up a logic for propositions and then of determining whether the propositions correspond with the relevant segment of actuality. Rather things *say* their logic; the empiricist equipped with his powers of observation and his knowledge of the rules of logic is in a position to listen to what actual things say, and this given him his correct propositions. Logic, in other words, tells us how language can say what it says correctly; how what is being *said* can properly represent what *being* says.

What is set forth here is not Wittgenstein but something of what can be done with Wittgenstein. The following discussion is aimed to develop and present some oblique inferences from Wittgenstein's second published work. When a reader who is located somewhere in the world of abstraction looks at the work of a philosopher who is somewhere else, angles of reference are likely to emerge which neither of them had foreseen. Then, too, it often may be that in this case we keep up with the differences only in order to reinforce the similarities. No more apology need be made for the argument except to add that it is hoped that in this way some advances may be the result.

The work is in the main an elaboration of three theses. These are: (1) that philosophy is an activity, not a static set of beliefs; (2) that this activity consists in examining the contents of the natural languages in order to get rid of the false philosophy and so discover the logic by means of which they correspond to reality; and (3) that the categories of philosophy so discovered are again activities (or methods); they are transparent, and we look *through* them rather than *at* them. We may best begin our discussion by considering inferences from these theses taken separately.

(1) The aim of philosophy is "to show the fly the way out of the

fly-bottle" (103) [1]. The use of the proper description is to get rid of explanation (47); we wish the logic to fit the facts in such a fashion that nothing stands between us and the facts. For a conception is not an object but a grammatical movement. Philosophy is something that we do, not something that we accept or reject. Just what it is that we do, or rather try to do, will be made evident as we proceed.

Meanwhile it may be instructive to point to an analogue. Did not Wittgenstein, Paul Klee and Gertrude Stein employ the same method in philosophy, in painting and in literature, respectively? Just what this common method is was best stated perhaps in its most general terms by Klee: "It is a great handicap and a great necessity to have to start with the smallest. I want to be as though newborn, knowing nothing absolutely about Europe; ignoring poets and fashions, to be almost primitive. Then I want to do something very modest; to work out by myself a tiny, formal motif, one that my pencil will be able to hold without any technique. One favorable moment is enough. The little thing is easily and concisely set down. It's already done! It is a tiny but real affair, and some day, through the repetition of such small but original deeds, there will come one work upon which I can really build" [2].

Of Wittgenstein it can be said that he has set a predicament in motion. To suffering epistemologists who feel that the interference of ways of knowing in what is known must of necessity be fatal, Wittgenstein promised a remedy. The therapy he suggested is one that can be practiced only by the patient and is, moreover, one involving a long process. Yet it offers hope at least, and is a method of working our way out of the difficulty in which Kant has reminded us we shall find ourselves. Kant wished us to embrace the forms of intuition and the categories, and to accept bravely the limitations they impose, even though they prevent us from knowing the real object. Wittgenstein wanted us to take notice of the elements of whatever philosophy we hold but only in order to banish them. To learn, in other words, what it is that constitutes our limitations is to be able to work toward

---

[1] All references in the text unless otherwise noted are to page numbers of the first edition (Oxford 1953, Blackwell).
[2] *Paul Klee* (New York 1946), Museum of Modern Art, p. 8.

getting rid of them and so to approach the real object with the minimum amount of interference.

(2) Activity is to play the "language-game" (5). The language-game is also a logic game. Here Wittgenstein is advancing a thesis not too far removed from the viewpoint of Hilbert: "if anyone utters a sentence and *means* or *understands* it he is operating a calculus according to definite rules" (38). We are told explicitly that "logical investigation explores the nature of things .... It takes its rise .... from an urge to understand the basis, or essence, of everything empirical" (42). The activity of philosophy will thus consist in a grammatical investigation to uncover the nature of empirical things by means of logic.

The awareness which we have of the mechanism of language means an interference with the awareness of the world. This is evident when we know that we are using one language as opposed to another. Wittgenstein has found it necessary to back up from the problem presented by the necessity of constructing the logically perfect language, a problem set forth in his first book, to the antecedent task of doing away with the obstructions preventing its solution. The analysis of language is negative, not positive; it is neither intended to discover anything nor to create understandings but only to get rid of misunderstandings (43). The positive logic of empirical situations is hidden. The language by means of which we get rid of misunderstandings is ordinary language (46). Our misunderstandings are ordinary ones; they are so common that we make them but do not know them. The analysis of ordinary language is the method by which we make ourselves know our ordinary, which is to say false, beliefs.

Predecessors and parallels are not wanting for the negative method which Wittgenstein proposes to the philosophical investigator. Perhaps the citation of one of each will suffice.

The predecessor is Plato. The method of Socrates which is known as *elenchus* is well described by Richard Robinson as "examining a person with regard to a statement he has made, by putting to him questions calling for further statements, in the hope that they will determine the meaning and the truth-value of the first statement" [1]. Note especially, that "Most often the truth-value expected is falsehood; and so 'elenchus' in the

---

[1] *Plato's Earlier Dialectic*, second edition, (London 1953, Oxford), p. 7.

narrower sense is a form of cross-examination or refutation''.

The parallel is with Freud. The method of psychoanalysis is to make the patient who is suffering from a neurosis aware of the false or contradictory beliefs which he unconsciously holds and which dictate his emotions and perhaps also many of his overt actions, on the assumption that when he is aware of their untenability he will be able to cope with them and perhaps even to get rid of them. This covert method of eliminating error, like the overt method of Socrates, substitutes nothing affirmative or positive, though of course the preparation for the freedom to receive truth assumes its existence.

Like Socrates, Wittgenstein assumed the metaphysics of realism behind his method. This ought not to be too surprising when we consider his antecedents and influences. He belonged to the British realists, through Moore and Russell. We should expect strong affinities with Whitehead who regarded a philosophical system as a high set of abstractions which could grip us without our being aware of it. Are we indeed so very far here from one side of Whitehead? The theory on which an analogy could be based is termed by Whitehead the "Fallacy of Misplaced Concreteness" and is to be found, among other places, in the third chapter of his *Science and the Modern World*. The abstract structure by means of which we view the world is confused with the world. Other views are possible, and a more transparent one which will occasion less distortion could be discovered. In this connection, at least, Whitehead, too, regarded philosophizing as a negative function undertaken in order to get rid of mistakes. Philosophy, he said in the next chapter, was "the critic of abstractions". Whitehead went on to construct a philosophy; Wittgenstein, in the work under consideration here, makes no such attempt. Wittgenstein, however, does develop and illustrate the method more fully than Whitehead did.

It must be emphasized strongly that the investigation proposed is not psychological. Psychology is specifically ruled out. When we talk about understanding we do not intend a mental process at all (61); understanding is a state, not a mental state (59). For the unconscious we use the term, disposition (59) or intention (181); we are probing beneath the surface but by means of grammar (168); belief itself is a kind of disposition (191).

There is no help for us from psychology, which is only confused and barren (232).

The escape from psychological involvement requires that we use words properly. This means that we must break through words in order to get at that to which they refer. The realist must also entertain the possibility of thinking without words. He is at the opposite pole from the Kantian-like symbolism of Cassirer, for instance. The absence of language from the highest type of thinking is illustrated in intuition or insight; here there are no steps. Even in the instance of logic, however, we are discussing possible states of affairs.

The empirical world is both what is the case and what is not the case; nothing stands still in existence. Hence the value to empiricism of logic, which can help us through thought to understand "what is not the case" (44). We must learn to distinguish between what is not the case and what is not possible or what is contradictory. The wall is now tan and we can consider it being painted blue; but it cannot be both tan and blue. The endorsement borrowed from tautology and the intent of non-trivial tautologies is required and serves to keep us within the bounds of logical security. Logic lies beneath the surface, not open to view (43). "It is the business of philosophy, not to resolve a contradiction . . . . but to make it possible for us to get a clear view of . . . . the state of affairs before the contradiction is resolved" (50). The bulk of Wittgenstein's book, then, is devoted to the empirical test of language: can it describe the simplest feelings and actions? Is it adequate for this purpose? Wittgenstein makes innumerable samplings. These are done in two ways: one is to sort out and examine the meanings and consequences of ordinary words and phrases; the other is to imagine how things could be with respect to language (230), because "to imagine a language is to imagine a form of life" (8).

(3) We may for purposes of brevity refer to the third thesis, which is the most important one, as the transparent ontology. Very pure theory must for logical reasons consist in no theory at all; only, we do not start there but instead work our way toward there, and it is in this working of our way that the activity of philosophy consists. Philosophy "leaves everything as it is" (49); we do not disturb anything, we only make pictures of how things

are. Compare this, for instance, with Descartes' view of conscious-
ness as a diaphanous medium analogous to light. Only, this time
there is a vast difference, for it is by means of logic that we shall
be enabled to see clearly and distinctly. And we shall obtain our
view, as we shall presently note, by regarding the structure of
language – its grammar – as a picture of the world.

Philosophy is the effort to see things as they are. To some
extent it fails and we measure the degree of failure. In viewing
nature through an ontology, we must find out the angle of
distortion in order to make the proper allowances. How much
surface dust should we expect on the lens, etc.? We must take
account in our philosophical investigations of the fact that our
own considerations are visible: to what degree do the means we
employ to see the world interfere with our seeing, so that we can
subtract them from the total picture? In order to be successful
at this game we shall have to rid ourselves of our ontological
categories. But we need to make certain before we do so that
they are in need of elimination, for they constitute our main line
of defense. It is only the proper ontology after all which in passing
casts the least shadow.

Wittgenstein's biggest point in both of his books (though
perhaps he would not have put it exactly in this way) is that when
the true propositions of philosophy correspond exactly to the
conditions of being, the propositions will become transparent
and only the being will be evident, so that philosophy itself
will seem to have disappeared. It is the ambition of Wittgenstein
to establish through a very pure theory the transparent ontology.
When philosophy understands other things correctly, that is
because there is no philosophy in them. The philosophy of
science, for instance, will consist in understanding science
correctly, and not in constructing a philosophy of science to
be regarded separately, after the way of philosophy. In our
understanding of the external world we wish as little interference
as possible occasioned by the mechanism of understanding. The
problem posed in this ambition is a delicate one calling for
enormous subtlety and precision.

In the meanwhile, however, this is far from a statement of the
true situation. What we are faced with may be termed premature
ontological systems. These we need to break up into single ideas

for purposes of testing. What is required is the reduction to simple names (21). When we begin with names, we know that our procedure is empirically reliable (27) and logically primitive. For we have only chosen the counters to be employed in our logic-game (24). Every word is a name and not merely those which stand for actual physical objects or for their collection, 'chairs' as well as 'this chair'. In this view we are committed to the realist's assumption that relations exist externally to and independently of the knower. Prepositions, then, are names of relations; conjunctions are, too; articles are names of numbers; verbs are names of actions; and so on. 'Above' describes a position; 'and' refers to togetherness and is exemplified when objects are spatially juxtaposed; etc. We may find that we shall have to put them together in different ways. An analogy is the method which Peirce termed experimentation with mental graphs (the observation of abstract pictures). This is a process of necessary fragmentation and fractionation. In this way we work toward very pure theory. A consideration of the categories could be a starting point. To what extent are they mutually exclusive and exhaustive? Take the Cartesian *res cogitans* and *res extensa*, for instance; under which of these should we classify the proposition? What did Spinoza gain by following Descartes into thought and extension, when *res extensa* was a nominalizing shift from the Platonic "Idea" and the Aristotelian "formal cause"? But there is another way. We can work more constructively, for example, by collecting all the information of a metaphysical nature that we need, and translating all the pieces into the same philosophical language.

The angle of distortion that we have observed in the case of Descartes is not confined to names. It is also to be observed with principles. For we find groups of distortions that bear a family resemblance. Let us consider such a one. We shall label it the axiom of pre-eminent reality. For it is found among all the philosophies which assume or admit a difference in degree of reality. Let us consider in this connection the quarrel between nominalists, idealists and realists. Wittgenstein himself attacks the nominalists for "interpreting all words as *names*" (118). It is a controversy not over the state of things but only over words (122). Wittgenstein in the last reference chooses the solipsists to represent the nominalists (he might as easily have chosen the materialists).

We could go on with the argument. Perhaps we should select one instance and do so. Take the solipsists, for instance. If one of them should say, 'the world is my idea', we could reply, 'very well, but tell me, what is your idea of the world?' And thenceforth we would be concerned with whether his account was true or false, complete or incomplete, adequate or inadequate, and not particularly with what is involved in his having it as an idea. We are going to be concerned, in short, with the self-consistent (and, it is hoped, empirically supported) structure, and not with the authority of its promulgation or with its genesis or history. These would all be irrelevant to its criteria and antecedent to its value, as well as beside the fact. "That is the truth", says Jurgen to the King Gorgyrvan Gawr, "whoever says it".

Wittgenstein's early influences, we have noted, were Moore and Russell. He may have acquired from them the highly sensitive and tentative version of metaphysical realism which underlies his work. This would be not a highly substantialized realm of essence but instead a range of recurrence, not a realm of existence but a range of transient elements, together with a highly elusive principle of interaction; but the whole structure so delicate that the mere names with their historic associations seem crude and misleading by comparison. Hence what we are given is not a bald philosophy but a tour around it and a view of its landscape, without once coming into contact with the delicate filaments of the theory (18). The presentation of realism becomes a matter of movement; the recurrent elements return us to the transient ones, and vice versa. Metaphysics, then, is a movement among the categories, not a fixed assembly. The categories themselves are paths, not points. They are not locations at which to stop, only places to turn. The "infinitely fine network" of the *Tractatus* has become a fluid set of points, a sort of topological philosophy required by standpointlessness.

Some philosophical systems resemble formal gardens, others are more like jungles. We make up the pattern with the simplest pieces, but the pattern after all can be too simple. We shall find that the natural ones are more complex and also more magnificent as well as invisible. In philosophy what man discovers ought to be what he himself has left untouched; that is the message Wittgenstein is trying to bring us, or, perhaps more accurately, to show us. It is a method which could be employed even in societies where the scientific method has not yet found its way of coping with the extenuating circumstances. The natural society is the cultural ideal. We shall find that man has discovered the pieces but not the secret of how they are put together. There are subtleties in the field of certainties. These occur in connection with the fitting of data corresponding to the absolutes of sensation into structures prescribed by the absolutes of mathematical tautology. In combining the two sorts of absolutes the absoluteness itself has had to be abandoned. We have left only absolute-guided probabilities. We are committed to the delicate business of the fitting.

How can this best be done? Fortunately, we have already at hand a method which has been used extensively even if never formalized. We have the study of paradigmatics, the technique of model-construction. In philosophy our metaphysical systems are models. We should observe them more carefully. We need, so to speak, a phenomenology of the paradigms – paradigmatic phenomenology. They disclose new relations and suggest novel values.

One convenient way of looking at models is to talk about systems. In philosophy ideas have a summation in a system, although this is not always admitted by those who treat of ideas. But as Wittgenstein wrote, "the most general remarks yield at best what looks like the fragments of a system" (228). To concede ideas but not a system is as though we were to admit destinations but not destiny.

Wittgenstein's method in his second book seems to indicate the replacing of philosophy by a kind of aimed or purposive casuistry. It is overlooked by most of his followers that he is intending systematic philosophy. To play the language-game with him is to clear the ground of misunderstandings in order to make way for the proper understanding, which would require no screen at all. We want to achieve what Peirce termed the vagueness of generality without the mechanism responsible for the vagueness.

If fame consists in a sufficient number of misunderstandings, it is a mistake to read the work of a great thinker until we have got rid of some of the misunderstandings. It is perhaps the only way to save the very pure theory. One could perhaps tell best what one looked like by having children by a number of different women, and then comparing their faces after discounting what each mother had contributed individually in the way of features. It is interesting to watch Wittgenstein's emphases reflected in the work of his followers. Those who would eliminate philosophy in favor of science offer a poor tribute indeed to the man who in his first book tried to restore to philosophy a position of its own; while those who would reduce philosophy to the analysis of meaning commit an act of subreption in view of his second book since they offer an interpretation which manages to conceal behind the means which they recognize the end which he sought. He liberated philosophy from science (with which it cannot have the proper relations if it is not free), and he made the categories more permeable and movement among them more fluid.

We have returned to our starting point. It may be, in the manner of Wittgenstein, that the present interpretation, too, is to be discounted. And at the end of his book (230) has he not suggested how this might be done for all attempts to account for the world?

There is little doubt of the cryptic note in all of Wittgenstein's work; it is the kind of writting which lends itself quite easily to many sorts of interpretation.

There are, of course, ancient precedents for this, too. According to Plato, the true philosophy cannot be expressed in words [1]. Plutarch said that Aristotle had "more abstruse and profound theories" which he "reserved for oral communication to the initiated, and did not allow many to become acquainted with" [2].

The aim which he set himself so far as we can tell was the construction of a logically perfect language. The idea was Frege's. "The logically perfect language should satisfy the conditions, that every expression grammatically well constructed as a proper name out of signs already in use shall in fact designate an object, and that no new signs shall be introduced as a proper name without being secured as a reference" [3]. "A logically perfect

---

[1] See Epistle VII, 341C–D.

[2] *Plutarch's Lives*, "Life of Alexander" (London 1948, Dent), 3 vols., vol. ii, p. 468.

[3] *Translations from the Philosophical Writings of Gottlob Frege*, ed. by Geach and Black (Oxford 1952, Blackwell), p. 70.

language would be one in which sense and reference exactly coincide". [1] The logically perfect language would lead to a standpointlessness in philosophy, akin to that achieved in general relativity physics by means of the tensor calculus. The method selected to achieve this aim was of an unusual subtlety and complexity. All previous philosophers had given their abstract points and illustrated them afterwards. In the *Philosophical Investigations* the situation is exactly reversed: we are given a series of illustrations from which we are supposed to derive for ourselves the abstract points. It is as though one were to lay out an entire philosophy but do it entirely in parables. Folk tales have something of the same character, for the analogical properties of Wittgenstein's illustrations do not lie entirely on the surface.

The world is either simpler than the mathematicians suppose or more complex than the philosophers have made it out to be. "If there are logical objects at all – and the objects of arithmetic are such objects – then there must also be a means of apprehending, or recognizing, them. This service is performed for us by the fundamental law of logic that permits the transformation of an equality holding generally into an equation. Without such a means a scientific foundation for arithmetic would be impossible" [2]. Wittgenstein in his second book attempted to exemplify the analysis of language in the simplest terms. He began with a language game with the fewest number of elements, but it should be noted that he did so in the most complicated kind of language. The appeal to ordinary language is an appeal to naive experience and immediate perception. If one could regard what Wittgenstein was doing as having been done in the object-language, and of how he was doing it as having been in the syntax-language, then the object-language was held down to the utmost simplicitly, while the syntax-language was allowed to proliferate into the most complex linguistic forms. But, remember, the aim of philosophy is to teach us how to subtract from our perspective the degree of distortion resulting from the acceptance of a given metaphysics and a given epistemology, for any assumed philosophy determines the point of view and the point of view is necessarily as exclusive

[1] *Ibid.*, footnote p. 58.
[2] *Ibid.*, p. 181.

as it is inclusive. Thus to see the world steadily and to see it whole all that we need to do is to get rid of every and any perspective. But what is the perspective behind the syntax-language?

This is a difficult question, but one thing is sure. The esoteric philosophy is – no philosophy. Become aware that you already have a philosophy, then get rid of the philosophy you have because it represents a limited and partial point of view, and then you will see the world more nearly as it really is. But to take these steps it is first necessary to go through the mazes of technical philosophy.

A professional philosopher, then, ought if possible to determine his own position, not in order to defend it but only in order to deduct it. As a professional philosopher, Wittgenstein tried to get rid of the metaphysical realism which Russell had taught him to want to get rid of. The result in Wittgenstein was not to turn back to the German tradition of metaphysical realism, two of whose members, Meinong and Frege, had originally influenced Russell, but instead to construct a method whereby philosophy could be properly applied in practice, a method of transparent facilitation for the institution of philosophy.

Like most men who try to found a school themselves, Wittgenstein was a failure as a teacher. It is evidently too early to undertake in one's own lifetime to set one's ideas going. For Wittgenstein's followers, the linguistic analysts, are teaching – inadvertently – the exact opposite of what he himself professed. For where he tried to show that the metaphysics implicit in ordinary language is wrong, they try to show that philosophy is wrong when it goes beyond ordinary language. Both Wittgenstein and his followers in England emphasized language, and concerned themselves with it, but despite the apparent similarities they did so for quite different reasons. For Wittgenstein, language is of interest for he wishes to get rid of the false philosophies it contains. His followers, on the other hand, wish to get rid of philosophy by reducing it to language [1].

---

[1] If the linguistic analysts are far from Wittgenstein, how much further are they from the early Russell. In the *Philosophy of Logical Atomism* of 1918 (chapter V), for instance, he said, "It is exceedingly difficult to make this point [i.e. that 'existence-propositions do not say anything about the actual individual but only about the class or function'] clear as long as one adheres to ordinary language, because ordinary language is rooted in a certain feeling about logic, a certain feeling that our primeval ancestors had, and as long as you keep to ordinary language you find it very difficult to get away from the bias which is imposed upon you by language".

The distinction between the Wittgenstein of the *Philosophical Investigations* and his followers is more marked still.

Where Wittgenstein was interested in attitudes he was also aware that these indicate the presence of beliefs; he was probing through the attitudes for the metaphysical beliefs which underlie them. His successors, the linguistic analysts, are concerned merely with the analysis of attitudes; they are looking through language for the attitudes language betrays, and that is all. What was a method for Wittgenstein is an end for them.

Again, Wittgenstein was concerned to discuss peripheral matters, whereas they are not. He was willing to discuss nominalism, for instance, and besides his method in general exactly what it was he was trying to do with it, whereas they are not.

In sum, he was a much broader thinker than his followers are, which is only to be expected. To take any philosopher too seriously, that is to say, to be willing to do only what he has done, is to impose upon oneself the restrictions which he neither felt nor had so far as we can tell; Wittgenstein did not limit himself to what he did, for he did what he did quite freely and not within the bounds of self-imposed restrictions. And so to use what he did as a set of limitations is, in a way, to differ sharply with him.

It is not true, then, to say that the subject-matter of philosophy is its own methodology. Philosophy as a whole cannot be confined to the way in which it deals with its subject-matter, on the assumption that this *is* its subject-matter. Such an investigation has been neglected from time to time, and it ought to be included under the scrutiny of philosophy; it is true that philosophy ought to pause now and then to examine the efficiency of its methods of investigation. But having looked to the sharpness of its tools it ought then to put them to work, and not be led off into assuming that sharpening its tools *is* its work.

BIBLIOGRAPHY

Ayer, Alfred J., *Language, Truth and Logic* (New York 1946, Dover)

Bergmann, Gustav, *The Metaphysics of Logical Positivism* (New York 1954, Longmans, Green)

Birkhoff, Garrett, and MacLane, Saunders, *A Survey of Modern Algebra* (New York 1948, Macmillan)

Bridgman, P. W., *The Logic of Modern Physics* (New York 1928, Macmillan)

Carnap, Rudolf, *Der logische Aufbau der Welt* (Berlin 1928)

Carnap, Rudolf, *Formalization of Logic* (Cambridge 1943, Harvard University Press)

Carnap, Rudolf, *Foundations of Logic and Mathematics* (Chicago 1947, University of Chicago Press)

Carnap, Rudolf, *Introduction to Semantics* (Cambridge 1946, Harvard University Press)

Carnap, Rudolf, *The Logical Syntax of Language* (New York 1937, Harcourt Brace)

Carnap, Rudolf, *Meaning and Necessity* (Chicago 1947, University of Chicago Press)

Carnap, Rudolf, *Philosophy and Logical Syntax* (London 1935, Kegan Paul)

Carnap, Rudolf, *The Unity of Science* (London 1934, Kegan Paul)

Cohen, Morris R., and Nagel, Ernest, *An Introduction to Logic and Scientific Method* (New York 1934, Harcourt Brace)

Feibleman, James K., *An Introduction to Peirce's Philosophy* (New York 1946, Harpers)

Feigl, Herbert, and Sellars, Wilfrid, *Readings in Philosophical Analysis* (New York 1949, Appleton-Century-Crofts)

Flew, Antony, Editor, *Essays on Logic and Language* (Oxford 1951, Blackwell)

Flew, Antony, Editor, *Logic and Language*, Second Series, (Oxford 1953, Blackwell)

Frege, Gottlob, *The Foundations of Arithmetic* (Oxford 1950, Blackwell)

Geach, Peter, and Black, Max, Editors, *Translations from the Philosophical Writings of Gottlob Frege* (Oxford 1952, Blackwell)

Goodman, Nelson, *The Structure of Appearance* (Cambridge 1951, Harvard University Press)

Joad, C. E. M., *A Critique of Logical Positivism* (Chicago 1950, University of Chicago Press)

Joad, C. E. M., *Guide to Philosophy* (New York 1936, Macmillan)

Joad, C. E. M., *Philosophical Aspects of Modern Science* (New York 1932, Macmillan)

Kattsoff, Louis O., *Logic and the Nature of Reality* (The Hague 1956, Martinus Nijhoff)

Kattsoff, Louis O., *A Philosophy of Mathematics* (Ames, Iowa 1948, Iowa State College Press)

Klee, Paul, *On Modern Art* (New York 1946, Museum of Modern Art)

Kraft, Victor, *The Vienna Circle* (New York 1953, Philosophical Library)

Laird, John, *The Idea of Value* (Cambridge 1929, University Press)

Lazerowitz, Morris, *The Structure of Metaphysics* (London 1955, Routledge and Kegan Paul)

Mises, Richard von, *Positivism* (Cambridge 1951, Harvard University Press)

Moore, G. E., *Principia Ethica* (Cambridge 1929, Cambridge University Press)

Muirhead, J. H., Editor, *Contemporary British Philosophy*, First Series (London 1925, Allen and Unwin)

Muirhead, J. H., Editor, *Contemporary British Philosophy*, Second Series (London 1937, Allen and Unwin)

Peirce, Charles S., *Collected Papers* (Cambridge 1935, Harvard University Press)

Plutarch's *Lives* "The Life of Alexander", (London 1948, Dent)

Quine, Willard Van Orman, *Elementary Logic* (New York 1941, Ginn)

Quine, Willard Van Orman, *From a Logical Point of View* (Cambridge 1953, Harvard University Press)

Quine, Willard Van Orman, *Mathematical Logic* (Cambridge 1947, Harvard University Press)

Reichenbach, Hans, *Symbolic Logic* (New York 1947, Macmillan)

Robinson, Richard, *Plato's Earlier Dialectic*, Second Edition, (London 1953, Oxford University Press)

Russell, Bertrand, *Analysis of Mind* (London 1951, Allen and Unwin)

Russell, Bertrand, *A Critical Exposition of the Philosophy of Leibniz* (London 1937, Allen and Unwin)

Russell, Bertrand, *Human Knowledge* (New York 1948, Simon and Schuster)

Russell, Bertrand, *An Inquiry Into Meaning and Truth* (New York 1940, W. W. Norton)

Russell, Bertrand, *Logic and Knowledge* (London 1956, Allen and Unwin)

Russell, Bertrand, *Our Knowledge of the External World* (New York 1929, Norton)

Russell, Bertrand, *The Philosophy of Logical Atomism* (Minneapolis No date, University of Minnesota)

Russell, Bertrand, *The Principles of Mathematics* (London 1937, Allen and Unwin)

Ryle, Gilbert, *The Concept of Mind* (London 1949, Hutchinson's)

Schlick, Moritz, *Gesammelte Aufsätze* (Wien 1938, Gerold & Co.)

Schlick, Moritz, *Problems of Ethics* (New York 1939, Prentice-Hall)

Schilpp, Paul A,. *The Philosophy of Bertrand Russell* (Evanston, Ill. 1944, Northwestern University Press)

Stevenson, C. L., *Ethics and Language* (New Haven 1944, Yale University Press)

Tarski, A., *Introduction to Logic* (New York 1946, Oxford University Press)

Urmson, J. O., *Philosophical Analysis* (Oxford 1956, Clarendon Press)

Weinberg, Julius Rudolph, *An Examination of Logical Positivism* (London 1936, Routledge and Kegan Paul)

Weiss, Paul, *Man's Freedom* (New Haven 1950, Yale University Press)

Whitehead, Alfred N., *Adventures of Ideas* (New York 1940, Macmillan)

Whitehead, Alfred N., *An Enquiry Concerning the Principles of Natural Knowledge* (Cambridge 1955, Cambridge University Press)

Whitehead, Alfred N., *Science and the Modern World* (New York 1931, Macmillan)

Whitehead, Alfred N., and Russell, Bertrand, *Principia Mathematica*, Second Ed., (Cambridge 1925, Cambridge University Press)

Wisdom, John, *Other Minds* (Oxford 1952, Blackwell)

Wisdom, John, *Philosophy and Psycho-Analysis* (Oxford 1953, Blackwell)

Wittgenstein, Ludwig, *Philosophical Investigations* (Oxford 1953, Blackwell)

Wittgenstein, Ludwig, *Tractatus Logico-Philosophicus* (London 1922, Kegan Paul)

INDEX